COMPENDIUM

Spiritual Care
through Muslim
Ethnographic Stories

MIND OF THE MODERN SUFI

Dr. Yunus Kumek

Second Edition

Sage Chronicle^λ
publishing house

Cover image: Carpet Design with the Courtesy of Masjid Al Salam,
  Buffalo, New York; Photo by Y. Kumek
Interior background: Shutterstock.com

Sage Chronicle $^{\lambda}$
p u b l i s h i n g   h o u s e

www.sagechronicle.org
3380 Sheridan Drive, #240
New York 14226
contact@sagechronicle.org

Published in the United States of America.

بِسْمِ اللهِ الرَّحْمٰنِ الرَّحِيمِ

A small gift for my Dear friend John.

Dr. Y. Kumek
Shoeshore
Buffalo, NY
Sept 7, 2022

PREFACE

This book brings into our contemporary life important Muslim teachings in a one-page story format. Each story has the first paragraph as the story and the second paragraph as the meanings and interpretations of the practice. The stories in the book aim to use contemporary life encounters with the meanings and interpretations in Islamic practice. These stories have been compiled and contemporized from ethnographic field work in different Sufi communities of New York, Boston, Pittsburgh, Chicago, Toronto, Istanbul, and Cairo.

The book uses a simple transliteration scheme from the original language of Arabic without going to the details of academic transliteration scheme. When there are names or referrals to God then the words are capitalized such as the Divine. The abbreviation used for the Prophet Muhammad is the Prophet. The footnotes with numbered superscripts give the immediate relevant information for the unfamiliar English reader. The endnotes with lettered superscripts give the information for the reader who is familiar with the teachings and readings in Sufism. The references with numbered and parenthesis superscripts allude to the notions in practice as some examples of these practices in the literature. The suggested readings are examples of some classical and contemporary work about the topic for interested readers. The glossary and index in the book can hopefully make it easier for general readers of English.

The short stories and anecdotes in this book can bring important and practical aspects of these teachings in our practical life. This book can be valuable for different level readers such as the Muslims, Christians, Jews, Buddhists, Hindus, and people who especially value spirituality and experiential knowledge and believe the mysteries of life beyond the seen and human control. Regardless of different naming of the deity as Allah, God, Adonai, or the notions of Nirvana or Samadhi, in this book, one can realize the similarity of common and intersecting points of spirituality or religious experience among different traditions.

The word "Sufi" or character of "Sufi" does not imply a group or sect in this case, but used to depict a self-reflective personality or a character trying to have a spiritual Muslim care in daily practices. So, each time you see the Sufi character, you can imagine and replace it with a "Muslim". It was also easy for me especially for Western audience just to denote everything as one character as Muslim without changing genders and trying to find 500 different Muslim gender names in more than 500 stories.

This book can be a valuable supplementary text in the disciplines of psychology, counseling, anthropology, philosophy, and religion.

Yunus Kumek, PhD
Lecturer in Muslim Ministry
Harvard Divinity School
Spring 2021

CONTENTS

Contents

xi

Contents   xiii

COMPENDIUM

Spiritual Care
through Muslim
Ethnographic Stories

MIND OF THE MODERN SUFI

1.   The Sufi and the Upside Down Bug

One day, the Sufi was walking with his kids. There were a lot of bugs. As they were walking the Sufi was thinking. Then, the Sufi saw a bug upside down struggling to get back up. The Sufi continued walking. After walking a mile, the Sufi felt something uneasy in himself. He said to himself "what is happening?" Then, he thought about the bug and realized he should've helped it. After a few minutes of search, he went back and found the bug at the same spot where he saw it and it was still struggling to change its position. The Sufi helped it to turn from its back. He felt much better and left.

IN PRACTICE

It is important to detect one's spiritual problems, diagnose, and treat them accordingly. A lot of times, the person may not know the cause of spiritual discomfort, uneasiness, fear, anxiety, or distress. The person can make the problem worse by ignoring it or treating it the wrong way. Therefore, in practice the famous saying "know yourself to know God"[1] alludes to this notion. In the above story, perhaps the Sufi was distracted while thinking and walking with his kids. When he had a glance at the bug, he did not internalize this creation's pain. But the image stuck in his memory and transformed into a discomfort in himself. Later, as the Sufi thought and reflected on his discomfort, he then interpreted that the source of distress was his unconcerned attitude towards the suffering bug.

Discussion Question

► How can a person practice the awareness of their inner conversations?

2.   The External, the Internal, and the Purpose

One day, it was dark and rainy outside. The Sufi went to a social fitness club. As soon as he went inside, everyone was so cheerful. The lighting in the building was so bright. People were drinking coffee and enjoying their conversations at each corner. Everyone looked well dressed, happy, and smiling. Then, he thought about his solitude, loneliness, and silence. He then was reflecting moments in temple, mosque, or in different places of meditation. Then, he asked himself: what is the difference? He said: This is the external. I don't know how these people are when they are with themselves in silence, which is the internal, the real self, and the purpose.

IN PRACTICE

It is important to know that the internal engagements are the essence that make one's purpose in life. This does not mean the person should be in gloomy environments to engage with oneself with prayers, chants, reflection, and self-accountability. The person can use all the means that would help for the real purpose when being in nature and in different environments. As in the above story, at a smaller scale, a person can be happy in a nice social club with all cheerful, fine people and places. One should know that the universe itself is a social club if one knows how to engage with it[2]. In other words, we are given a system, structure, and beings that everyone is cheering, chanting, and appreciating in their position with God. In this sense, a person, not recognizing this disposition with God, may not have a real purpose although he or she may look happy. For the real sense of loneliness and self-reflection, there may be enormous internal spiritual bleeding such as depression, anxiety, and unhappiness.

Discussion Question

▶   What is your real-self?

3.   Friend or Companion

One day, the Sufi was thinking the difference between the words friend and companion. She said to herself, "I think companion is the person who you hang around with. Friend is a person that you go beyond companionship and there is a closer relationship."

IN PRACTICE

It is important to choose with whom one should hang around. Because the presence of others and their conversation can affect the person's spirituality positively or negatively. Therefore, the people who were around the Prophet were called companions, sahabah. They were with the Prophet as much as possible to receive the constant positive spiritual flow into their hearts and minds. The words, "hang around" and "conversation" also from the same word of sohbah meaning conversation and lecture. In other words, the words sohbah and sahabah are from the same root word. On the other hand, the only Friend, Khalil[1] should be God in one's relationship[3]. In this relationship, the Friend does not leave the person and will always be there if the person is fulfilling the requirements of this relationship.

Discussion Question

▶   How do you contemporize the understanding of friend and companion at our times?

---

1. Khalil is from khullah, genuine love and companionship.

4.   Life, Purpose, Worries, and the Sufi

One day, the Sufi was worried as she was getting older. She was worried about her life and her purpose. As she was thinking she did not feel good about the things that she wanted to accomplish. She was getting older. Her body was getting weak. She said to herself "I know I am going to die soon. So, what should I do?" She looked at her heart and said "I know. I will do my intention for doing good and work towards it as best as I can."

IN PRACTICE

One of the spiritual diseases that generally accompanies people is the forgetfulness of death.[2] Or, it is defined as the sickness of desire for a long life. As everyone is going to die, it is important to make preparations for it. It is not only physical preparations of preparing a will or graveyard arrangements. But it is the arrangements of one's intentions, efforts and spiritual struggle in their relationship with God. In the above story, the Sufi alludes to this fact that with her intention about the goals for the good that she was not able to accomplish, she decided to make intentions about it and work towards it [4]. God rewards the person according to the good intention and sincere efforts but not the outcome of their efforts.

Discussion Question

▶   How or why our concern change as we age?

---

2. Tul-u amal: desire for long life.

5. Balancing Ascetic Life and Social Life

One day, the Sufi was enjoying his prayer. He was taking so much pleasure from it. As he was praying, his mom called him for assistance for a minute. The Sufi immediately stopped his prayer and went next to his mom. His mom was happy with the Sufi. The Sufi said to himself "although I was enjoying my prayer and it was very hard for me to break it, if God would be pleased I would do it."

IN PRACTICE

The ascetic life through prayers, meditation, and solitude is encouraged with checks and balances. The full asceticism or monasticism through disconnecting oneself fully with their familial and social responsibilities is discouraged by the Prophet[5]. In other words, one can practice solitude or limited retreats with the intention of benefitting oneself and then going back to people for being more beneficial. There are a lot of genuine Sufi teachers who prefer not to socialize but enjoy their prayers and meditation of God in solitude. However, they still socialize due to the rights of others on them such as family or students. In the above story, one can especially see the case of a mother as a person is required to stop one's optional spiritual engagement if their mother is calling. As suggested by the Prophet[1], there were pious individuals who did not fulfill these kinship and social relations and therefore, they were tested with trials and difficulties by God.

Discussion Question

► Is ascetic life rare at our times? Why?

6.   Mother Sufi

One day, the Sufi was thinking why are his kids more attached to their mom than to him. Then, he was thinking all the difficulties of the labor that his wife went through. Then, she had the struggles of breastfeeding and suckling. She was constantly being worried about them. The Sufi said to himself "I think, I understand. It is payback time."

IN PRACTICE

According to the practice, both parents, father and mother have rights in their children. The children are expected to take care of them and be nice to them even in the ages and times of being grumpy. The practice puts special emphasis for children to be extra nice to mothers. According to some interpretations of the Prophet, mothers have three times more rights on children than the fathers [5] [6]. In addition, even though a person may not get along well with their parents, children are still expected to keep nice, gentle, and kind in their treatment of them in order to please God. This instruction is stated numerous times in both the scripture and sayings of the Prophet[6][5].

Discussion Question

▶   What are the factors that affect parent–children relationship?

7.   Sufis from Different Cultures and Learning

There was a Sufi who used to choose different Sufis as friends from different cultures. He used to hang around each day with a Sufi from a different culture: an American Sufi, an Indian Sufi, an African Sufi, a Turkish Sufi, and an Arab Sufi. One of his friends realized this and asked the reason. The Sufi said: I learn something different and new from each of them. They all understand and practice being close to God similarly but also differently.

IN PRACTICE

In the journey of spiritual path, the person can benefit from different people with different perspectives. A person who may not have the complete knowledge but can be strong in genuine practice can bring different perspectives. A person who may know the knowledge using the mind constantly but lacking in practice can bring different perspectives. Each culture can bring different embodiments of the same teachings of spirituality. In this perspective, it is a very unique experience to learn the spiritual practice from different people with different cultures as mentioned in the above story. Genuinely similar values are embodied differently in different cultures.

Discussion Question

▶ Why do some people view cultural diversity as richness and some as a possible source of problem?

8.   Some Things Aren't Always as They Seem

There was a Sufi who used to drink coffee every day in a paper cup. As usual one day, she picked a paper cup from its package to pour the coffee and it looked different than the normal paper cups. The Sufi said to herself "maybe this is a special paper cup. Maybe, it will last longer than the other ones." As soon as she poured the coffee in the cup she started screaming. The coffee was dripping from the bottom. The Sufi said to herself "good-seeming evils!"

IN PRACTICE

It is important to realize something that what may look good, nice, and beautiful can be bad and evil in its essence [7]. On the other hand, an evil-seeming incident can be good in its essence for a person. Therefore, one should not be misled with appearance as mentioned in the above story.

Discussion Question

▶   What is your experience with evil or good-seeming incidents?

9. Sufi's Promotion

There was a Sufi working in a company. She wanted to talk to her boss about a promotion. Therefore, she was seeking a good and happy time to approach her boss. One day, right before Thanksgiving, she came and asked her boss for a promotion at work. Her boss was in a happy mood because of approaching Thanksgiving. The Sufi got her promotion and said "Alhamdulillah, Thank you God."

IN PRACTICE

God is always merciful, forgiving, and appreciates the person's repentance and gratitude. There are also special times when the mercy of God is extra showering on people. In these times, the prayers, requests, and needs are especially fulfilled by God [8].

Discussion Question

▶ What is the wisdom of having special times, hours, or days in religious practices?

10. The No Wife-No Life Man and the Sufi

There was a man in the mosque who used to always come to the Sufi and complain and say "no wife, no life!" This man was not able to get married. He used to always complain about life, his brothers, and his poverty. It was the same story every day. As this man used to approach the Sufi, the Sufi used to pretend as if he was busy praying and reading the scripture. One day, there was another poor man sleeping in the mosque. This man, no wife-no life came to the Sufi again and said: "look if I had money and car, I could have helped this poor man. But I don't have anything. What can I do…" The Sufi felt bad and sad.

IN PRACTICE

It is important to sympathize with people even if it may become difficult at times. We don't know each person's real situation, only God knows. One of the prayers that Sufis constantly ask from God is that "Oh God, show us the realities of the things." In other words, evil-seeming something may be good for the person and on the other hand, something good may be bad for the person in its true reality.

Discussion Question

▶ Is it easy or difficult to sympathize with people? Why?

11. Life, Pain, and the Gain

One day, the Sufi saw an old man crying in the mosque and praying. The Sufi knew the man. The man did not have any relatives or family. He was going to have major surgery the next day. The Sufi was holding himself hard not to cry about this scene. Then, the Sufi said to himself "Allah is more merciful than me and everyone. There is a pain but inshAllah always gain if it is done with pure intention."

IN PRACTICE

Sometimes, the evil and sad-seeming incidents can break our hearts. Sometimes a memory or a bad experience can make our hearts contract. One should remember to turn every opportunity of pain, evil, or good-seeming incident as an avenue to increase one's relationship with God. Because this is the final and ultimate purposeful engagement that would pay back in this world and after death. In the above story, the old man transformed his pain into a fruitful relationship of attachment and going back to God and crying. The Prophet mentions that the power of tears genuinely flow in relationship of God. The fire of hell cannot touch these eyes in the afterlife [9].

Discussion Question

▶ Why are tears very important in practice?

12.   Meanings, Feelings, Intention, and the Sufi

One day, the Sufi did not feel good. She was thinking of the meaning and her intention in life. She was thinking about death. She was thinking about meeting the loved ones after death but she still did not feel good. She did a little bit of reflecting on herself. She said to herself "what is bothering me? Ok, I found it, my purpose, my goal in life. The things that I was not able to accomplish." Then, she said to herself "at least, I made the intention if I die."

IN PRACTICE

It is very important to have high goals, a purpose to do good in life and to please God. Doing good comes with worship, practice, and learning on the path to God. There are afterdeath narrations in the Quran and from the Prophet that the person begs to God to come back to the world one more time in life after death in order to do good or more good. But when a person dies, there is no coming back. In this perspective, the Sufi in the above story was getting these feelings of self-accountability and self-reflection. She was able to convince herself. Ultimately, God rewards the purpose of one's intention even if the person was not able to accomplish what he or she intended.

Discussion Question

▶   Why is the regular practice of self-reflection important?

13. The Disputing Sufi

One day, there was a Sufi. She had a dispute with her husband. She felt that she was right. She felt as usual uneasy and asked forgiveness from her husband. Then, she felt better and relaxed.

In practice

It is important not to have any ill feelings towards another person. The Prophet mentions that one cannot enter Heaven until one removes these feelings from one's heart[5][6]. In this perspective, the Sufi implemented this teaching and felt better.

Discussion Question

► How can carrying negative feelings for others hurt the holder of these feelings?

14. The Old Sufi's Struggle

There was an old Sufi who used to go the mosque and pray. One day, it was raining and the roads were muddy. While he was walking slowly due to the physical problems of old age, he fell down in a puddle of mud. Then, he went back to his home and changed his clothes and walked back to the mosque. Satan was watching the Sufi. While the Sufi was going back to the mosque, he fell down again in a puddle of mud. Then, he went back and changed his clothes and walked back to the mosque. Satan was still watching the Sufi. Then, the third time, he was about to fall down in again a puddle of mud. Then, Satan in the form of a human came to the man and helped him not to fall. The old Sufi thanked and said, "can I know your name?" Then, he said "I am Satan." The old man said: "Why did you help me?" He said: "The first time you fell down and went back home to change your clothes and went back again with all this difficulty. God forgave all your sins due to your sincere intention and effort. The second time you fell down and went back home to change and went back again with all this difficulty. God forgave all your families' sins due to your sincere intention and effort. As you went to your home for the last time, I was afraid that God was going to forgive everyone due to your sincere effort. Therefore, I wanted to help you to go to the mosque so that it would not happen."

IN PRACTICE

It is important to remember that the struggle is more important than the outcome for God. If one has the right intention and struggle, then the person is using the right vehicles to journey on the path.

Discussion Question

► What is the importance of intention and struggle in practice?

15. Divine Guidance of the Sufi and the Mind

There was a Sufi who had a major change in her life. She was getting the signs of this change prior to its occurrence. She was thinking what is the Divine Expectation from me? What would be the Divine Guidance? As she was thinking, she said to herself "I should still follow my mind. Because I don't know if it is really a divine guidance or a temptation from Satan."

IN PRACTICE

It is important to always use the mind as a compass. One should fulfill the reasons perfectly as if the person could be called a materialist or giving too much value to reasoning. But in its essence, the person knows that by following the means, reasons, and mind, the person respects the order and structure that God created and established. In other words, according to some Sufis, following the means and mind is another way of praying to God.

Discussion Question

▶ How should be the balance of heart and mind?

16.   The Angry Divorced Woman and the Sufi

One day, there was an angry woman that the Sufi met at work. The woman started telling her life story to the Sufi. She raised her children in the best schools. She spent all her life taking care of her children and husband. Her children left her. Her husband left her. She was angry. The Sufi felt sad. The Sufi was thinking and said to herself "the best way is to listen and not to say anything."

IN PRACTICE

Sometimes, the evil-seeming things can happen in one's life. Those are the times and opportunities for people to make self-reflection and self-accountability in the short life span of humans. Depending on the spiritual level of the person, these times can make the person either more agitated or more strong on the spiritual path. An agitated person can become angry with everything. Or, a person can use these times as spiritual opportunities. This can make the person stronger, less dependent on people, and more dependent on God, Who never leaves the person and Who is the real Friend.

Discussion Question

> ▶ How can one use their weak moments as an advantage to spiritually excel?

17. Life, Power, Evil Beings

One day, the Sufi felt uneasy. She said to herself "There are evil people and unseen evil things. Life is difficult. I don't have any power." She felt anxious, depressed, and sad. Then, she started praying. A few minutes later, she was feeling so good and powerful. She said "Alhamdullilah, there is nothing of which to be afraid."

IN PRACTICE

It is important to keep regular daily practices of prayers, litanies, and chants. The cycles of events in the day can alter the spiritual mode of the spiritual traveler. If there is no daily practice of worship and prayers referred to as wird, the person cannot be immune to the temptations, bad thoughts, and evil beings. In the above story, the Sufi engaged herself immediately with prayer as soon as she was going through the cycles of spiritual contractions and fear.

Discussion Question

▶ Why are daily practices of prayers, litanies, and dhikr critical for spiritual soundness?

18.   Sufi's Change of Life

One day, the Sufi was thinking about the sweetness of prayers, reflection, and reading the Quran in seclusion. The Sufi took so much pleasure from it. She did not want to involve or socialize herself with people. Then, she remembered the teaching of the Prophet about being with people and being patient with them and at the same time maintaining the sweet relationship with God. The Sufi said "this is so hard to do and it is so painful. I am tired of being hurt. I am tired of being around the people." Then, she forced herself to change and adapt to being with people. She was still in a sweet relationship with God.

IN PRACTICE

It is really sometimes difficult to socialize or even to see people. These spiritual seclusion moments can last for days, weeks, months, even years. At these times, one is expected to use the faculties of mind with the normative teachings of the Prophet and the scripture. As in the above story, the change for the Sufi was hard. But, she correctly engaged her mind to implement the change although her heart was still with God. This was difficult, but this is one of the ideal goals to reach in the practice of one's faith.

Discussion Question

▶   How can a person live a balanced social life without hurting others?

19. Focus, Achievements, and Time

One day, the Sufi was thinking about time. As she was getting close to death, there were still a lot of distractions in her life to achieve what she wanted to achieve before death. Then, she felt uneasy, pained, and stressed. She said to herself "what should I do?" Then, she prayed to God and asked for relief from stress, pain, and uneasy fearful feelings. Then, she said to herself "I should stick to my intention, try my best and be regular on the path until I die."

IN PRACTICE

It is important to focus in practice to achieve the spiritual goals as well as the worldly goals leading to benefit others. The essence of prayers and chants is to remove all the distractions in daily discourses and reconnect with the One and Only God. This focus gives the person empowerment. This empowerment can lead to achievements in both spiritual and worldly engagements with blessings from God.

Discussion Question

▶ How can one's unachieved goals be a source of stress? How can one remove this source of stress?

20.   Achievements, Loss, and the Sufi

One day, the Sufi was thinking. She was receiving all the worldly achievements. She said to herself "Is it something that God is happy about, or could it be a spiritual plot?"

IN PRACTICE

World achievements are not the signs of spiritual achievements. Sometimes, it can be the opposite. One's spiritual goal or purpose can be trapped in the success, recognition, fame, and power. But in reality, this can be points of loss in the spiritual journey. Therefore, it is very important to carry doubts and skepticism with the questions as the Sufi mentioned above "Is it something that God is happy about, or could it be a spiritual plot?"

Discussion Question

> ► How can one define a spiritual achievement?

21. Harvard Shuttle and the Sufi

One day, the Sufi was in Boston. She saw a shuttle. On the shuttle, there was a banner saying "Harvard loves you." The Sufi was thinking. Harvard is just a name of a university. People work there, teach, and learn. It is not a person. How can something abstract love me?

IN PRACTICE

In our daily discourses, the abstractions or embodiments can make us assume constructions of things, objects, plants, animals, and people. It is important to give the true value of everything in their proper place in reference to their purpose of creation and their relationship with God. Although the above statement can be a figurative language of embodiment, the Sufi points out an important concept that there is an assumption that is expected from the person. This assumption is to construct Harvard similar to a person who can love, feel, see, or touch which is not correct. In practice, it is important to establish the authenticity of the meanings in accordance to the definitions in scriptures and sayings of the chosen ones, the prophets or messengers. If not, the person can be living in a self-constructed imaginary or dream world but when one faces reality, the personal devastations or destructions can be unavoidable.

Discussion Question

► What makes things illusion or real?

22. Difficulty of Being a Real Human

One day, the Sufi was thinking the difficulty of being a real human. The person should not oppress, backbite, lie, always be nice, smile, be appreciative, and truthful. As he knew that it is the right thing to do but it was so difficult to practice. Then, he said to himself "Alhamdulillah, there is the teaching of Astagfirullah."

IN PRACTICE

It is important to increase one's ethical and moral levels through spirituality and practice. It is also important to realize the difficulty of perfecting these as the person is constantly changing bodily and spiritually. A strong spiritual connection is expected to increase true ethics and morality in oneself. Even in this cases, if there are black holes of mistakes and oppressive moments, it is important to ask forgiveness from people and God by genuinely chanting by Astagfirullah. The normalization of this teaching is important in practice therefore the Sufi says "Alhamdulillah."

Discussion Question

- ► How can one be a real human according to the teachings of the practice?

23. Worlds of Pens

There was a Sufi who went to the worlds of pens. There were a lot of pens used by humans for different purposes. All the pens used to die and finish their lifespan in a few months. He then found and met with a pen that was used to write the Quran. The pen was not finishing and the ink was still there, one year, two years, and so on. The Sufi said to himself: "I think the pen does not want to die because he enjoys writing the Quran."

IN PRACTICE

Similarly, one can want to live long to do good, to enjoy prayers and the Quran. Although for a person on the path, death is not ugly or evil but going back to the Beloved, God and being with role models, prophets, messengers, and saints in the afterlife is preferred.

Discussion Question

▶ How do you view dying? Do you prepare yourself mentally and emotionally for the time of death?

24. The Easiness and Difficulty of the True Relationship with One God

One day, the Sufi was thinking about the easiness and difficulty of the true relationship with one God. She said "it is very logical and easy to worship, pray, and ask from only One God. Although, it is very difficult to implement if I have fear of others or I become happy when people praise me."

IN PRACTICE

In reality, this is the true struggle until one dies in order to elevate one's status with only One and Unique Creator, God. Although it is assured in the scriptures that God is only One and Unique, the humanly encounters show that there are problems in the real application of this core notion. In other words, as suggested by the scriptures, the person is expected only to have love and respectful fear from God. Then the person should not be happy when the people praise him or her after an achievement. In reality, the person does not know if God is pleased with this person or not. Therefore, regular prayers and chants such as la ilaha illa Allah, there is nothing to be attached but except God, are key practices to establish and perfect this understanding until one dies.

Discussion Question

 ► How can one achieve the true level of detachment from everything except God?

25. Institutional Reality and Changing Identities

One day, the Sufi saw a course in the college course catalog named "institutional reality." Then, she smiled to herself and said "they are teaching how to protect yourself at work by having another identity. I don't know if it is worth it."

IN PRACTICE

It is important to live one's life to face oneself in the silent moments and in solitude. In other words, changing identities can sometimes hurt the person at the times of self-reflection. In this case, changing identities can entail being nice, just, kind, moral, and ethical to one group of people, but not being that way to another group of people and that is a problem. Practically speaking, it is as if the person is nice and kind to their colleagues and superiors at work but not nice to the people below them in rank. Or, if the person is a nice, ethical, and moral person at work but opposite at home. These changing identities can hurt and be very painful at the times of silent, and lonely moments especially when one is approaching death after retirement. All the unjust, unfair, unkind, immoral, and unethical memories can torture the person. Therefore, in this short span of life, it is always suggested to live an ethical and moral life without changing the identities at work, at home, or at any other venue or occasion. This is all about one's respect to one's true and genuine self and to God. If the true and genuine self is dead, the person can still physically be alive but changing identities may not hurt the person anymore and even can be disguised with formal trainings as the course title above alludes to "institutional reality." Ethical behavior should be embodied in the self as a virtue.

Discussion Question

▶ How can one carry a true and genuine self in all different endeavors of life?

26. Justice or Just-Us

There was a Sufi. He once had a friend who used to work at the court. He said to Sufi: one day, I was working at the court. A few lawyers were talking about a plaintiff and defendant. The plaintiff had a good lawyer but defendant was not able to afford a lawyer. The lawyers were chatting and sarcastically said to each other "this defendant does not have a lawyer. He will see if it is the justice or just-us." The Sufi smiled but was very disturbed.

IN PRACTICE

In the evil rendering of life, one can remember that there are things that we can control and there are things we cannot control. Even if one cannot do anything about an injustice or oppressive attitude or action, one should not side but have a feeling of disgust against this evil. As one can see the reaction of the Sufi to the above case that occurred.

Discussion Question

▶ How can one shun oneself from siding injustices even though the person may not have any power to affect a situation?

27. Disciplining for Different Levels

One day, the Sufi was with her son. Her son used to jump around, make noises, and disturb others. The Sufi was trying to gently and softly calm her son down. She was afraid that others would be annoyed. She said to herself, "it is very delicate to gauge people at different levels. Kids are kids. Accepting them with their child-like behavior. On the other hand, adults are often annoyed with every noise, sound and disturbance."

IN PRACTICE

It is very important to recognize everyone according to their level. If one expects something from a person of a different level, the person can possibly break one's heart and future spiritual and physical potential for growth.

Discussion Question

▶   How do we actualize understanding people with different age, gender, and ethnic identities?

28. The Patient and the Sufi

One day, the Sufi visited a friend in the hospital. Her friend had cancer and just had surgery. When the Sufi saw her in the hospital, she had deep pain and sadness. Although the Sufi can try to understand reasons beyond the situation, she still felt pain and disturbed as a human.

She then said to herself, "what can I do to remove this pain?" She decided to go to mosque and pray. She felt better with the engagement of prayers and discharge.

IN PRACTICE

In life, there are times that incidents can affect and disturb us more than others. One should always be prepared for these "hard hitting" incidents. If the person practices worship, prayers, and chants regularly, they can pay back the person when disasters happen. In the above case, the Sufi had an exit point by going to mosque, praying and being by herself and God. If the person does not know how to exit from these moments, there can be potential negative energy that can hurt the person.

Discussion Question

▶ How can one develop a spiritual mechanism to cope with evil and good seeming incidents?

29. Harshness, Teaching, and the Sufi

One day, the Sufi invited a friend to his home. Her friend was a nice fellow but she believed in discipline and a little bit harshness in the upbringing of kids. The Sufi's kids knew the friend. As soon as she came, all the kids were scared and behaving well. The Sufi was thinking "which one is better? A display of softness but sometimes the outcome of bad treatment by the kids, or, discipline with a little bit of harshness but no outcome of bad treatment from the kids?"

IN PRACTICE

The ideal is to treat everyone especially the kids with kind, gentle, and loving attitude. The Prophet as the role model was the peak in this trait. The women, children, and everyone were very comfortable around the Prophet. On the other hand, there are some teachers in the practice that they believe that the notion of discipline or adab should also entail some fear to stop the bad behavior so that there is respect. During our times of changing values, the latter approach with discipline is getting more criticism by Westerners. But one should review this notion of teaching with discipline especially in Eastern cultures and even in religions such as Buddhism. The discipline and respect has been implemented differently historically than in our times.

Discussion Question

► How do you understand the Eastern and Western cultures in child & parent and student & teacher relationships?

30. Changing Personalities

One day, the Sufi was working on her project. She was happy that she could focus, think, and generate new approaches to accomplish her daily work. As soon as she finished her work, she now needed to make a few phone calls and send a few e-mails. She felt that she needs to be in nice, kind, and in caring mode. Then, it was almost three in the afternoon. She was trying to change her mental and spiritual mode to be lovely and smiley for her husband and kids. Then, it was the prayer and chanting time. She started praying. She was thinking of all these modes of changing personalities and their difficulties. Then, she said to herself: "it is possible but not easy, Alhamdulillah."

IN PRACTICE

It is important to be fully in the space and time. Due to changing venues, sometimes one can have spiritual and social accidents. In these accidents, people can find the person rude, harsh, and not caring. It is important to accept the difficulty of changing personalities while changing venues and time. One of the ways to make it easy is to establish constant prayers and chants during the day. This can help person to focus, self-reflect, detach, and discharge spiritual toxicity.

Discussion Question

  ▶   Can a person only assume one personality? Why?

31. Internal World, External World, and the Difficulties of Interaction

One day, the Sufi was thinking of the beauties of the internal world: silence, reflection, thinking, and solitude. She was taking so much pleasure. Then, she started thinking of the ugliness of the external world: talking, marketing, socializing, and pretending. She became so disgusted. She said to herself: "how do I make the transition from one to another? It is always so difficult and painful."

IN PRACTICE

This is the real struggle. Being with people and being patient with their external affairs but at the same time truly being with God through prayers, reading, chanting, reflection, and thinking. Two worlds can be most of the time different and opposing each other. Therefore, the person in practice lives in the moment for the sake of the future. In other words, the person can be with people for the sake of God that when the person meets God after death, he or she can sincerely state that this person was being in the world for God's pleasure. The pain is over and the person is now with God. God can reward this person for his or her sincere effort in the world.

Discussion Question

▶ How can one solace oneself about the unknowns of future by making an intention of living their life in order to please God?

32. Cancer, Funeral, and the Sufi

There was a person who used to smoke. The Sufi knew him. He got sick and had lung cancer. The doctors told the family that he would die soon because he had a high stage cancer. The Sufi visited the person, made some prayers, and tried to show sympathy to the family. When the Sufi went home, he mentioned about his visit to his kids and discussed the shortness of life, the importance of time, and the weakness of humans. A few days later, the Sufi got the sad news that the man died. The Sufi's kids happened to know about the sad news as well. Everyone was affected.

In practice

Death is reality. Preparing oneself before death is a mindful discourse that people are expected to take. Here, although it is important, it is not physical means of preparation such as will, funeral arrangements, or letters to the loved ones but the real preparation of meeting with God. Sometimes, God gives tribulations, sicknesses, or difficulties as the final performance of the life journey to elevate the person's status before meeting with God. Although people may cry in evil-seeming incidents, it is like a wedding day, as Rumi says, "for the ones who are longing and preparing to meet with God."

Discussion Question

▶   How can a person make preparations for their death?

33. The Clear and the Mystical Teachings

One day, the Sufi was thinking about starting a venture. She got all the signs that she should start immediately. Then, she realized that it was a Tuesday not Wednesday. Then, she was thinking if she should follow the mystical signs which tell one to start the venture on Tuesday. Or, if she should follow the clear signs and should start on Wednesday. She said: "if there are clear ones, those are preferred over the mystical ones." Then, she decided to start her new venture on Wednesday.

In practice

When heart and mind contradicts it is important to follow the mind. In other words, if there are clear teachings and guidelines of the religion through scripture and the practice of the Prophet, then the person is expected to follow the clear ones over the mystical ones. If there are no clear ones, or there is a room for interpretation due to lack of clear ones, then the mystical signs can play an important role. In the above story, there is an understanding in the tradition that the Prophet used to start new things on Wednesdays [10]. Therefore, the Sufi took that route instead of her personal signs.

Discussion Question

▶ How do you understand the concept of contraction between heart and mind?

34. Little Minds Thinking Big

One day, the Sufi went with her four-year-old to a science museum. There were skeletons of dinosaurs and other fossils. Her four-year-old son was amazed and asked questions constantly. The Sufi was surprised about the quality of the questions from a four-year-old. She said to herself: Wow, a person can start the journey even if they are only four years old. The important part is how to gauge and help them.

IN PRACTICE

It is important realize to that sometimes little minds can really think big. In this process of imagination, if they are not engaged correctly, after years of childhood and adulthood, these memories and conversations can come back to the person. These memories can be sometimes fake, illusion, or it can be something positive in one's relationship with God. In other words, the personal religious experience can start from early childhood years with understanding the nature, art, and sounds. On the other hand, there are some Sufi scholars who try to limit the kids' exposure to visual and audio related items such as pictures or music. Their reasoning is that a child may not know how to transform those meanings from these visual and audio sources into meanings. Therefore, these sources can become isolating in their construction of a positive relationship with the Divine.

Discussion Question

▶   How do you relate your childhood religious experience to your current religious practice?

35. Anger, Difficulty, and the Sufi

A month passed. The Sufi was so nice to her kids. She has not been angry. One day, the kids as usual did something annoying and not respectful to their mom. She burst out with anger to them. Then, after a while she calmed down. She said to herself: "I was doing fine for some time and didn't get angry but controlled my anger. What happened to me? I lost myself again." She went back to her kids and discussed the reason why she got angry, gave advice to them, and asked also forgiveness from them.

IN PRACTICE

It is good to give advice. How to give the advice can be more important than the content of the advice. In other words, it is very challenging to give advice without being angry but genuinely relating the message in a way that others don't get offended. This communication and attitude can become more challenging with the people that we see every day at work or at home. It is also important to regret how we talk or feel about others. Therefore, it is a virtue to say one is sorry and ask forgiveness from the people if there is any possibility of breaking their hearts.

Discussion Question

▶   Do you practice self-reflection often?

36. Spiritual Hunting with Distractions

One day, the Sufi was working on spiritual hunting and search. In other words, she was trying to engage with prayers, chants, and reading the scriptures, the Quran, and the hadith. She was trying to reflect, understand the meanings, draw and contemporize these meanings. She used to call this spiritual hunting. She forgot to turn off her cell phone. While in her deep meditation, she heard text messages coming constantly from her phone, she said to herself "if I look at the screen, I will lose all the mode and stage that I build up." Then, she ignored them. Yet, she wondered whether it was something of an emergency. Then, after she was done she checked her phone. It was not something important, she said "Alhamdulillah, thanks to God."

In practice

It is important to engage fully and focus in spiritual discharge and charge moments. One should really know how to disconnect from one's surroundings. Most of the spiritual advancements come, appear, and are given by God in those moments of focus. These times may not be long. But it takes warm-up, peak, and cooldown periods in these spiritual engagements. It is very similar to physical exercise. In the above story, although the Sufi had responsibility towards others, she still continued in her engagement. She was still disturbed in case it was something of an emergency.

Discussion Question

▶ How do you interpret the phrase of "spiritual hunting"?

37.   Life, Desires, Pleasures, and Death

One day, the Sufi was thinking of life and her desires. She wanted to take pleasure by following her desires such as eating or having fun. Each time she attempted something she remembered death and she was not able to take much pleasure. Then, she said to herself "what should I do?" She was contemplating this for a while. She stood up and she prayed. She was feeling better. Then, she started eating a nice meal while her mind and heart engaged with God, and an internal chant. She said to herself: "Wow, I still take pleasure from the meal. Maybe this is the secret."

IN PRACTICE

One can transform worldly pleasure into infinite pleasure by relating them with God. In other words, if someone wants to enjoy something for the sake of its pleasure then when this thing finishes it may be a source of pain for this person. But, if one knows how to connect immediate pleasures of world to spiritual enjoyments through prepositions such as "with, to, or from" God, then the person can fully take taste from them. In other words, when a person appreciates all the pleasures in the world in their relation with God, the person knows that due to this appreciation, God will give more in the world and after death. So, the pleasure does not become bitter with the thoughts of its ending and with the thoughts of death as in the above story.

Discussion Question

▶   Do the thoughts about death make your enjoyment in life bitter? Why?

38. Nights and Sleep

One day, the Sufi was thinking about his sleep. He said to himself: "I am sleeping so much at night, 11 p.m.–6:30 a.m. It is a waste of time although I get up to work in the early morning fresh, perform and enjoy my work. He said to himself "what should I do? every day, I have the same problem, too much sleep!"

IN PRACTICE

Sleeping is good as long as it is done in balance and moderate way. Similar to eating, a person can make an intention to sleep so that he or she can be fresh to worship God and to increase closeness to God. On the other hand, there is an encouragement to use a portion of the night in prayers and worship because nights are special in one's relationship with God. Most of the people on the path try to implement the Prophetic suggestion of waking up in the last third portion of the night, a few hours before sunrise and engaging oneself in sincere, genuine, and solitary worship of the Divine.

39. People, Disappointments, and Dilemma

Each time the Sufi socialized with people, she would regret it. She used to blame herself: "I don't know why I came here. I told myself, staying by myself, worshipping, chanting, and reading the scripture is much better than being under the siege of the looks of people in social gatherings." The Sufi was again in disappointment. She was also in dilemma between solitude and service to others by socializing.

IN PRACTICE

Solitude can be enjoyable with worship, chanting, and reading the scriptures, increasing one's mindful and spiritual knowledge and experience. When the person socializes, a spiritually active Sufi should constantly be monitoring one's inner feelings and thoughts as they may increase when being with others. In other words, an exercising person can have a fast blood flow. If the exercise is not done according to the suggested ways of fitness trainers, then the person can have a heart attack and die. Similarly, when a person is with others if the feelings and thoughts are gushing to the person such as arrogance, thinking bad about others, vanity, jealousy, etc., they should be immediately caught and removed with "astagfirullah" according to the suggested ways of spiritual trainers.

40. Cats, Dogs, and the Sufi

There was a Sufi who went to visit her friend in Turkey. As she was wandering around the streets in Istanbul she was astonished about the wandering cats and dogs on the streets without leashes or owners. She then asked her friend: "Can these dogs be harmful without any leashes or without owners?" Her Sufi friend said: "they are just living with us. They are part of our life."

IN PRACTICE

There are a lot of Sufi stories about dogs and cats. The barking dogs at the times of call to prayer in Muslim countries is a very observable incident. The classical interpretation is that dogs can see the satans running therefore they bark. There are a lot of cat stories visiting the mosques. The Prophet gave a nickname to one of his close friends the title of "father of cats", "Abu Huraira." Abu Huraira loved the cats and spent a lot of time with them. Abu Huraira also spent most of his time with the Prophet learning from him. Therefore, many of the narrations and practices[3] about the life of the Prophet had been recorded and transmitted by Abu Huraira.

---

3. Hadith.

41. Fame, God's Pleasure ,and the Sufi

One day, the Sufi was thinking about the fame, recognition by people publicly, and recognition by God secretly. She looked into her heart and ego. She found that her ego wants people's applause and recognition. At the same time, she felt that her heart wanted recognition and pleasure of God. Then, the Sufi said to herself: "but they don't go together, either one or the other?" She was thinking this dilemma within herself but couldn't solve it.

In practice

Fame can be a poison in the genuine spiritual path of establishing a sincere relationship with God. If God is pleased and happy with this person, the person can be famous. Still, this fame can take the person away from God if the person does not know why he or she is doing what she is doing. On the other hand, there are a lot of secret saints that only God knows and loves. In this case, the person can be a little safer than the poisonous strikes of fame and people. In this regard, the person on the path should dislike being praised by people.

42.   Trials, Position of the Heart, and Detachment

One day, the Sufi was thinking the wisdom behind trials, hardships, and difficulties. Then, she met a friend who was living a very rich and nice life but not attached to her possessions. Later, she met another friend who was poor, sick, and always fearful of becoming even poorer and losing what she had. Then, the Sufi looked at the two cases and said to herself: "I found it. It is detachment from what you have."

IN PRACTICE

A person can be rich or poor, having an easy life or difficult life. It is not important. The important part is the position of the heart if changing as a sign of attachment to them. If a person's heart is the same in the happiest times of his or her life and the same in the most difficult times of his or her life, then this person is detached from everything except the fulfilment of the choice of God. This state is called zuhd. If it becomes a constant trait of a person then it becomes a spiritual station. Then, this is the real joy, happiness, and heaven for the person in the world.

43.   Heaven 1, Heaven 2, and the Sufi

The Sufi was enjoying life with detachment and was always pleased with God. She was always thankful and grateful to God. She was so happy in all times of difficulty or joy. Then, she said to herself, "I am already having my first Heaven in the world. After death, I hope I will be in the second Heaven."

IN PRACTICE

There is the state and station of gratitude.[i] When the person reaches this level, everything becomes equal, the sadness and happiness. The state can be temporary. The state can be permanent in Sufi terminologies. Then, it is called station.

44. Cat Hanging around with Humans and the Sufi

There was a cat who used to hang around with humans. She did not like to hang around other cats because she found them very annoying. This cat always saw humans perfect and wished that she was a human like them. When a person entered the house she used to come next to them and hug them. The Sufi understood this situation and told the cat "It is not as you think."

In practice

One of the sicknesses of the heart is that we don't like to be who we are, but we want to be like others. God gave us so much. Thanking and appreciating increases the bounty. In the Quran,[ii] it is mentioned that if the person thanks and is appreciative for all the bounties, then God will increase them more. In the above story, the Sufi felt that his cat was in the same position. He tried to tell her that the humans are not all perfect with their evils and their diseases of the heart.

45. Quotidian Refreshing Rituals, Exceptions, and the Sufi

One day, the Sufi was going to travel. She thought about missing her daily regular, quotidian prayers, chants, and meditation with God. This routine practice of rituals was so critical to the Sufi. She was really concerned about this. Then, she started her travel. While in the plane, in the airport, and on the train, she was successful to find a corner to establish her virtual spiritual space to continue her regular spiritual habits. She completed it and said "Alhamdulillah, thank you God, You gave me the ability even while traveling to be attached to You."

In practice

The daily regular prayers, chants, and meditations are very critical. This is called Wird or Awrad in practice. There is a saying that "if there is no wird there is no spiritual refreshment and spiritual discoveries."[iii] In this perspective, a person's day has a meaning with its discoveries and spiritual searches. If there is a day without this, this day can be considered as wasted.

46. Patience, Difficulty, and the Sufi

One day, the Sufi was traveling with her family. It was a long trip to another country. The trip was so tiring. The kids were crying. It was so difficult to go to the bathroom. The husband was complaining and saying "I am not going to travel again. It is so difficult." The Sufi took a deep breath and continued chanting and praying to God for easiness.

IN PRACTICE

Traveling can be a piece of torture from hell as mentioned by the Prophet.[6]iv Patience can be defined as not acting with negative motions in times of difficulty. One of the ways to implement patience is engaging oneself with prayer and chanting as mentioned in the Quran. Complaining does not help but can make the person more miserable.

47. Heart Diseases, Detection, and the Sufi

One day, the Sufi was praying in a park. Her kids were playing. There was another family and a small girl. The Sufi gave one candy to all her children. Her kids came and asked her for seconds, she said "no." Then, a small girl came to the Sufi and asked for a candy. The Sufi gave her a candy. Then, after the girl finished her candy, she came and asked for another one. The Sufi was thinking "what should I say? I have a few more candies left. They are expensive". The Sufi told the small girl to wait. The Sufi was looking in her bag to see if she can give something else to the small girl. Realizing this the small girl's mother came and got very angry at the small girl. The Sufi felt horrible and said "my stinginess!"

IN PRACTICE

Like the above story, the Sufi immediately tried to detect her spiritual disease in the incident instead of blaming the mother. In spiritual endeavors, it is a level to know one's own spiritual disease. Then, one can work on his or her disease. Stinginess is a disease that sometimes may be hard to detect. Stinginess is a sign of attachment which can be the opposite of the positive spiritual state of detachment.[v] Every positive spiritual state can be the opposite of a spiritual disease.

Discussion Question

▶ Is it difficult to detect one's own spiritual diseases? Why?

48. Easiness in Practice, and the Effect of the Place

One day, the Sufi went to very high spiritual place, the holy sites.[vi] Everyone was praying. He found praying and all spiritual engagements very easy compared to other places. Then, he said to himself "Wow, it should be the effect of the place!"

IN PRACTICE

The positive spiritual places filled with angelic beings and other spiritual creations of God that can make the invisible medium very easy to engage with prayers and to be happy. Holy sites are the utmost experiential places for millions of people praying together 24 hours a day for hundreds of years. The build-up of positive angelic and spiritual beings can make this place unique and very easy to practice. On the other hand, the places of evil and bad engagements can make the person engage oneself with ill thoughts, depression, even committing an evil action.

49. The Children as Blessing but Not as a Trial

One day, the Sufi woke up and heard the kids screaming. She said to herself "again the same, dealing with their screaming and giving me hard time before they go to school." Then, she remembered the teachings about children in the Quran and from the Prophet that the children can be both trial or blessing. Then, she said to herself "I hope they become blessing for me and not a trial."

IN PRACTICE

It is important to know that every engagement, affiliation, or accumulation can be a blessing or trial. Wealth, children, position, beauty or health, or even spiritual engagements can be blessings or trials or tests. Therefore, it is always important to ask God to transform all evil and good seeming engagements, affiliations, and accumulations as a true blessing in this life and afterlife.

50. The Physicist Sufi, Superconductors at Zero, and the Self

There was a Sufi who was thinking about the law of superconductors at absolute zero. There is no friction at this temperature. He said that when the person is at absolute zero, humble, and then, one can go beyond one's friction of the ego and self.[4] Then, there is the superconducting and happy person in this world and afterlife. There is no friction of the nafs.[5]

IN PRACTICE

There are different levels of self. The initial self is called raw self.[vii] The person with this type of self can always run behind his or her desires. In other words, the desires of this self can control the person by giving orders. As the person goes to different spiritual trainings, the person can start not listening to the orders of the self. The person can act with the guidelines of the mind, heart, the Scripture and the Prophet. In this journey, there is one of the higher stages of the self. At this stage, the person gets full spiritual freedom[viii] from the imprisonment of the evil self. In the above story, this could be equivalent to the superconducting case in spiritual physics.

---

4. Nafs.
5. Raw Self or ego acting towards evil with spiritual sickness.

51. The Sufi with Bald Head and Long Hair

There was a Sufi who was thinking about the effect of spirituality with long hair and shaved hair. He said to himself: In both cases there are super different effects. Long hair increases softness and spiritual inspirations. Shaved hair increases justice and mindfulness. A Sufi can live in-between both worlds.

IN PRACTICE

The person should have a balanced state of mind and heart. The Prophet used to have sometimes long hair and sometimes shaved hair. The Quran mentions after the pilgrimage shaving hair and shortening it can give security to the person and remove one's fears. On the other hand, the Prophet and many companions had long hair.[5] The Prophet narrated also about the curly hair of Jesus.[6] [5]

52. The Sufi and the Kufi

The Sufi had long hair. He put on the Kufi, the head cover, on his head. Each time he put on the Kufi it was slipping and falling so easily. The Sufi was tired of this. Then, he decided to shave his hair and put on the Kufi. He shaved his hair. Now, when he put on the Kufi it was stuck to his head so hard. When the Sufi wanted to take off the Kufi, it did not want to come off easily because the sharp shaved hair held the Kufi tight. The Sufi became tired of this as well.

IN PRACTICE

It is important to balance heart and mind. According to some mystics, long hair represents spirituality,[11] the heart and the full detachment. On the other hand, the bald or shaved head can represent the realms of the mind, reasons and following causality. An ideal person is expected to have both states in practice. The Prophet used to have both long hair and shaved head.[6] [5] [9] [12]

53.   The Life, the Kids, and the Trials

One day, the Sufi had a disagreement with her daughter. Her daughter was in her teenage years and acting as if she knew everything. The daughter did not want to socialize with her parents in public. The Sufi mom was getting super annoyed with her daughter's attitude. She said to herself, "what should I do? I should act rational but I can't stand it." She went and prayed in solitude for guidance.

In practice

It is important to realize expected problems with age, culture, gender, and kinship relationships. The Sufis try to act with wisdom to minimize times of anger that one can say "I wish I didn't do this." Although it is very difficult to maintain peace of mind in the issues and attitudes of children but it is still expected to act with wisdom, patience, and counsel.

54. Optimizing the Time before Death

One day, the Sufi thought the cycles of sleep, chats, eating, and engagements that do not have immediate spiritual production. Then, she said to herself, "how can I optimize my time?" She then followed less sleep, silence/purposeful talk, and less food. She felt good. She said "this should be the key."

IN PRACTICE

Three rules of less or minimum are applied for sleeping, eating and talking. A person who is successful in three minimums can go steadily upward in the journey.[13]

55. Departure, Crying, and the Sufi

One day, there was a Sufi who did not want to visit the holy sites. His other friends used to visit the holy sites every year but he did not. When he was asked the reason he said, "I don't want to cry when I am departing from the holy sites."

IN PRACTICE

Even spiritual attachments can cause pain. This pain can be the powerful and the positive. The pain of seeing the Loved One and missing God is a very noble and high level of pain. God appreciates this suffering in high magnitudes that humans cannot count.

56. Poverty, Happiness, and Connection

One day, the Sufi visited a poor town in Cairo. She found that everyone was happy although they were poor. She went to their mosque. She found that everyone was praying, chatting, and smiling. She said to herself, "that should be the reason."

IN PRACTICE

The religion is the key to establish happiness in one's life. External welfare does not bring permanent tranquility in the heart although the person can have immediate and temporary effects. People's genuine religious prayers can make the person have a heavenly life in the world while others may be feeling bad about them due to lack of their social and economic conditions.

57. The Sufi Having Egyptian Coffee

One day, the Sufi was in a coffee shop in Cairo. The Sufi enjoyed different types of coffee in Egypt. While he was drinking coffee he was chatting with the store owner. The owner mentioned that the Elite Egyptians prefer Starbucks over local coffee. The Sufi said "I don't know why people always want what they don't have."

IN PRACTICE

The positive attitude of what one has, is the first step of gratitude and thankfulness to God. In this sense, positive local or hometown support for the ownership of a business market can be similar to someone having what one has in the spiritual journey with the attitude of gratefulness and thankfulness.

58. Thirsty Child and the Sufi

One day, the Sufi was traveling with her child in the car. Her child got thirsty. Then, he asked to his mom, "can I have some water?" His mom said, "Ok, when we stop at a gas station, then we will get a bottle for you." The kid was very thirsty. He kept asking every other minute. His mom kept saying, "Ok, I will get it soon." The kid said, "sorry, I forgot that I asked before." A minute later the kid came with the same question. The mom said to herself, "I should stop immediately or he will keep asking."

IN PRACTICE

When a person is thirsty, the need for finding water becomes so urgent for him or her. This urge can make the person want to get water as soon as possible. Similarly, if the person does not need to have a spiritual path, he or she cannot benefit from great teachers or from great experiential sessions of meditation, prayers, and retreats.

59. Checking the Heart

One day, the Sufi visited a poor city in Cairo. The Sufi was staying in a nice, expensive hotel. She went outside to take a walk. There were a lot of beggars coming and asking money from the Sufi. The Sufi tried to keep always some money for the poor in her pocket. As she was giving the money to one beggar, other beggars came and asked for more money from the Sufi. The Sufi said her money was finished. The beggar insisted. The Sufi felt uncomfortable. The Sufi for a minute made self-reflection on her heart to check if there were any judgment feelings towards the beggar. She said "Alhamdulillah but it was not easy."

IN PRACTICE

It is important to check one's heart constantly. Any type of arrogance, judgement of others, feelings of superiority, disgust, or ridicule are some examples of dangerous cases for the heart. In the above case, the Sufi tried to help people without judgment but with empathy of their situations. In the case of one beggar insisting about more money, she tried to neutralize her heart not to have any type of bad feelings towards the beggar. The real state of the heart can be with detachment of worldly endeavors although the Sufi stayed in an expensive hotel. It is not the physical or external detachment but detachment of the heart from everything except God.

Discussion Question

► How one can make the habit of checking their hearts? Is this difficult?

60.   Funeral, Crying, and the Sufi

One day, the Sufi came to his home. He heard his wife crying in the room and talking on the phone. As soon as the Sufi overheard the word "funeral," he understood what was going on. Without going to the room next to his wife, the Sufi sat and engaged himself with his regular daily routine of meditation and prayer. Then, his wife came from the room and told the news about their loss. The Sufi said: "We belong to God and will return back to God."

IN PRACTICE

It is important to have a daily routine of meditation, prayer, and reflection time. This becomes more critical when someone is hit with an evil-seeming incident. At these times, this routine practice of the person makes the person collect oneself spiritually and keep the spiritual composure and calmness. In the above story, instead of rushing to his wife about the loss, the Sufi first rushed to God for self-spiritual strength to help others. After empowered with his daily routine practice of meditation, prayer, and reflection, he then helped his wife.

61.   The Best Place in Town: Graveyard

One day the Sufi went to a town in Cairo to visit a family member. The town was so overcrowded with people, buildings, and cars. The streets were not clean. Cars were beeping relentlessly. After a few days, the Sufi got the bad news that a family member died. Then, he attended the funeral and went to the graveyard for the burial. The graveyard was so nice. There were olive trees. The Sufi felt very peaceful and calm there. Then, he said to himself, "this is the best place in this town."

IN PRACTICE

The graveyards are residences of people who can hear others but cannot talk. The calmness of the graveyard can be due to the high spiritual level of the deceased with God. It is recommended to visit the grave of the Prophet in Madina. The visitors anonymously report the utmost calmness of the atmosphere around the grave of the Prophet. Oppositely, if there is a grave of an evil person it is suggested not to stay around it but pass it as soon as possible. It is recommended to plant trees in the graves. As the trees are living beings they pray, chant, and glorify God. When the deceased person in the grave hears the chants, prayers, and glorifications for God, he or she feels better.[14][15] Therefore, it is also suggested to read the scripture and prayers when one visits a grave.

62. Heart, Changes, and Level

One day, the Sufi visited her hometown. She saw her family and friends. She visited the places that she used to hang around. All the memories were so nice. The time for departure came. The Sufi felt some uneasiness in her heart. Then, she said to herself, "my low level." Then, she engaged herself with prayer, reading the scripture and chants until uneasiness in her heart was gone. She said "Alhamdulillah."

IN PRACTICE

It is important not to attach anything to one's heart. This is the ideal level. If there are some traces of attachment such as feelings of uneasiness or sadness as in the above story, one can engage oneself with prayers, the Quran, and chants until those feelings are removed. In practice, a true happy life is only attained by full detachment and discharge of the heart from everything except God.

63. Nights and Purpose

One day, the Sufi woke up in the middle of the night to pray to God. Everyone in the house was sleeping except the Sufi. She started praying in solitude. She thought about her past life, where and with whom she spent time. She thought about the remaining portion of her life, how and where she should spend her efforts. She then renewed her intention and purpose and said, "I started this journey to please God and I should end it in the same manner."

IN PRACTICE

It is important to finish the journey with the same good and high intention that the person started in the beginning. There are a lot of people who start with the good intention but lose it in the remaining portion of their lives. Constant self-reflection to diagnose one's intention, position, and purpose is very critical along the journey. Nights are very paramount for this purpose. When the person wakes up after sleep, being fresh and while everyone is still sleeping, the person can pray, cry, and do self-reflection. The Prophet always performed night prayers when everyone was sleeping.[6] ix Therefore, a lot of friends of God excel in the spiritual journeys at night.

Discussion Question

▶   Why is it important to check the intentions before the actions?

64. Chats Leading to Disturbance

One day, the Sufi was chatting with his mother. As the Sufi did not like to talk too much so as not to make mistakes and displease God, he said to himself, "this is my old mother, let me chat a little bit to entertain her." The Sufi started chatting with a normal chat similar to others. Talking about weather, food, kids, and people. The Sufi became a little bit uneasy while the topic was about people. He was trying to not backbite or talk bad about others. As the conversation continued, the Sufi said something about a person that disturbed him so much and he said to himself, "I wish I did not talk and as usual observe silence instead."

IN PRACTICE

Silence, smiling, and greeting people are some of the encouraged ways by the Prophet.[5][6] It is expected that if a person talks then they should have a reason. Any talk or conversation without purpose can lead to uneasy states of heart due to sins such as backbiting of others, showing signs of arrogance, etc. It is very difficult to balance the two modes of social life compared to introvert life with oneself. The Prophet showed a good model of this balance. He used to always smile and greet people. Everyone was very comfortable around him. On the other hand, when he talked it had a purpose. His speech was very concise, to the point, and at the same time, dense in various meanings. There are a lot of narrations that people could have counted the number of words that he used while he was talking[6].

65. Balance between Solitude and Social Life

One day, a Sufi felt very lonely in her spiritual journey. She normally much enjoyed solitude but also the responsibility of teaching others and learning from others. She then felt uneasy. She said to herself, "what should I do?" Having students always brings arrogance. Learning from others in social gatherings always brings the possibility of spiritual messiness. Then, she said "I need to do it if that is what the Prophet did and suggested."

IN PRACTICE

There are some who don't care to have students but only their sweet relation with God. Although these people exist it may be rare and not be the case for all. The general rule is that it is important to give back in terms of teaching and other means of service to our fellow humans. As the Sufi mentioned, teaching sometimes can bring unwanted guests of arrogance and reputation due to the followers or students. Nevertheless, the person is expected to perform self-accountability to get rid of these diseases. Because all the good is from God and all the evil looking incidents come due to humans' acquirements. On the other hand, the Sufi mentioned about the problem of spiritual messiness in social, good encounters of learning. This is in comparison of the times of focus to the times of solitude. One should craft his or her abilities to balance and to transform oneself from times of spiritual messiness to spiritual focus. Although this may not be easy, it is the essence of lifelong spiritual struggle.

Discussion Question

▶   How can one make a balance between social life and solitude?

66. Life, Responsibilities, and Balance

One day, the Sufi thought about all the responsibilities towards her children, family, friends, and other humans. Then, she said to herself I need to keep and maintain these responsibilities to please God. The balance is very difficult without breaking hearts and fulfilling these responsibilities.

IN PRACTICE

Transition between worldly and spiritual affairs can be difficult. There is a level that a person can live among people of the worldly affairs but his or her mind, heart, and spiritual can be with God. This is the ideal goal to achieve. Prophets are examples of this model. Even in the various passages of the Quran, the people who challenge the prophets present this argument that, how can a person eat and drink like us and claim that this person is a messenger from God. This person represents all the spiritual affairs as a role model. In the Divine wisdom, God sends us these messengers and prophets as role models to show difficult level of being with God while among people. This is the goal to achieve and it is possible.

67. Darkness and Belief

One day, the Sufi felt uneasy about his life. As soon as he engaged himself with prayers, reading the Quran and chants, he felt good. As soon as he stopped this engagement, he felt much in spiritual darkness and distress again. He said to himself, "what is the solution?" Then, he said to himself, "the challenge is being with God while among people in worldly affairs."

IN PRACTICE

A person who is engaged with the remembrance of God in any form such as prayers, reading the scripture, litanies, and divine chants, can refresh their heart with ease and tranquility. This fact is stated in the Quran as "Only remembrance of God calms the hearts."[x] It is sometimes difficult to embody the times of calmness and tranquility with the changing states of the heart in distress and contraction. It is suggested that the person immediately go back to their regular rituals such as prayers, readings, litanies, and chants at these times of darkness and distress.

68.   Out of Trouble Man and Marriage in Heaven

There was a poor wise-fool that the Sufi used to know. Each time the Sufi met this man he said "Alhamdulillah, thank God, I am out of trouble." The Sufi used to call him "out of trouble man." One day, the Sufi attended a funeral. He saw the out of trouble man at the funeral and gave him a ride after the funeral. While they were chatting in the car, the Sufi asked him: "are you married?," he said "no, I am not now, but inshAllah, I will be in Heaven. I am looking forward to it." The Sufi said: "what a level!"

In practice

It is suggested to get married. There are always exceptions to general rules. There are people who may not be married due to dedicating one's life for learning, praying, and teaching. They may feel that if they get married they may not fulfill the rights of a spouse. As in the above story, there are a lot of wise ones who may have a high spiritual level with God and they may disguise their identity by acting foolish sometimes. They are called wise-fools. The wise-fool in the above story did not get married in his life and perhaps dedicated his life to worship and solitude with an intention of getting married after death in Heaven.

69. Anger, Ugliness, and the Mirror

One day, the Sufi got angry with his kids. He used to immediately rush to the mirror to look at his face. Again, he went and looked at his face. It looked so ugly. He then kept looking until he calmed down. He said: "a'uzubillahi min ashaytani rajim." He felt better. His anger was gone.

IN PRACTICE

One of the bad spiritual states is not purposeful and egoistic anger. There are times anger can be praiseworthy but it is rare and not the dominant norm. When the person is angry, the person ruins all his or her spiritual states. In the above story, the Sufi looked at his face to see the ugliness so that he could use it as a means of calming down. As anger is considered from Satan, in these bad states, one can reflect these ugly and satanic expressions in one's face. One of the Prophetic suggestions against anger is the talismanic expression of "a'uzubillahi min ashaytani rajim" in order to avoid the temptations of Satan.

70. God, Humans, and Measure Stick

One day, the Sufi got angry with his kids. They did not listen to him although he had been advising them constantly. He got angry because he remembered when they were babies. He used to change their diapers, carry them on his shoulder, and feed them. Now, his children do not appreciate their father. Then, he said to himself, "God does not have any children. We are all creation from nothing. The Creator over creation has more rights than parents over children. I now understand how God is so Patient, Forgiving, and Forbearing compared to us, lowly humans as parents."

IN PRACTICE

It is important to remember that God creates everything for a reason, purpose, and with wisdom. The kinship relationship between children and parents can be an example of a measuring stick for one's relationship with God. God requires in the Quran and in the scriptures to appreciate, to be kind, and gentle to one's parents. When one develops the notion of thanking and appreciation with people especially with the ones to whom the person is much in debt then, a person naturally develops an appreciative relationship with God. The Prophet mentions that a person who does not thank people for their favors would not thank God[12].

71.   Different Names of God and Daily Affairs

One day, the Sufi was traveling with her son. They were in the plane. The plane was taking off. Her son said, "mom, I need to potty, I can't hold myself." All the seatbelt signs were on and no one was allowed to get up. The Sufi said to her son, "repeat the Name of God, Al-Qabid." The kid starting saying it. After a few minutes, the boy said, "I don't need potty anymore." The mom said, "Alhamdulillah."

IN PRACTICE

There are different names and attributes of God. One can approximate one's correct understanding about God by studying these Divine Names. Therefore, there is an encouragement to memorize and to chant those names constantly in different encounters of life as in the above story. The Sufi knew one of the Names of God is Al-Qabid, the Contractor or the Holder. In this helpless situation, she told her son to chant this Name. Then, the boy's urge was held back by reciting this Name of God. A person can have prescriptions of different Names of God in different situations similar to a prescriptive medicine with the correct number of repetitions.

72. Hugging, Anger, and Child

One day, the Sufi father got angry with his kids. The youngest went to him and started hugging and kissing his dad. He then started kissing and hugging him too. The Sufi then said to himself, "I was angry but I am not anymore. What happened to me?"

IN PRACTICE

It is important to be insistent and demanding in asking forgiveness from God. The Prophet mentions that when a person prays and asks forgiveness from God he or she should be firm and insistent.[1]xi God can do anything. There is no human association of anger for God in practice. Anger is something negative and a defect in human discourses. Instead, one can use the word God's displeasure.

73.   Controlling the Heart and Thoughts

One day, the Sufi met a person who was mean to others about their faults and was not respectful in religious matters. After a year, one day, the Sufi was invited to a social gathering. The Sufi was not sure if he should go or not. He did not have a clear intention for why to participate in the gathering. Then, he decided to attend and happened to meet the same mean and disrespectful person in this social gathering. The person was paralyzed. The Sufi felt bad for him and tried to stop his thoughts and disposition of his heart about the possible reasons for this person's difficulty.

IN PRACTICE

It is really important to make intention as to why to do something or not. Mere intention of having fun or no intention can put the person in jeopardy with one's relationship with God in case something happens. In the above story, when the Sufi attended the gathering and saw the person who used to be mean and disrespectful, his immediate and uncontrolled urge was to relate what happened to him with his prior improper disposition with people and religion. Now, the Sufi put himself in a difficult self-control position fighting against and stopping these thoughts coming to his mind and heart. In practice, a person does not judge others especially with their difficulties. There are a lot of incidents that if people judge others, the same problems and issues can occur with them.

74. Cheap Paper Cup and the Sufi

One day, the Sufi was drinking coffee. She used to drink coffee in a paper cup and reuse the paper cup again. One day she had a drink of coffee then the following day, she washed the used cup. She spent a lot of time cleaning it for a drink of a new fresh coffee. As soon as she poured the coffee there were some drips from the coffee. The Sufi looked at the cup and said, "it probably dripped while I was taking a sip." Then, she took another sip with care but again there was a drip. She said to herself, "I need to be more careful where I touch my mouth to the cup with my lips." Then, the third time she took a sip with a super extra care, and there was a drip again. Then, she observed the bottom of the cup. She identified the leak and said to the cup: "what a cheap paper cup!"

IN PRACTICE

At times a person gives much value to a practice or an unauthentic or invaluable teaching. A person can spend years on following or doing a practice with a good expectation without realizing its true value. A bad disappointment can occur due to wasting all the efforts after a long time. Therefore, it is important to give the correct value to everything. An authentic teaching, a reliable teacher, or a genuine practice will not disappoint the person in this life and after.

75. Self-Control, Willpower, and Environment

One day, the Sufi planned to spend some time of the day with his kids and family at home. He said to himself, "whatever the kids do I won't be angry." Sure enough, he lost himself again and got angry. He immediately rushed to the mosque for prayer, meditation, and reading the Quran. Immediately after an hour of engagement with prayers, he immediately felt his real self of calm and peaceful self. Then, he asked to himself, "who was the person at home? Was it me or someone else? Now, I can go back home and handle inshaAllah the challenges better."

IN PRACTICE

Self-control with willpower is important. As humans, there is limit to everything. One of the suggestions is to change the environment if the person is sucked into an environment where one cannot be his or her real-self. As in the above story, although it was a little bit late, the Sufi changed his environment and rushed to mosque for prayers before more damage was done due to his anger. As soon as he engaged himself with his genuine relationship with God, his normal desired self, returned to him. Once the person restores this positive potential energy, he or she can go back to the difficulties of life to help others in their journeys.

76. The Unusual Men and the Rebellion

There was an extreme cold warning that no one was advised to go outside due to the case of freezing and frostbite. The streets were all empty except a few unusual men. The Sufi looked out the window. He recognized a few of those people. Those were the ones who would normally not go out to walk but at the times of storms and difficulties, they would go out to show their strength and rebellious nature. The Sufi looked and smiled, "I wish they acted with their mind and followed the warnings. It takes a few seconds to lose your organs and life in this extreme freezing temperatures."

In practice

It is important to follow guidelines. A person cannot act bold and safe when there are a lot of warnings for spiritual traps. There are some who may not follow what they are instructed but follow the opposite due to their rebellious nature. Similarly, in relation with God, when God put guidelines of do's and don'ts, there would be still ones who would act oppositely. In this case, it is very dangerous to be at the opposite position which may ruin one's life in this world and after death.

77. Natural Disasters and Important Places

One day, the Sufi heard that there would be a big storm. Everyone was going to market to buy more food and watching the news about the approaching disaster.

The Sufi immediately ran to the mosque to pray. She did not leave the mosque until the disaster was over. Everyone was stressed and uneasy but the Sufi was in peace and happy. The Sufi said "Alhamdulillah."

IN PRACTICE

All difficulties can be easy if the person knows how to handle them. In the above story, the Sufi practiced the way of the Prophet that when there was a possibility of disaster or calamity the Prophet used to pray until it was over.[6][5] Sometimes, people may not know how to respond to disasters. As there are physical preparations needed such as buying food or checking candles in case of power outage, the person also may be more importantly preparing oneself spiritually to connect with the One, God Who is All Powerful and Who can change anything at any time.

78.   Irregular Prayers of Difficulty and the Sufi

One day, the Sufi was in the mosque. She realized that there was a person who never came to mosque but came only in difficult situations in her life. The person talked to the Sufi and asked some advice. The Sufi said to her, "I wish you came regularly and not only when you are in difficulty because this will give more strength, hope, and ways to handle your difficulties."

IN PRACTICE

The regular small steps are more important than bigger irregular steps. In other words, a person can be super pious once or twice a month for a week. Another person can be mediocre in one's relationship for a few minutes daily. The latter would be in better position in one's spiritual strength and stability compared to the first one as suggested by the Prophet.[6]xii

79. The Lonely Wise-Fool

There was a lonely wise-fool who used to come to mosque. Everyone used to make a joke of him. He did not show up for a few weeks in the mosque. Then, one day in a very cold weather he came to the mosque. He did not properly dress to protect himself from the freezing cold weather. While he was leaving the people advised him not to go out without any gloves or jacket that he may get sick and even die. The wise-fool got very angry and said, "I have been in my home for a long time and no one asks me. Why do you care about me now?"

IN PRACTICE

It is important to check on people as we are all humans. People get lonely, depressed, and need company. A simple phone call, or a quick visit can prevent terrific spiritual depressions and dead ends.

80. Nights, Sleep, and Dreams

One day, the Sufi woke up very disturbed. She was disturbed about the time that she spent and how much she wasted a lot of it while sleeping. As she was getting older, she did not want to waste her time in her remaining life sleeping and doing nothing. Then, she went to her teacher and shared her problem. Her teacher said to her, "before sleeping read some of the chants and when you wake up immediately start with chants and glorification of God. Then, hopefully, you will feel better and the time in-between two states, before and after sleep with chants will be considered as if you are in worship by God during your sleep."

IN PRACTICE

It is important to value time in its reference to one's time, in the efforts of establishing a relationship with God. The Prophet suggested chants such as 33 times SubhanAllah and 33 times Alhamdulillah before sleeping. The person's last engagement in life would then be the effort of connection with God before sleeping, an imitation of death. Similarly, the Prophet used to say, "Thank you God for making us alive again after our death, the sleep."[6]

81. Guidance, Uncertainty, and the Journey

One day, the Sufi woke up and said to herself, "people think that I am pious and spiritual." She thought about the spiritual journey and death. She had this fearful, uncomfortable feeling about the uncertainty of completing the journey with the death in the state of guidance from God. Then, she immediately added a prayer to her prayer list from the prayers of the Prophet "Oh God, do not deviate our hearts after You have guided us, and give us from Your Infinite Mercy and Blessings. Indeed and for sure, You are the Generous Endless Giver of All Blessings and Bounties. Amen!"[xiii]

IN PRACTICE

Positive uncertainty is called the safety measure of the path.[6] A person can be easily trapped in spiritual holes if this safety measure is not present. In other words, when a person has the feelings and thoughts of, "I am safe and saved." This is the point where one loses. Therefore, the person should constantly ask God to stay on the straight path when one starts the journey as suggested above which is the prayer both in the Quran and the prayers of the Prophet.

---

6. Tamken.

82.   Being with Old Friends, the Journey, and the Progress

One day, the Sufi went to visit her old Sufi friends. She was enjoying her time as they were talking about some Sufi topics in the journey. The Sufi realized that her old friends are still at the same spiritual level. When the Sufi gave her disposition about the topic discussed, her friends realized that the Sufi was gone so far at a much higher level. Then, the Sufi realizing this said "Astagfirullah, this could be a trap!"

IN PRACTICE

It is important to desire progress in the spiritual journey in one's relationship with God. Everyone has a different pace in the journey. Some may not do much progress but preserve what they have. Some will go back. Some will stay with not much progress. Some will excel much in the race of the journey. It is very critical to increase the self-reflection, repentance, gratitude, and humility for God. If not, the progress itself can have some black holes like traps to suck the person in that the person may not realize. Some of these black but invisible holes can be the feelings of arrogance, superiority, and vanity. In this perspective, in the above story, when the Sufi realized this she immediately asked forgiveness and repentance to God by saying "astagfirullah."

83. The Divorce

One day, the Sufi was upset with his kids and family. He woke up in the morning and said to himself "it is the weekend, everyone is home, I should not be angry." He then decided to leave home and go to the mosque to pray for spiritual strength and help from God. The mosque was empty except there was a man that the Sufi did not see before. The man was praying as well. After completing the prayer, the Sufi had a chat with the man. The man said: "I am going through a divorce. Please make dua, pray for me." The man was married for 22 years and he had seven children. The Sufi tried to counsel the man if there was a way to save the marriage. The man said, "I want to get out of it and be with God. Before I die, I want to do what I want to do, I am 55 years old." The Sufi said, "ok, can you be a shadow man at home and keep the marriage and still spend your time in worship of God." The man insisted that it was not possible. The Sufi said to himself "subhanAllah, God sent me a person to help me and be patient in my problems."

IN PRACTICE

It is always encouraged to run to God in times of difficulty and uneasiness. Both the man and the Sufi ran to the mosque to pray and ask for help. The Sufi took a lesson for himself from the man's situation because this man was going through divorce. It is important to prevent something disliked like divorce if it is possible. If it is not possible by all means, then God allows the divorce but it should be the last resort, not the first one. It is important to realize that one can worship and spend time with God while still having social and family engagements although it may be sometimes difficult. Therefore, it is ideal to keep both but not sacrifice one or another if possible.

84.   The Women in the Graveyard

One day, the Sufi went to a graveyard outside the city. The graveyard was in an isolated area from the town. The Sufi went there to visit the grave of a deceased friend. There was no one in the graveyard except a woman walking there. It was unusual to see someone without a car walking inside the cemetery. The Sufi went next to the grave of his friend. He did some prayers and read the chapter of Yasin from the Quran. After the Sufi was done, he started walking to his car. The Sufi started driving. Again, the Sufi saw the woman walking. The Sufi said to himself "let me check if she is ok." He stopped next to her with his car and said, "are you ok?," the woman took the sunglasses from her eyes. There were tears and she said, "yes, I come here a few times a week to visit my dad and I talk to him." The Sufi said, "I am sorry for disturbing you," then he drove away.

In practice

It is important to visit the deceased and pray for them. There are people who are at higher spiritual states that can be aware of the deceased person's affairs in the grave. There are incidents that while the Prophet was visiting or passing a graveyard, he reported what the person was doing in their grave.[6]xiv [5]xv The Prophet also mentioned that when a person visits a grave and greets the person the deceased person hears but cannot respond.

85. Gourmet Coffee Making

One day, the Sufi was in a good spiritual state. She said to herself let me make gourmet coffee today. She first reflected on the smell and taste of the coffee while she was chanting. After a while, she put the coffee in the machine and poured water in its container and did some chants on it. Then, she opened the coffee machine lid and started smelling the coffee before brewing it. The coffee smelt really good. She enjoyed smelling the coffee for a few minutes while she was doing her chant on it. Then, she said, "bismillah" and hit the switch button. As the coffee was brewing, a nice coffee smell was coming and the Sufi was enjoying it while she was doing her chant. The drips of coffee into the coffee pot, its fresh brewing smell, and the chants of glorification and gratitude for God, all were super enjoyable. Then, the last drop came into the coffeepot. The pot was full with the coffee. Now, the Sufi was thinking about the nice fresh coffee. How she would drink it and how the coffee would pass through from her mouth, throat, and stomach. It has no calories so she didn't feel any guilt. Then, finally, the Sufi took the first sip of it while she was chanting. It was an unexplainable experience!

IN PRACTICE

It is important to focus on all details of spiritual engagement. One can call this awareness, mindfulness, or being fully present. Regardless of the terms, the spiritual sciences develop by detailing the experiences. When the travelers follow the main guidelines structured by the Quran and the Prophet, then experiences are detailed by the scholars. A spiritual science with a methodology develops over time that people have used for centuries.

86. Alone in the Cemetery

One day, the Sufi wanted to attend a funeral. He unfortunately missed the funeral prayer but promised himself that he should at least attend the burial in the cemetery. As he was busy that day, he left his work to drive to the cemetery which was far from where he was. By the time he reached to the graveyard, the burial was completed, everyone left except a few people. The Sufi parked and walked to the freshly buried grave, everyone left the graveyard except the Sufi. The Sufi saluted the deceased person and thought about the past memories and how the Sufi used to chat with him. The Sufi felt sad and started reading prayers and chapters from the Quran, especially the chapter of Yasin. Then, the Sufi made his farewell salutation for his friend in the grave and left the graveyard.

IN PRACTICE

It is very rewarding by God to attend the funeral prayers and burial ceremony in the graveyard as testified by the Prophet.[6]xvi [5]xvii Perhaps, it could be due to the reason of remembering death and doing some self-accountability before one dies. Or, it can be that people tend to avoid the sad events like funerals in their enjoyable life engagements. Therefore, when a person attends a funeral or burial ceremony in graveyard, God rewards for the fulfillment of their responsibility for their loved ones. It is also suggested to salute the deceased when entering and leaving the graveyard as the deceased can hear the person but not talk as testified by the Prophet.[5] The deceased person is thankful for the visitors especially when they pray to God for him or her as in the story above.

87.   Two Dogs, the Old Fox, and the Fish

One day, the Sufi had a dream. There were two dogs, an old fox, and a gentle fish. The first dog attacked the old fox. The old fox tried to defend himself but it was very difficult. The fox was old, weak, and thin. Then, the other dog attacked the gentle fish that landed on the shore. The poor fish tried to defend herself but it was useless, the dog already started eating the fish but the fish was still trying to defend herself. The Sufi woke up in the middle of night from the dream, startled and uncomfortable. Then, next morning, the Sufi went to her teacher to ask the meanings. Her teacher said: "The old fox is your husband. The fish is you. Dogs are your children. Your husband needs to use his wisdom and mind as the old fox when he deals with children. At the same time, it seems that the children may be mistreating you. You and your husband need to work together to prevent that and act as a team to raise them with wisdom. The children have a lot of energy as the dogs want to attack and eat as in the representations of the dream. Always God knows the best and true meanings." Then, the Sufi went to talk to her husband for counsel.

IN PRACTICE

It is important to interpret the messages from the dreams. The Prophet used to ask people after the early morning prayer[xviii] if there was anyone who saw dreams and needed interpretation.[6][xix] There are a lot of guidelines of a true and authentic dream depending on the time, context, and the spiritual state of the person. Authentic dreams are other signs from God to guide people. It is important to ask interpretation of one's dreams from experts in this field and ask the people who would always consider the best interest of the person.

88.   Driving and Moving Objects

One day, the Sufi was driving. She looked out of her window. She said to herself, "things appear to be moving." Then, she stopped. There was a big rock on the road. She said, "let me try to move this rock." She tried a few minutes but she couldn't. She said to herself, "well, I can't move this rock like this. Let me try to reverse my car and go back and find another side road." As she was driving on the reversed gear, she realized that the rock seemed to be moving and going further from her. She said to herself, "If I can't move something away from me then I can move away from it. The result would be the same."

IN PRACTICE

It is important to change environments and be with good people. Sometimes it is very difficult to change oneself, similar to the moving the rock as in the above story. Changing others is not even a discussion. In this case, changing environments such as "moving on" to the good environments of dhikr, remembrance of God and prayers can make a change in oneself. This approach can be sometimes easy and the result can be the same.

89. Fame

One day, the Sufi was thinking, "Why is fame such a bad thing in practice? I think fame can be used for good purposes. If a person is famous, then he or she can do good things for others and people can imitate them." Then, she thought about Satan. Satan is the most famous. I don't want to be famous like Satan. Then, the Sufi said, "what is the definition of fame?"

IN PRACTICE

Everything is performed with the intention of only and solely pleasing God. Fame is defined in the Oxford dictionary[2] as "the condition of being known or talked about by many people, especially on account of notable achievements." Asking for fame is useless and dangerous in practice. Therefore, there are a lot of Sufis that purposely block the ways of being famous. They want to live and be buried anonymously but only known by God but not by people. If a person becomes famous without desiring and asking, it is a very daunting task to maintain sincerity on the path in one's relationship with God. It is not impossible but not easy.

90. The Bad News Giver: Did You Know What Happened?

One day, the Sufi saw a man in the mosque. For the Sufi, this man's title was "bad news giver." Each time the Sufi saw him, he would give tragic news by stating, "did you know what happened?" Then, he would report for example, "there was an accident on the highway, people died." Or, "There is a snowstorm coming tonight, there is a traffic ban," and other news. Each time the Sufi heard about it, he used to not be disturbed but focus on his prayers, chants, and meditation.

IN PRACTICE

It is important to prepare oneself about the outcomes of one's life journey. One day, a person came to the Prophet and asked, "When is the end of world and accountability in front of God?" The Prophet replied to him and said, "what did you prepare for it?"[5] It is more important to have a schedule in one's relationship with God rather than elaborating on the unseen or unexpected events called "news." Therefore, a person who is at a spiritual level of neutrality,[xx] is not much affected with the news of evil or good-seeming incidents.

91. God, Humans, and Lies

One day, the Sufi thought about how to best pray to God. First, she uttered some divine phrases of glorification,[7] appreciation,[8] proclaim of Oneness and Uniqueness of God[9] and then asked forgiveness.[10] In the second stage of her prayer, she asked from God for the good that she wanted for this life and afterlife. She both started and ended her prayer with salutation and appreciation to all teachers especially for the Prophet.[xxi] Then the Sufi said, "God is Perfect, the Creator, without any need. Humans are the creation with needs and weaknesses."

IN PRACTICE

It is important to realize the boundaries of one's relationship with God. God is not like humans, although we tend to sometimes use a language of similitudes to make things understandable in our human world of communications. These similitudes are okay as long as the person knows that they are only similitudes or metaphors. These are the boundaries. Passing the boundaries in our human mind can put the person easily in jeopardy of confusion, not genuine knowledge and loss of mind and heart. As in the above story, there are etiquettes of asking from God. First, one proclaims the truths and facts about God with Divine Phrases of glorification, appreciation proclaim of Oneness and Uniqueness of God and then asks forgiveness. Then, one can ask their need with always remembering the Prophet and other teachers in the beginning and end of the prayer as appreciation. The Divine Phrases are all facts about God. If it is used for humans, then it would be lies as humans are weak and in need. Therefore, arrogance is the biggest lie for humans in front of God.

---

7. SubhanAllah
8. Alhamdulillah
9. La ilaha illa Allah
10. Astagfirullah

92. Cooking and Talking

One day, the Sufi attended a spiritual gathering. There was a hard-pressed person in life with some hardships in this gathering. The topic was about the concept of destiny and one's relationship with God. Although the Sufi was holding himself not to talk and be in silent mode, there was some misunderstanding about the concept of theodicy so he felt that he needed to express his stance and explained the ideal expected disposition of a person in these discussions. After he left this gathering, he felt uneasy. He said to himself, "I hope I did not imply anything that would make that hard-pressed person guilty and worse. I wish I didn't talk as I promised myself before."

IN PRACTICE

It is really difficult to keep the balance of talking and silence. When a person talks it is expected that the person ponders well before putting thoughts into words. In this case, using a language and voice tone without irritating others are similar to heat, fire, or an oven. Having empathy for others is the spice of speech. However, the main ingredient of talking is the addressing to one's own self or ego in order to better it but not to better the other person. In this regard, the Sufi had a hard time balancing all these critical elements as mentioned in the above story.

93. Finding Yourself

One day, the Sufi was thinking about the concept of understanding oneself. She said to herself, "how can I understand myself?" She was thinking about the answer of this question for many years. She had a very busy schedule. Over the years, she changed her schedule a little bit and started spending time with herself, praying, reading the Quran and reflection in solitude. As time passed in these lonely moments, she started discovering what makes her happy, sad, and what makes her body uncomfortable and comfortable etc. One day, she said to herself, "now, I think I am discovering myself."

IN PRACTICE

It is very important to know who you are. If the person knows himself or herself then this is the first step knowing God and establishing a true relationship with the Divine. In the solitude moments of prayers, reading the scripture, and chants a person tries to discover his or her real self with the guidance of God through the teachings of the scripture and the Prophet. In practice, it is important to take oneself or ego[11] similar to dealing with a separate individual. As a person knows another person over time, knowing one's own self can take time. Once the person knows oneself then the person can go the next step of training the self or ego.

---

11. Called nafs in practice.

94. Astagfirullah

One day, the Sufi had an uneasy feeling in her heart. She felt uncomfortable. Then, she started chanting the phrase astagfirullah, and starting crying. After a few minutes, the Sufi was feeling better. She said "alhamdulillah, thank you God."

IN PRACTICE

When a person is in uneasy dispositions of heart, one can chant the phrase astagfirullah which means "oh God, please forgive me with my all renderings and engagements with my eyes, ears, organs, mind, heart, thoughts and feelings." The Prophet mentions, "there are times where some sort of shade is in my heart, and I seek forgiveness from God hundred times a day." [2] xxii Although the Prophet had a very intimate and unceasing relationship with God even during his sleep, protected and guided consistently by God, he also asked forgiveness from God as a human for possible undesired renderings. In the above story, the Sufi did not know the source of the problem but immediately tried to solve with the engagement of this chant. It is important to have the awareness of one's heart. If there is anything undesired in it, the person should remove these feelings, thoughts, and rendering by asking for forgiveness as a means of cleansing one's heart. It is well known in practice that asking forgiveness from God cleans the heart especially with the chant astagfirullah.

95.   Loud and Silent

One day, the Sufi attended a circle of meditation and chanting. People were chanting loudly. The next day, the Sufi attended another circle of meditation and chanting. People were chanting silently. The Sufi said to herself "wow, a person can have a choice depending on the personality and state of mind and heart at that time or day."

IN PRACTICE

There are both perspectives in loud and silent meditation and chanting. In both cases, there can be advantages. When a person is in a group of loud chanting, they can have the spiritual uplift of the audible and sensible medium. When a person is in a group of silent chanting, they can have the spiritual uplift of the sensible medium. One should remember that sometimes loud chanting can be a disadvantage due to the high pitch or loudness making it difficult for others to concentrate. As the Prophet reminded one day to people that when chanting they should not feel the need for loudness because God is All Hearing, All Present, and Close. God is always with the person.[2] xxiii

96. Going Back and Back

One day, the Sufi made something that was considered sin or a displeasure of God. He promised before to himself that he would not do it but he did it again. He was ashamed of himself in front of God. God gave him so much. He said to himself, "how would I face God?" He went for praying. Then, he started crying and asked forgiveness and said: "Oh God! Where can I go? There is no one who can forgive my bad and ungrateful treatment towards You. Please forgive me. You are the Most Forgiving. You like forgiving. You are the Most Merciful and the Most Compassionate."

IN PRACTICE

It is important to constantly go back again and again to God until one dies. There is no one who can help a person in reality except God. If God wants and accepts then, others follow as means. If God does not want to accept although others seem to comfort the person, there is in reality no one that could help this person. In the above story, the Sufi embodied a prayer suggested by the Prophet, "Oh My Sustainer and Nourisher, I oppressed myself many times with sins, rebelling against You. No one can forgive those sins except You. Please forgive me with a forgiveness from You. Have mercy on me. Indeed, and certainly, You are the Most Forgiver, Accepter of Repentance and the Most Merciful and the Most Gracious." [2] xxiv

97. Pain and Mistakes

One day, the Sufi thought about the mistakes that he made in his relationship with God. Each time he did something wrong to hurt the relationship, he had an immense pain with disgust and self-blame. Then, he tried to stop himself at a limit not to be pessimistic and lose his relationship with God. He said to himself, "It is very difficult to keep balance on the path."

IN PRACTICE

It is important to go back and ask forgiveness for the evil-seeming renderings of a person in one's relationship with God. There is no number or limits of going back because there is no one to go back in reality except God. The inner feelings should accompany the person with self-accountability and unpleasant feelings such as disgust about one's self. Sometimes, a person can have dangerous temptations and can become doubtful and unenthusiastic about going back to God. This is a very dangerous limit that the person can pass and have evil temptations that make the person see themselves as a loser and become pessimistic in their relationship with God. The balance should be self-accountability with full blame, humbleness, and humility but at the same time having a full belief that God's mercy is Infinite and God can forgive any person regardless of the enormity of the sins of that person.

98. In Charge

One day, the Sufi thought about the overwhelming responsibility of being in charge. "I am in charge of my tongue, my body, and my mind. I am in charge of my kids. I am in charge of responsibilities at my work and my social life. Too many things, to many responsibilities, and it is very difficult to manage all."

IN PRACTICE

It is not desired to be in charge of something or someone. However, if a responsibility is given although the person avoids it, then it is expected that the person fulfills it as satisfactorily as possible. Being in charge of something or someone brings accountability in front of people and God. A good fair ruler or a spouse in a family can help others and attain very high level in one's relationship with God. Oppositely, oppression and unjust treatments in family life can make one's accountability very challenging and difficult in front of God.

99. Intention and Difficulties

One day, the Sufi attended a difficult religious gathering. He forgot to make his intention before attending. During this gathering, people were discussing religious matters in impolite etiquettes. The Sufi tried to contribute with his "two cents" but was not sure if it would be useful. The Sufi did not feel well as usual and left. He said to himself, "why did I come here?"

IN PRACTICE

It is important to make your intention before you do anything. Sometimes, things may look straightforward but even in these times, it is important to renew and repeat one's intention to get the highest benefit. Sometimes, the person may be in unpleasant situations that one may not expect. If the person had a good intention in these cases then still, the person is rewarded by God due to one's intention. In the above story, the Sufi had a problem with himself that he forgot to make an intention for attendance of the gathering. When he encountered a difficult and unpleasant environment he went back to his intention to seek comfort and relief but he realized that he did not make an intention before his action.

100. Jury Duty

One day, the Sufi was called for jury duty. Like everyone, she went to the court. There were a lot of people as jury candidates waiting in the room for initial selection process. It seemed that most of the people did not want to be there and wanted to see if the judge would excuse them. The Sufi said to herself, "how can I disconnect with my surrounding and transform this room to my worship place?" Then, the Sufi made the intention and prayed to God for this transformation and started engaging with her prayers while waiting for hours. Others were complaining but the Sufi said "Alhamdulillah" to God for this transformation.

In practice

It is important to realize one's physical conditions and accordingly ask from God the means for spiritual transformation. Sometimes, it is difficult to disconnect oneself from one's surroundings due to various distractions, although it is not impossible. Making the intention and asking help from God are the key first steps as the Sufi did in the above story. After, one can engage oneself with chanting, prayers, and readings. If the person is flowing in this engagement, the transformation is successful. That is great. If not, the person should not force themselves but possibly refresh themselves with wudhu, or pick a chant that is easy to recite.

101. Lawsuits and Ethics

One day, the Sufi was called for jury duty. The case was about a lawsuit. The Sufi did not know much about lawsuits and he did not feel good about it. He always thought that lawsuits were an unfair way of acquiring money from people. Then, he said to the judge, "I think, I have a biased opinion against lawsuits." The judge said, "why?" The Sufi said, "I don't believe that the people do wrong and negligence on purpose." The judge said, "you are dismissed for your jury duty." The Sufi then started thinking and said to himself, "did I do something right? What if there are lawsuits which are necessary" He kept thinking…

IN PRACTICE

It is important to think before you utter words. The Sufi was not sure about his stance about lawsuits until the judge dismissed him from the jury duty. Then, he started elaborating about it. One of the biggest issues in front of God is the unfair accumulation of wealth. Although people like it, but when it becomes a norm in a society, then it can endanger the pillars of social, ethical, and religious core teachings. On the other hand, lawsuits can make people check and balance their practices. In spiritual path, one can call check and balances as self-reflection to better oneself. Therefore, in this case, lawsuits can become favorable in social life as a means of practicing self-reflection.

102. Sleep and Complications

The Sufi had some sleeping problems lately. As he woke up, he did not feel good, he kept having headaches and bad dreams. It was again night time and the Sufi was getting ready for sleep. He said to himself, "again I will be in pain when I wake up with discomfort. What should I do? Should I see a doctor?" Then, he remembered the prophetic suggestions before going to sleep and used the bathroom for relief, made wudhu, washed up, and went to bed and started reading some supplications. Finally, he laid down on his right side and slept. He saw a nice dream and was feeling very good in the morning and said "alhamdulillah."

IN PRACTICE

It is important to follow the Prophetic suggestions in every detail of life to take oneself out of the burden of decision-making. In other words, when the person needs to decide life details without guidance of the Prophet, it is possible that the person can make unnecessary and unfruitful wrong decisions. In this case of sleep, before going to a doctor or asking medical help, the Sufi remembered to practice the Prophetic suggestions about the manners of sleep. At the end, he saved himself from the trouble of medical visits with the help of some simple and blessed suggestions of the Prophet. This does not mean that one should not seek medical help if there is a need; however, sometimes a simple approach can solve a problem without complications.

103. Throat and Silence

There was a Sufi who used to not talk in the morning. When he used to go to the mosque, he used to keep silent until the afternoon. If the people came and tried to talk to him he used to show his throat and tried to talk to them with sign language. As time passed, there were some brothers who were concerned about Sufi's throat. They came to Sufi and tried to give him herbal medicine and long advice about how the Sufi should really take care of his health. The Sufi was listening and nodding his head. The Sufi said to himself, "maybe, I should have just said them that I don't want to talk in the morning, but then they would find me weird."

IN PRACTICE

In practice, there are travelers on the path that they don't want to engage with the worldly issues until they are charged with spiritual equipments in the morning. The Sufi in the above story was one of them. The Sufi did not want to talk but enjoy silence until a certain time of the day. However, he did not want to disclose this with others. It is sometimes difficult to seem normal among others while the person may not enjoy or dislike others. It is still important not to seem weird or abnormal in order to attract attention. Sometimes attention can bring undesired disturbance by others but if it comes then it is important not to be affected with the feelings of superiority, difference ,and arrogance.

104. Coffee Cup Size

There was a generous Sufi who used to give people regular light coffee in small cups for free. The coffee was so light that it tasted more like water. As soon as the people took a sip, they used to say, "this is the best expresso that I have ever drank in my life." The Sufi used to say to each person that it was a regular light coffee but not expresso. Then later, she got tired of correcting people about this. Now, each time they say, "this is the best expresso that I have ever drunk in my life," then she started smiling and told herself that, "everyone is tricked by the cup size."

IN PRACTICE

It is important not to be tricked with the external. Since expresso coffee is served with small cups, people assumed and directed their judgment even after tasting the light coffee that they were drinking expresso. Sometimes, our judgments are so strong that there are clear guidelines but we act blindly. Similarly, in spiritual path, knowing God and destroying all the negative or wrong judgments can be sometimes difficult but not impossible. As soon as some people, hear the words God or religion they immediately can have the impulses of prior built-in notions without considering what they are presented now.

105. Spiritual Discoveries

There was a Sufi who used to attend a lecture of another Sufi at night. The first Sufi used to work on different issues of heart and mind during the day. She used to pray, think, and take notes of her spiritual discoveries. At night, when the other Sufi was giving a public lecture, she used to mention explicitly the first Sufi's spiritual discoveries. The first Sufi over time normalized this and kept this secret with herself and told herself, "in spiritual life, abnormal becomes normal with the Grace of God."

In practice

It is important to realize that when the person is on the path trying to keep steadfastness and continuity, there can be some spiritual openings and discoveries showered by God. In this journey, abnormal for others can become normal for this traveler. It is mentioned in a Prophetic tradition that God orders one of the angels[12] to give the right inspiration when the person walks on the path with humility. All those inspirations and discoveries are from the Grace of God. The person should be careful and humble. He or she should not be trapped with the temptations of superiority due to these spiritual discoveries and bounties.

---

12. Name of the angel is mulhim.

106. Sufi's Prayer and Regret

One day, there was a poor but pious Sufi. She had some family friends who used to come and visit her. The Sufi started having bad and unbearable family problems. Then, the Sufi prayed to God, "Oh God, whoever is causing these problems take care of them." Then, after a while she heard that the family friend who was coming to her house and causing problems with her family was now going through divorce. The Sufi said to herself, "what did I do? I wish didn't pray."

IN PRACTICE

It is very dangerous to make the friends of God upset and sad. They don't do anything physically but pray to God for their difficulties. In this regard, the people has been generally very careful when they are dealing with the friends of God because their prayers are immediately accepted as they have a high status with God. In the above case, the Sufi had someone who used to come to their home and cause some regular problems in her family. Then, the Sufi prayed to God and the prayer was executed but the Sufi was upset with herself.

107. Loving-Warning and the Traffic Ticket

One day, the Sufi was driving and thinking about a Sufi teacher. The Sufi seemed to have bad feelings and had some disagreements about an issue with this Sufi teacher. As soon as he was engaged in those thoughts while driving, a police car put his lights behind the Sufi's car to pull him over. As expected, the Sufi got a ticket and he said to himself, "each time I have bad thoughts about a teacher I get a ticket, this is not surprising."

IN PRACTICE

It is important to control oneself, even one's thoughts, about the teachers and the real friends of God. Sometimes, if there are two people who are both friends of God, there may be some loving warnings for the ones who may not have good feelings towards the other. This loving-warning can be a type of difficulty like a traffic ticket or unpleasant incident that the person may be disturbed in one's flow of life. In these cases, one should be thankful to God because there is a loving-warning to the person similar to a relationship between the child and the mother. God is above from all these representations yet the person can humanize some evil-seeming incidents in life encounters.

108. Intellectualizing the Religion and the Etiquettes

One day, the Sufi was thinking about intellectuals and their basic premise of using their mind. She said to herself, "one can use their mind until a certain point. The essence is the attitude of etiquette and respect but not the mind."

IN PRACTICE

This is the key point: the essence of religion is the attitude of etiquette and respect[13] of God. If a person does not have the boundaries of etiquettes of thoughts and emotions that humans are limited creations like others, then it is very easy to mentally and emotionally wander around in prohibited poisonous wrong and dark lands similar to black holes in space. In this regard, the chant SubhanAllah constantly reminds this to the person. These erroneous wanderings also require constant corrections and repentance with the chant, astagfirullah as well. When a person is at this level of understanding, then it is suggested to thank God due to this spiritual level with the chant, alhamdulillah. Therefore, knowing the guidelines of the path is important as the useful and beneficial knowledge is important as reminded by the Prophet.[5] These are the main areas where philosophers and some religious folks in the West have possible issues due to the lack of: 1) etiquettes with God; 2) knowing one's limits as humans in this relationship; 3) not accepting and submitting themselves to the guidelines as the cornerstones.

---

13. Adab

109. Proud Sufi

One day, the Sufi was reading in the Quran. He read the verses[xxv] about some people's arguments on why God did not send angels as messengers but humans. God mentioned that if God would send angel messengers then they would be in the form of humans. Then, the Sufi said to himself, "why are people not happy for being human but want something else? I am proud to be a human being. Thank you God, alhamdulillah."

IN PRACTICE

Accepting who you are is the first step to excel. In this case, humans are weak, needy, and are the creations of God. Once the person maintains this perspective with humility and humbleness then, the person can find power in his or her human traits in their relationship with God. Most of the problem occurs when humans don't want to accept this reality in their relationship with the Creator. They try to disguise themselves in some clothes even sometimes they don't realize it. The worst cloth is the cloth of arrogance, superiority, and power while in reality the person is weak, needy, and poor. This lie puts most of the people in trouble in their relationship with God in this life and after.

110. True Gratitude

One day, the Sufi was thinking, "why I cannot embrace thanking God fully? It should come naturally as if I am breathing air into my lungs. It should not need any effort."

IN PRACTICE

In practice, everything starts with an effort and imitation. Sometimes a person may be thanking God and saying Alhamdulillah yet still, can have some stingy thoughts or frictions in their inner self. Over time and by practice, the embodiment of natural thanking can follow. The expressions of "what a little in number the people of thankers!"[xxvi] Or "what little in quantity is the habit of thanking"[xxvii] are repeated in various places in the Quran in order to allude humans' ingratitude and unappreciative attitudes towards God. The Prophet also indicates that, "the person who does not thank God does not thank people,"[12] or vice versa. God increases the happiness and peaceful blessings in this world and after when the person is always in the state of thankfulness, alhamdulillah.

111. No Police Land

One day, a man went to a town. There were no police or law enforcement. People used to freely steal and kill. This man was startled and asked one of the locals, "why are there no police in this town?" The local man said, "no one wants to be the bad-guy enforcing the rules and laws. Therefore, no one wants get that job although they are paying good."

IN PRACTICE

It is important to recognize rules and accountability in one's relationship with God. Most of the time we hear a lot, "I don't want to be the bad guy." In one's relationship with God, God is All Merciful and Caring and Loving. One should recognize that there are people who are at different levels. A higher level person would fulfil God's commands because this person loves God. Another level person, perhaps lower, would fulfill God's commands due to accountability after death. Both are fine and acceptable. What is unacceptable is that representing the understanding of God as only "Loving" but not "Accounting." This sole perspective can lead people at different levels and different times to a similar attitude of the people as in no police land in the above story.

112. Good Deeds and Language

There was a man who came to the mosque and started talking to another man sitting. The man took a few minutes listing his past good deeds that he did for the sake of God. The other man was looking at this man's face and smiling. After a while, the man stopped talking. The other man smiling said, "I am sorry, no English!"

IN PRACTICE

It is important to keep one's good deeds private and secret if one has done them for the sake of God. The pleasure of God requires sincerity. Sincerity requires the absence of others applauding words or attitudes toward the action. Therefore, showing off is considered disbelief when a person does a good deed to be praised or known by others. It doesn't matter much if people know it or not. People can say, "great job!" Then, a misleading and a fake satisfaction can be there. Yet, when God is pleased with the person, the satisfaction is fulfilling in this world and after death. In the above story, the man had a useless conversation whether the other person understood him or not.

113. People's Sensitivity and Culture

There was a Sufi who did not like to talk to in the mornings. When he used to go to mosque, he used to prefer silence. A man from a different culture came one morning to the Sufi to visit him in the mosque. This man loved the Sufi very much. He was upset to the Sufi. He said to him, "what did I do to you? Why you are not talking to me?" The Sufi handed him some coffee and wrote on a paper that "the Sufi loves him too but now he is busy, he can't talk." The man was still upset, but kept talking to the Sufi and complaining about the Sufi's silent treatment. The Sufi kept the silence, put his head down, and listened to the man. After, the man left the Sufi said to himself, "I should be more sensitive of different cultures. Not everyone understands what I am doing."

IN PRACTICE

Silence is the default mode of a person that's not talking. Especially, there are ones who are on the path who prefer to be silent in different times of the day such as mornings until they finish their daily dialogue with God called wird. At these times, the person wants to focus on their relationship with God without any external even internal disturbances of thoughts or feelings. When people are engaged at these times, some Sufis cannot fully pay attention to the etiquettes of social interactions. An outsider should always maintain good thoughts about others, in this case about the Sufi in the above story. Yet, at the same time, the Sufis should try to recognize the cultural and social sensitivities of people to prevent more evil that may lead to more disturbing headaches later.

114. Ant and the Sufi

There was an ant who was going for pilgrimage. A Sufi saw him and asked him:

Sufi: Where are you going?

Ant: To the holy sites.

The Sufi laughs and says:

Sufi: I don't think you will make it. The holy sites are a thousand miles away from where we are right now.

Ant: I know that, but I have the intention.

The Sufi feels so ashamed about the ant's answer and declares the ant to be his teacher.

IN PRACTICE

Intentions precede actions. If a person intends always for the good and beneficial, God rewards the person according to the person's intention. If a person prays or gives charity to the poor with the intention of showing off to people or to gain some worldly benefit, the person can get what she or he wants in the world, the tag. After death, the person can be punished due to not acting sincerely. Also, in practice, Sufis commonly observe nature, animals, and plants and try to learn from them to increase their spiritual development.

115. One Dollar Coffee Machine

There was a poor Sufi in a mosque. He bought a small coffee machine for a dollar and he put it in the mosque. While he was staying in the mosque, he was drinking coffee by himself. If other people came to the mosque he used to give the leftover coffee to them. As time passed, people started respecting him because he was so generous and giving coffee to everyone. The Sufi gained a reputation as the "respectable coffee maker of the mosque."

IN PRACTICE

Similarly, our egos are similar to cheap coffee machines. As the ego gets responsibility and recognition by God, it gains value. Power, responsibility, and positions bring recognition. If one wants to be recognized by God, a person should maintain humbleness and appreciation of the Divine.

116. Coffee Machine and Serving

As people were coming to the mosque, everyone was asking for coffee from the famous Sufi coffee maker. The Sufi was getting upset. He was being disturbed while he was praying as people were coming and asking coffee from him. One day, he decided to put the coffee machine outside at the serving table. If people want it, they can make their own coffee and they won't disturb the Sufi. People started making their own coffees without disturbing the Sufi. The Sufi said to himself, "I don't care if someone steals the coffee machine, I can buy another one. It is cheap."

IN PRACTICE

Likewise, our egos are cheap coffee machines. If we don't hoard it for ourselves but give it away to serve others to please God, a cheap self can have a high value. If we try to hold our egos tightly the disturbances will increase. Therefore, one should let it go in order to taste the pleasure and satisfaction of serving others.

117. Cookies and Scripture

One day a Sufi was reading and memorizing the scripture, the Quran. He spent a good amount of time with the sacred Book. Then, he took a break for coffee. As soon as he went next to the coffee machine, he saw his favorite cookie next to the coffee machine. He said to himself, "There is no one in the mosque except me. Who brought this cookie? I know this cookie is not local. You need to order it online." He indulged in deep thinking . . .

IN PRACTICE

Sometimes, miracles can be called cookies. Cookies may come in different forms as someone engages oneself with practice, reading the Quran, memorizing it, praying, or fasting . . .

The question is: Is the cookie healthy? Meaning that, is it an encouragement by God on the path? Or, is it a test or trial from God to see if the person on the path will be arrogant by claiming supernatural incidents and try to be superior to their fellow human beings.

118. Sufi Argues with His Wife

One day, a Sufi was in an argument with his wife. During the fight he decided to discuss some of their marriage problems.

Sufi: I need to meet with you to talk.

His wife: You are probably going to tell me how bad I am!

Sufi: Probably, you already told to your friends and my kids how bad I am, so you took the precedence. Congratulations!

His Wife: You claim to be a Sufi and you think about your reputation. Shame on you!

Sufi: You think you are pious. Please stop pretending to be pious and naïve.

Sufi was now thinking. He said to himself, "I am now heading toward a dead end. I am already receiving a lot of texts from her on my phone. If I don't say anything then she will think that she won and I will hear about it for the rest of my life." He was thinking, "What should I do?" Then, he said to his wife:

Sufi: I wanted to meet with you to tell you how much I appreciate you and I love you. That was the reason . . .

The argument was over. Sufi said, "Alhamdulillah (thanks to God), that was a good thought that Allah gave it to me. I was heading toward a dead end."

IN PRACTICE

In Sufi marital relationships, the spouse is always right. The husband's position is to always be silent and passive in any disputes, forgive, don't make a big deal, and move on.

119. The Best Voice

There was a man in the mosque and he thought he had the best voice when he used to sing to call people to prayer.[14] As soon as he would sing the prayer call, the people in the mosque would leave the mosque in order to not hear his voice until he was done. They waited outside and then came back. He actually had a very bad voice. One day, this man came to the Sufi in the mosque and brought the recording of a famous prayer singer and said, "Can you please listen to this famous singer in the Kabah and tell me who sings the prayer call better? Me or him?"

IN PRACTICE

Sometimes, the spiritual diseases can become the character of a person if there is no fellow friend telling the person of his or her mistakes. Therefore, it is a practice to have friends, not wives or husbands, to tell you your mistakes rather than simply praising your achievements. One Sufi says, "I love a friend who warns me about a scorpion on my chest. Why should I get angry with her?"

---

14. Adhan.

120. Looking at the Mirror

There was a messy Sufi who did not like to look at the mirror. He used to think, "When I see myself in the mirror, it really makes me uncomfortable—the messy hair, untrimmed moustache, uncombed beard, and un-ironed shirts." He used to avoid looking at himself in the mirror.

IN PRACTICE

Similarly, our internal messiness is ugly in its essence. Allah created everyone physically beautiful. Arrogance, hatred, anger, and jealousy are the essence of ugliness. If the person does not have mirrors to reflect on those, then that is the real problem.

121. Sufi and Value of the Book

There was a poor Sufi in a mosque to whom people used to give money for his survival. One day, a man was reading an historical rare prayer litany book. This Sufi saw this book and approached this man.

Sufi: Can I buy this book from you?

The man smiled sarcastically to the Sufi and said: "I know that you don't have money. How can you pay for this book?"

The Sufi showed a miracle and put his hand in his pocket and took out fresh bills worth a thousand dollars all bunched together and gave them to the man.

The man was shocked and said: "Here is the book. It is a gift from me. I don't want the money."

IN PRACTICE

In this story, one can understand that the market value of the book was a few dollars but the Sufi was willing to give thousands of dollars to get the book. The book was about prayers and the divine expressions of different prophets such as Abraham, Moses, Jesus, Muhammad, and other saints of God. In Sufism, anything valuable in the relationship with God has a very high price. Sufis don't value anything related to this world but rather the Divine.

122. Evil and the Sufi

One day, a person saw a Sufi in the mosque praying. He approached him and said:

The man: I want to talk to you about something important.

This man was so disturbed by the problems in the world—its injustices and evil.

He continued and said: I am so disturbed by what is happening in the world!

The Sufi smiled and said: Is this the reason that you wanted to talk to me?

The man said: Yes.

The Sufi said: Did you first ask the same question to Allah for an answer?

The man did not respond but did not seem happy with the Sufi's answer either. Understanding this, the Sufi continued:

Look! I understand you want to do something. Right?

The man said: Yes.

The Sufi: How do you do it? You have ideas, then you put them into action, right?

The man: Yes.

The Sufi: So, ask Allah to inspire you with the right and fruitful, and good ideas about what you want to do.

The man seemed a little bit more convinced with the Sufi's logic.

IN PRACTICE

In Sufism, doing good with the inspiration of easiness from Allah is very important. One can ask God to make it easy for the right choice in decision-making. In practice, there is a constant dialogue that is expected between the Divine and humans.

123. Number of Angels and the Sufi

There was a Sufi in the mosque. A man knew him and said to himself, "Let me ask him a question and tease him."

The man: How many angels are in the mosque now?

The Sufi: There are currently 84 angels.

IN PRACTICE

Some of the Sufis can alternate their positions with the unseen and seen world. These alternations can be due to the high quality and quantity of their engagements with the prayers, chanting, and reading scriptures. Although normal people can think that they are weird, these Sufis may not recognize their own abnormality when interacting with others.

124. The Door and the Responsibility

Everyone was coming to listen to the Friday sermon in the mosque. The Sufi was in the mosque as well. He was sitting next to the outside door. The famous assistant priest of the mosque was sitting next to the Sufi. As people were coming inside they were closing the door and locking it by mistake. Each time, the priest was getting up and unlocking the door and telling the people to leave the door open. Another man came in and did the same as the others, closing the door which would then lock itself. Another, another, another . . . The poor priest was getting annoyed and getting up and sitting down . . . The Sufi was watching and smiling . . .

IN PRACTICE

Similarly, there are people who work in the churches, mosques, or temples. They may be externally close to worshipping God but they are actually very distracted and very far away from God. Sometimes the closeness can make the person blind. It can have an opposite effect. A person looking to the brightness of the sun can become blind. Satan was very close to God but lost. Similarly, some Sufis believe that God is so obvious that if people cannot see God then it is because of the blindness due to the clear brightness.

125. Death and the Sufi

There was an announcement in the mosque: "One of the famous members of the mosque died." Everyone was upset and disturbed. The Sufi was smiling. He said to himself, "What a lucky guy! He is going to meet with God. I don't know why these people seem to be so upset."

IN PRACTICE

Death is not a pain or evil but the joyful moment of meeting with God. As long as the person is always eager to meet with God and pleased and appreciated God all his life, then God also wants to meet with this person. In one of the famous sayings of the Prophet Muhammad, God will treat the person in the way that she will expect to be treated in the afterlife.

126. Coffee Machine and Generosity

There was a poor Sufi in a mosque. He bought a small coffee machine for a dollar and he put it in the mosque. While he was staying in the mosque, he was drinking coffee by himself. If people came to the mosque he used to give the leftover coffee to them. As time passed, people started respecting him because he was giving coffee to everyone. One day, a person brought some cookies and put them next to the coffee on the serving table. The following day, a person brought crackers. Every day now there were some drinks and food in the mosque.

IN PRACTICE

The best way of teaching in practice is being an example rather than preaching to people. The starter of a good action receives from God each individual's rewards as well.

127. Sufi and His Sufi Mother

The Sufi was talking on the phone with his mother who was in another country:

> Sufi Mother: How is the weather over there? Is it winter or summer?

> Sufi: It is summer for the person who always follows the path of God. It is always winter for the person who is not on the path.

> Sufi Mother: What do you mean? I don't understand.

> Sufi: Did you eat garlic or onion?

> Sufi Mother: How do you know? I ate onion.

IN PRACTICE

Garlic, onion, or any bad smell or bad words or actions will repel angels and make spiritual understandings and inspirations difficult. Therefore, in the story above, the Sufi deduced his mom's inability to grasp the spiritual understandings to her engagement with something unpleasant. He was inspired by God to guess about it and he was correct.

128. Sufi and Garlic

There was a Sufi who used to like garlic sausage a lot. One day, he had an important meeting regarding a job interview. Before the meeting, to make him happy, his wife prepared for him the food that he liked the most: garlic sausage. He ate and he was so happy and ready for the meeting. He went and did the interview. He was answering all the questions successfully but he did not feel right and the interview was over. He didn't get the job. He said to himself: "Garlic sausage. I am not going to eat it anymore."

IN PRACTICE

The angelic beings do not accompany the person if there is a bad smell due to food or anything. The Sufis try to minimize their time in the bathroom due to these reasons. In the above story, the Sufi understood that although everything seemed to be normal, his inability to control himself when it came to the smelly food made him lose the angelic blessings.

129. Sufi and the Elevator

One day, there was a Sufi with a bunch of people in an apartment elevator. The elevator stopped in-between the floors. Everyone was screaming, pushing the elevator buttons frantically. Some of the ladies were crying. The elevator was still not moving.

Sufi was smiling, waiting for people to calm down a little bit.

Finally, Sufi said "I am sorry; can I push the button?"

He then said: "Bismillah—In the name of God."

The elevator started moving.

IN PRACTICE

Everything works and moves with the name of God. The purpose of all prayers in practice and in one's life is to remember this simple but important fact.

130. Sufi and His Father

Sufi was a student in Boston. His family was living in New York. His father loved the Sufi so much that each time the father talked to the Sufi, he used to compose a song and sing it for his son on the phone. His brother and his mother were jealous about this and said: "Look, he doesn't compose any songs for us but only for his son."

The Sufi heard this and said to his mom and brother, "Names are not important but the characters . . ."

IN PRACTICE

It is common to write letters and compose poems and songs for the loved ones in practice, especially for teachers, friends, and family members. It is the expression of appreciation in words. In the above story, the Sufi was saying that it is not important to whom the song was composed but the content of it.

131. Sufi and Serving

As people were coming to the mosque, everyone was asking for coffee from the famous Sufi coffee maker. The Sufi was getting upset. He was being disturbed while he was praying as people were coming and asking him for coffee. One day, he decided to put the coffee machine outside at the serving table. If people want it, they can make their own coffee and they won't disturb the Sufi. Although the coffee machine is out on the serving table, people did not make their own coffee. Everything was next to the machine—the raw coffee, the filter, and water. If people came and asked for coffee from the Sufi, he showed them where the coffee machine was and they could make their own coffee. But, people still did not make it.

In practice

Similarly, people take pleasure when they are served. In Eastern cultures this concept of serving is very prominent in social and familial relationship. Although being served can lead a person to laziness and dependency, serving someone—giving or making something and putting together a dish to bring—is a common practice to increase brotherhood and sisterhood. There is a famous aphorism in practice that people are slaves of servitude.

132. Sufi and Serving Coffee

One day, Sufi made a coffee. He was smelling the nice, fresh coffee in the morning and taking pleasure from it. He took the pot and started pouring it into a small coffee cup. A few hot drops spilled, he burned himself, and all the pleasure was lost.

IN PRACTICE

Similarly, in the spiritual pleasure, a small—even tiny—drop of arrogance burns all the efforts on the journey. The Prophet says, "A person who has an atom's size of arrogance in one's heart will not enter paradise and smell the fragrance of it." The antidote to arrogance in the journey is humbleness and humility. One can enact this by constantly prostrating and bowing before God and glorifying God. Also, any thoughts or feelings of arrogance should immediately be addressed. If not, it can mutate into an unhealthy cell like a cancer.

133. Sufi and Her Pocket

There was a Sufi. As she put her hand in her jacket pocket, there were candy wrappers, candies, prayer notes, beads, a napkin, some coins, and other things. As she wanted to pray, she didn't want to be disturbed by knowing of the existence of all those things in her pocket. So, she took off this jacket and prayed wearing one with empty pockets.

IN PRACTICE

Similarly, the practice of detachment from the world during the prayers and chanting is very important. One cannot fully achieve the practice of spiritual emptying or discharging if mindful detachment is not present. According to some of the scholars, putting one's hands back in-between each movement during the prayers is the mental reminder of disgust and detachment from all worldly engagements.

134. Sufi and Oranges in His Pocket

There was a Sufi in Alaska. He used to pray in the mosque and loved to give oranges to the kids after each prayer. He used to put his hand in his jacket and hand out a few oranges to the kids. Kids loved him because in the middle of winter they did not know where the Sufi was getting the oranges. One day, kids and the Sufi were again in the mosque. The Sufi needed to go the restroom. He took out his jacket and put it on the hanger. While waiting, the kids were curious and wanted to check his pocket for the oranges. They put their hands into the pocket opening. There were no pockets—just a big hole where the pockets should be.

IN PRACTICE

It is an everyday incident to encounter different supernatural occurrences or miracles in a Sufi's life. Actually, for a Sufi nothing is abnormal on the path of the Infinite. They consider abnormal as people's lack of appreciation of the Divine.

135. Sufi and People's Jealousy

As the Sufi was spending most of his time in the mosque, everyone was getting annoyed with him. People were gossiping and saying, "We are working and this guy is spending all his time here, worshipping." His wife was getting annoyed with him as well because he was spending all his time with worship and she was complaining to him that she always wanted to worship like him but she was not able to do it. The Sufi realized this and said to himself, "What should I do before these people destroy me with their jealousy? I need to hide myself . . . "

IN PRACTICE

It is a very common historical occurrence that jealousy of people always puts the Sufis in jeopardy. Therefore, some try to pretend to be insane. Some leave people altogether and live in the mountains or in caves. Some try to pretend or take the title of being the cleaner of a mosque or a temple.

136. The Sufi and the Trip

Sufi's brother in-law came from California to Cleveland. The Sufi was living in New York.

He said to his wife: Why don't we visit your brother?

His wife: What a nice husband! Let's go!

Sufi: Do you want your sister to come too?

His wife: That is a great idea!

Sufi: How about your mom? Why don't you take her too?

His wife: Thank you, honey! You are so thoughtful.

A day later . . .

Sufi: Honey, I want to come on the trip with you but I don't want to disturb you. You can go as a family with your brother and mom, and chat about your old memories.

His wife: Are you sure? You don't want to come with us?

Sufi: Maybe not this time.

His wife: Okay.

IN PRACTICE

Sufis always prefer spending time with God. Sufi are very jealous about their relationship with God. Any engagement should be really something worthy to disturb these sweet moments of spending time with God in worship. In the above story, the Sufi taught that it was not necessary for him to go because his wife already had company.

137. When and Where to Die and the Sufi

The Sufi's wife in the above story always complained about his indecisiveness when it came to planning trips or vacations. When his wife suggested to the Sufi that they visit her brother, she already had backup plans. The Sufi used to change his mind a lot about going on a trip.

IN PRACTICE

Sufis often contemplate where and when they will die. Before engaging themselves with a trip or to any commitment, they may ask the following questions to themselves for self-reflection: Do I need to go on this trip? Will it benefit my relationship with God? If I die on this trip, what is my intention and how will I answer God? According to the normative beliefs, a person will meet with God in the way and the place where one dies.

138. Sufi and the Bitterness and Sweetness

There was a Sufi who used to eat sweet in the daytime and salty at night. When a person asked the reason he said, "The daytime is already bitter. I need to neutralize it with some sweetness. The nighttime is already sweet and I need to neutralize it with some bitterness."

IN PRACTICE

There is always longing for the Divine. Due to daily distractions, a person may not find avenues to concentrate on the worship and remembrance of God during the daytime. Therefore, it can be bitter for the ones who are disconnected with God. On the contrary, the nights are releases from worldly duties so there is more time to engage in prayer and remembrance of God. Therefore, it is sweet as long as one uses it to charge and discharge oneself in the spiritual path of God. In practice, worshipping at night has a high value for God.

139. Sufi and Hiding

One day a Sufi was hiding from the people in the mosque. In his hiding space, he was enjoying the prayer, reflection, and the divine experiences. A lady was in the mosque as well. When the lady saw this Sufi in his hiding spot, she started screaming and ran away. She thought that he was an abnormal being.

IN PRACTICE

Privacy within the public space is a key to maintaining constant companionship with God. If the person does not uphold this notion, he will suffer due to detachment from God. This is a big torture for the ones in practice. Therefore, there is a famous prayer from the Prophet Muhammad: "Oh God! Do not leave me alone even less time than a blinking of an eye."

140. Heart and the Sufi

One day a Sufi was not feeling well. He was trying to focus on his heart. As he looked within the details of his heart, he realized that he was longing for God. Then, he started reading the scripture and prayer and started crying. As he was crying, he started feeling better and said to himself, "Alhamdulillah, thanks be to God." Then, as he was engaged in crying, he felt dehydrated and wanted to drink coffee. He said, "Bismillah, in the name of God," and took a sip. While attempting the second sip, he spilled the coffee on himself and said, "Astagfirullah, forgive me God."

IN PRACTICE

In the teachings of Sufi practice, the heart oscillates in the state of spiritual contraction and expansion, as the names of God are the Contractor and the Expander. When the person feels in contraction in the state of heart, this is a signal or a call for the person to engage in praying and glorification of God through prayer, chanting, or reading the scripture. As the person transforms oneself to the expansion state of the heart, there is always an increased possibility of spiritual arrogance. Therefore, the traveler should constantly be in the state of alertness and humbleness with the notion of "Astagfirullah." In the above story, spilling coffee on oneself can indicate the representation of possible arrogance in mystical understandings.

141. The Sufi and the Sunglasses

There were two Sufis in the mosque. One was rich but used to buy cheap clothes. The other was poor but always wanted to buy expensive clothes. One day, the rich Sufi went to a dollar store to buy sunglasses. Then, he went to the mosque with his new sunglasses. The poor Sufi saw him with his new sunglasses and said: "You look very nice with your expensive Ray-ban[15] sunglasses." The rich Sufi smiled and took the sunglasses and gave them to the poor Sufi as a gift. The poor Sufi was so happy.

IN PRACTICE

Sometimes, on the spiritual path, a person can assume and put a value on something that is invaluable for God. The external can be deceptive when one assesses its real value. The people's attachment to the world, wealth, and luxury are examples of these incorrect assessments.

---

15. An expensive sunglasses brand.

142. The Sufi on the Beaches of Miami

There were two Sufi friends. One was a regular mosque attendee, spending most of his time in the temple, and enjoying the prayers and reading the scriptures. The other was spending most of his time on the beaches of Miami, enjoying the sun, and while enjoying, performing his prayers and readings from the scripture. One day, the regular Sufi wanted to visit the other Sufi. He was worried about his friend's spirituality because he was spending most of his time on the beach. The regular Sufi took a plane and went to Miami and found his friend on the beach. The regular Sufi was very uncomfortable because the beach was not like the mosque. He was walking and looking down and trying to find his friend and not be affected by the naked scenes of the opposite gender. Finally, he found his friend and immediately asked the question: "I really don't understand. How can you pray and read your scripture here?" His friend said: "They are not attractive. I don't look at them."

In practice

In normative teachings, an unwanted look, bite, or hearing can affect the heart of the person. There may be some exceptions to the general rule depending on the special circumstance of the person, similar to the story mentioned above.

143. Sufi and Eating

There were two Sufis—Mary and Kimberly. Kimberly saw Mary eating very slowly.

Kimberly: What are you doing?

Mary: Eating.

Kimberly: Why are you eating so slowly?

Mary: I am thinking and chanting before I take each bite.

IN PRACTICE

Eating is not a separate engagement but, while doing something, a Sufi can fulfill this need of eating. That is the best way. If one sets a separate time for eating, he or she may not get pleasure from it. It is okay to cook good food and it can take time. During the preparation, one can reflect on different types of food given by God. According to practice, eating can take time if the person is thinking on each bite and chanting on it, but at the end he or she can get more pleasure from it.

144. Sufi Who Talks a Lot When He Is at Fault

One day a Sufi was late to the class. The teacher was angry but did not show his anger. Sufi immediately engaged with the class discussion to pretend that he had been there since the beginning of the class. The other students understood this and were annoyed.

IN PRACTICE

Sometimes, the faults can paint the mind and the heart as a result of not accepting one's mistakes. A person on the path is expected to face all mistakes during the course of the day. It should be the accountability of all actions, words, sentences, sounds, sights, and tastes. At the end of the day, the person can self-evaluate all of his or her dealings and whether they were necessary or not. Then, the next day, the person can become more careful. At least he or she can eliminate some of them in the beginning of this new day. For some scholars, one's realization of his or her mistakes is also a positive achievement on the spiritual path. One of the worst levels of the spiritual path is not realizing one's mistakes or not being aware of them.

145. Death and the Sufi

One day the father of a person died and he came to the mosque. He saw the Sufi sitting and reading the scripture. The man said: "I can't sleep. I still think about my father. I don't have any one. I am all alone by myself."

IN PRACTICE

The grief of the loss is very painful. It is normal to be sad and have tears. In Sufi practice, it should be temporary. The grief for the loss should not take over and become dysfunction in the person's life.

Sufis don't see someone's death as loss but gain as one is finally meeting with the Beloved.

146. Being Lonely Among the Sufis

There were a few Sufis together in a temple. They were engaged in remembrance of God, chanting, and prayers. When there was a coffee break two Sufis were talking.

> John: How do you feel? I feel so content and peaceful after the chanting and it was a nice lecture. I got positive energy.

> Justin: I feel so lonely.

IN PRACTICE

One of the spiritual states in the practice is the state of escape or loneliness. The person in this state can desperately burn for being with God. Although the person may be a saint, this person may not be satisfied with the images, rather desiring the Essence. This stage also can be called union with God if it is not transitory, but remains a permanent spiritual state.

147. Backbiting and Arguing

The Sufi was sitting in the mosque. Some people were talking and laughing about the ugliness of a girl. Sufi heard this and was disgusted about their enjoyment of their backbiting, eating the flesh of their sister.[16] When the Sufi heard this conversation, he stepped away from them in order to not listen to them. Next morning, the Sufi entered the mosque. He saw the same people who were laughing, but now were arguing with each other and they were so angry with each other.

IN PRACTICE

The effect of something evil can manifest itself as another disturbance. The people talked badly about a poor girl and enjoyed it and now they are fighting with each other over some nonsense.

---

16. In practice, it is known that a person who backbites or gossips behind a person and takes pleasure from it for no purpose is behaving in a way similar to eating the dead flesh of that person.

148. Silence and the Sufi

One day a woman attended a Sufi retreat for self-discipline. She saw a friend of hers that she had not seen for a long time. Her friend asked how the Sufi was doing all these years. The Sufi started explaining in detail what had transpired in all those past years.

Finally, it was the Sufi's turn to ask the same question of her friend and said: "So, how have you been? What did you do all these years that I didn't see you?" Her friend replied: "I am sorry. I cannot talk because the teacher in the self-discipline retreat said that you can eat but you can't talk." The Sufi was so annoyed.

IN PRACTICE

There are three main principles on the spiritual path—minimizing talking, eating, and sleeping. In the above story, the teacher in the retreat let the new practitioners eat whatever they wanted but tried to discipline talking only as a method of teaching. In practice it is understood that the amount of talking, eating, and sleeping are all related. In this case of self-discipline training, the teacher focused only on habitual talking. The Sufi was annoyed because her friend let her talk without telling her of the teacher's recommendation at the beginning of their conversation. If the Sufi knew this, she wouldn't have engaged in talking and wouldn't have told her friend in detail about her life.

149. The External and the Daytime

There was a Sufi in the mosque. It was daytime. The weather was gloomy, rainy, and dark. He heard people screaming, fighting, and arguing in the subway station next to the mosque. The Sufi said to himself, "It is either Satan or the self or both."

IN PRACTICE

In Sufi teachings, one of the names of God is the External. God changes the weather, light, sun, night, rain, snow, hot, and cold. In each change, the spiritual state of the person can be affected. If the person is not on the path, all these changes can depress the person. God gives these changes so that the person feels the need to establish a positive meaningful relationship with God, the External. One of the ideal states of a spiritual traveler is that the external changes do not affect one's spiritual state negatively but help to increase the relationship with the One, the External. It is believed that the negative spiritual states of a person are caused either by Satan or the self of the person, or both. Satan or the untrained self or ego gives temptations to do evil. Then the person can execute it if he or she has a weak connection with the Divine.

150. The Internal and the Night

There was a Sufi. After the sunset, she used to gain her power of inspirations and crying. She used to feel different in her spiritual states compared to daytime. She used to allocate her time especially to writing poems, crying, and reading from the scripture at night times.

IN PRACTICE

In Sufi practice, nights are important avenues to establish a very private and secret relationship with the Divine. One can refer to this name of God as the Internal. God knows all the detailed feelings, emotions, and experiences of a person even though sometimes the person cannot differentiate and name them. According to one of the Prophetic traditions, God especially establishes a very intimate and powerful relationship with the person in the last one-third of the night. The person can get benefit of this relationship if the person is awake—not sleeping—and engaged in prayers, chanting, meditation, and reading the scriptures.

151. Required Divorce

One day a Sufi was giving a lecture about divorce. He explained different cases and their outcomes and finally he said, "The only required divorce is between Satan and the self or ego."

IN PRACTICE

In some of the Sufi understandings, the person's self, ego, or mind is a partner of Satan. Satan sends signals to the self and the self takes it[17] and likes to execute it. Some can say that the self and Satan are married because both work toward the path of destruction of the person. When a person starts a spiritual journey the person can aim to divorce Satan and be independent in order to end the abuse. After this divorce, Satan can get angry and can try to hurt this person but the person has the protection order from God through chanting, prayers, and blessings.

---

17. In some traditions, this relationship is depicted by the dwelling or receiver of the spiritual faculties of the person when Satan sends signals, lummahshaytaniyah.

152. Two Cats and the Sufi

There was a Sufi who had two cats and two children. Cats were brother and sister. This Sufi's children were a boy and a girl. The Sufi used to interact with the cats. The female cat was very polite and sensitive. On the other hand, the male cat was very harsh and aggressive. Therefore, the Sufi used to be very polite to the female cat and at the same time he was trying to teach some good manners with discipline to the male cat. The Sufi was thinking about this difference and realized that maybe he should raise his children similarly.

IN PRACTICE

Sufis generally observe different animal behaviors, the gender differences, the ego, the eating habits, and their reactions. They try to take some lesson from different animals in order to implement in their own self's spiritual discipline.

153. Cat, Mouse, and the Sufi

A Sufi had a cat in her house. Her cat's name was Sabir. She put that name to him because of his patience. One day, Sabir found a mouse at home and started chasing it. The mouse went into a hole. Sabir went outside the hole and waited there patiently until the next day when the mouse came out. Sufi was watching this and was amazed with her cat's patience and so named her cat Sabir, the patient one. She acknowledged Sabir as one of her teachers in learning patience.

IN PRACTICE

In Sufi practice, it is very important to observe everything—the animals, the objects, the plants, and the changes. Active and critical thinking is an expected methodology to increase one's knowledge on the spiritual path. The knowledge is useless unless the person benefits himself or herself.

154. Sufi and the Professor

One day a Sufi was giving a lecture on the concept of understanding submission, reliance,[18] and surrender in relationship with God. There was a professor who was sitting as a student in the class. The professor did not get what the Sufi was trying to say. A few years later, the Sufi received a phone call from the professor. The professor was crying and said, "I understand what you meant by surrender now. My wife had cancer. I was distraught. She was getting worse in front of me every day in the hospital. I couldn't help her. I thought that I was powerful and confident. She died. I submit and surrender." Sufi was sad.

IN PRACTICE

It is very important to embody the notion that all of a person's physical and spiritual power is from God. In other words, the person should believe and embody that one cannot even lift his or her arm or be in a good spiritual engagement unless there is a blessing and opening from God. There are phrases that people chant daily to instill this notion for the spiritual traveler. In the above story, the professor trusted and relied on his own power in his dealings with life and he suffered.

18. Tawakkul is translated as reliance.

155. Evil and the Pregnancy

There was a girl who used to go to church regularly. She got pregnant. It was very difficult to handle her labor pains. Finally, she delivered her baby. Now, she stopped going to church. She said to herself, "I have been going to church all my life. God did not help me when I was in pain during my labor. I am not going to go to church again."

IN PRACTICE

People have a difficult time when interpreting the evil, pain, and difficulties in life. One of the purposes of the spiritual path is to train the self and ego before encountering the tests of evil, or difficulties in life. If the person does not wear proper clothes in freezing weather the person can lose his organs and limbs. Similarly, there can be people going to church, mosque, synagogue, or temple. If the people do not acquire and embody the self-training of spiritual heart and mind through practicing different rituals, the person can alienate oneself from practice due to not going beyond with the meaning of symbols.

156. Bad Word and the Sufi

There were two kids who were memorizing the Quran. They were playing in the mosque and the Sufi was busy with his reflection. One of the kids said a bad word to another one. The Sufi called the boys and said, "Make a choice. Good word and bad word does not stay at the same time in the heart." A good word and a bad word cannot occupy the same place in one's heart at the same time. If you say a bad word, all the good words and your memorization will leave you.

IN PRACTICE

A person's intake of good food, good words, or good smells makes a good spiritual heart. One of the best good words is the word of God. The Quran is pure and clean. Therefore, a person cannot touch the Quran before washing oneself. A person will not be able to memorize something purely if his or her tongue and mind are engaged with anger, backbiting, jealousy, and anything that does not concern the person. This notion is much embedded in the advice of the Prophet for the ones who want to memorize the Quran.[19]

---

19. Tirmizi, M. 2007. *Jami At-Tirmizi*. Dar-us-Salam.

157. Bad Smell and Thinking

There was an insane person who used to pee on his clothes. With his smelly clothes, he used to come to mosque. People did not want to embarrass him. The places that he passed in the mosque used to smell bad. One day, this person came to the mosque and then left. The Sufi was praying and thinking "Alhamdulillah, he came but it does not smell bad." As soon as he had these thoughts, it started smelling. The Sufi smiled and said to himself, "My bad thoughts . . . "

IN PRACTICE

Sometimes if a person thinks badly about others, or has feelings of arrogance, the bad thoughts may transform into other forms such as bad smells. In the above story, the Sufi's bad thoughts about the person transformed into a bad smell. One day, there was a man who was backbiting about others. He threw up and some chunks of meat came up in his vomit. He went to the Prophet and said that he did not eat meat but he threw up and meat came out. The Prophet said, "That is the flesh of your brother that you backbit".[20]

---

20. Hanbal, Ahmad B. 2012. *Musnad Imam Ahmad Ibn Hanbal*. Dar-Us-Salam Publications.

158. Shouting and the Sufi

There were two people arguing and shouting in the mosque. A Sufi was in the mosque, too. As soon as the Sufi heard their shouting, he left the mosque.

IN PRACTICE

When there is shouting among people, then that environment is contaminated with bad spirits instead of the angelic beings. Actually, there are verses in the Quran [31:19] that discourage shouting as a way of communication. Bad spirits encourage bad words, shouting, anger, and physical harm. Angelic beings, the Quran, the chanting, and prayer inspire good words and peaceful feelings and tranquility.

159. Glass Cup and the Sufi Teacher

There was a Sufi who had a glass cup. He wanted to throw it in the garbage. When the Sufi teacher understood this he called the student and said: "My son, do not throw the glass to break it but gently put it down. If you get used to breaking things you will not be careful in breaking people's hearts."

IN PRACTICE

Being genuine to people is very important. God is always with the ones whose hearts are broken according to teachings in practice.

160. Sufi and the Ocean

One day, the Sufi was next to the ocean watching the professional divers. There were a few divers diving to very deep parts of the ocean and bringing out some pearls. The divers were connected with a rope to the ship. One day, one of the divers did not want to dive with the rope. He dived. Hours and then days passed but he did not come back. Then, they found out that he was dead. The Sufi was not surprised but sad.

IN PRACTICE

In the above story, the person maybe had a good intention but did not follow the rules and died. Similarly, in Sufi practice, the rope represents the pillars of the faith and practice. The goal is that the person expands on the pillars without destroying or removing the pillars. One of the main pillars is that God is One and Unique. God revealed the Quran. God states about the Divine Self that God is One and Unique in the scriptures. Some can rationalize this belief and some can submit and surrender to it. Sometimes, there can be renderings due to the problems of analogies and language. Therefore, Sufis don't think about the essence of God but they ponder on the attributes of God. Thinking about essence of God removes the rope in the journeys of spiritual excursions.

161. Man with One Leg and Man with One Eye

One day the Sufi was talking with her nephew on the phone. Her nephew lost most of his sight in one of his eyes. This was due to a tumor behind his eyes. Her nephew was upset. He used to be a good-looking man. While talking with her nephew, the Sufi saw a man with one leg using crutches and going to the mosque to pray. She said to her nephew:

Sufi: Do you prefer to have two eyes—one perfect and the other not seeing well—or do you prefer to have two perfect eyes but only one leg?

Nephew: It is tough. I prefer what I have now because I don't know if what you describe is more complicated or painful for me.

IN PRACTICE

Appreciation without any complaints in relationship with God is the key. The phrase Alhamdulillah (thank you God) represents this notion of appreciation in the relationship with the Divine in all circumstances. In the above story, the one-legged man was struggling to go to the mosque to pray to God in order to appreciate what he has. Sometimes, people look at what they don't have and complain instead of appreciating what they have and being thankful in their relationship with God.

162. Sufi and the Eyeglasses

One day a Sufi had a dream. In his dream, he saw that his cat jumped on him and grabbed his eyeglasses. The cat was holding the eyeglasses with his teeth. The Sufi grabbed his eyeglasses and pulled them. The cat was holding them tightly and pulling them to the other direction. The Sufi woke up and he said to himself: "What does this mean?" He was thinking and did not understand the meaning. A few days later, he finally made the interpretation as follows.

As the Sufi was on the spiritual journey he was trying to understand everything in life and beyond. But still, he was using some tools to see, understand, and experience. God was inspiring him through experience and angels to remove all of the tools for the pure objective truth. The cat in this case was representing an angelic being attempting to remove the eyeglasses from the Sufi. But the Sufi was still attached to the world and not focused on the manners of the spiritual path. He still wanted to use the tools or the reasons.

IN PRACTICE

Sometimes, the evil-looking incidents have a purpose in life. Sometimes they are coming with a good purpose similar to Rumi's violent guest poem. The person sometimes struggles and aspires to do something bad and there can be a blessed and merciful stopper that the person may not realize.

163. The Ant and the Carpet

There was a Sufi in the mosque. She saw an ant walking on the carpet. The carpet was nice and green with some designs. The Sufi said to herself, "Wow! This ant probably thinks that he is in a green ocean."

IN PRACTICE

In the above story, the ant was on a two-dimensional plane compared to the Sufi with a three-dimensional plane who can see the design of the carpet. The Sufi was above the carpet, looking down. In practice, it is understood and experienced that there can be millions of dimensions. Some mystics can experience some of them.

Similarly, the knowledge and experiences of the Transcendent, the High, God can sometimes be simplified and reduced to the human understandings of time and space. One should not forget that the similarities do not give the person the essence about the Divine. There is always room for error. Therefore, caution with possibilities and the statement of "God knows the best" is added in internal and external expressions.

164. Sufi and the Right Answer

There was a Sufi in the mosque. A man with inflexible beliefs came and wanted to do some missionary work. He wanted the Sufi to go with him. The Sufi did not want to go but he said to himself, "If I say that I don't want to go, he will argue with me and I don't want to waste my time." He said to the man "I will think about it . . . " The man left the Sufi alone.

In practice

It is always important to reflect and think well before uttering any words to any person. Therefore, Sufis prefer silence and purposeful talking if and when necessary. If they are put in a difficult situation of choice they try to use wisdom to minimize any evil and undesired effects.

165. Sufi and Choosing His Prospective Wife

There were two single Sufis who wanted to get married. They heard that there is a girl who wants to get married as well. The first Sufi who got the news said to himself, "I should not be selfish. I should have my friend first consider marrying her." He went and told his Sufi friend. His friend was not interested and he already had arrangements for another girl. The first Sufi said to himself, "OK, then maybe I should meet with this girl." Then, he happened to see this girl in the mosque and shocked, said to himself, "I will never get married with this girl. She is so ugly." A few years passed. He married this girl. After he had kids from this girl, he remembered his promise not to get married with this girl and he blamed himself and said, "My negative thoughts about others."

IN PRACTICE

Sometimes, in practice, the person can be tested with the things that he or she does not want. Therefore, the Sufis try to catch their bad thoughts before the opposite happens. This is a level in which the Sufis try to watch and be conscious about their thoughts.

166. Sufi and Not Flying

There was a Sufi man who went to the airport to take his brother who was flying to England. As his brother was going to the plane, he waved to his brother and said to himself, "I will never fly to England. It is such an ugly country." After a few years, he went to England and he liked it so much. He said to himself, "I should not have those thoughts in my mind."

IN PRACTICE

In the above history, the Sufi did not want to fly to England and had some negative thoughts about it. God made him fly there in order to rectify his thoughts about different places and people.

167. Sufi and Burping

There was a Sufi in the mosque. He heard an old lady burping constantly and she could not control herself. Sufi had a feeling of disgust. Immediately, he caught and stopped his thoughts and feelings and said, "Astagfirullah."

IN PRACTICE

In the above story, the Sufi was afraid that if he did not catch his negative thoughts and feelings about the situation of the old lady, he would face the same problem when he became old or sooner. In practice, a person can have instant negative feelings and thoughts toward others. Those are not harmful as long as they don't become permanent and they are terminated with certain mindful chants such as "Astagfirullah" which means, "Oh God, forgive me for my bad thoughts about others."

168. King and the Sufi

A king one day asks every inhabitant of his kingdom what they want. Everyone wants something different. Someone asks for pounds of gold. Another person asks for a lot of land with many fruit trees. A person asks for a number of cows, sheep, and chickens. A Sufi comes and asks for the king himself and the king is startled and asks, "Why do you want me?" He responds, "If I have you, whatever you own is mine." In Sufi tradition, the highest intention to perform chants, rituals, or service to other people is the pleasure of God. If one pleases God, God can give boundless rewards and pleasure from the Mighty Kingdom.

IN PRACTICE

In Sufi tradition, the highest intention to perform chants, rituals, or service to other people is the pleasure of God. If one pleases God, God can give boundless rewards and pleasure from the Mighty Kingdom.

169. Sufi, Change, and God

One day a Sufi saw her old friend with another person that she had not seen for a few years. After the greetings, her old friend started introducing her. The Sufi was a little bit uncomfortable because the Sufi was not the same Sufi that her friend used to know a few years ago. Every hour he was different.

IN PRACTICE

In Sufism, change and advancement on the spiritual path is good. Every day a person is expected to go further in the closeness and union with God. The only unchanged One is God. God's attributes are constant and unchanged—the difference between the creation and Creator.

170. Sufi and the Preface of a Book

There was a Sufi who bought a new book on spiritual advancement written by a famous teacher. The book was translated to English. The translator was a Sufi as well and also a student of the teacher. The translator wrote in the preface a very harsh critique for the ones criticizing the book without genuine intention and learning. The Sufi was shocked with this type of introduction in the preface. The Sufi was upset about it.

IN PRACTICE

The Sufi books are generally written for the ones who have sincere intention to learn and sympathize with the travelers. In practice, the traditional followers, simple intellectuals, or people with the diseases of the heart such as jealousy and arrogance may not be able to benefit from these writings unless there is a sincere intention.

171. Sufi and the Satan

One day the Sufi was praying at night in her home. Satan approached her to distract her from her engagement in prayer. After finishing the prayer, she said to Satan: "Why don't you make repentance? God's mercy is infinite." Satan said: "No, I will prove that I am right."

IN PRACTICE

Sometimes, intellectual discourses prevent the person from genuine learning due to the disease of "I will prove that I am right." In the scripture, one of the traits of a person is accepting the good, beautiful, and truthful whenever and whoever it comes from.[21] Then, God makes everything easy for that person.

---

21. Surah layl . . . (SaddaqabilHusna).

172. Sufi and the Handyman

There was a Sufi and a drunk, poor handyman. Sufi was trying to help him by giving him some work at his house and advising him on changing his bad and destructive habits. The handyman was coming to the Sufi's home. One day, the Sufi gave him a small loan so that the handyman could buy a car and not be dependent on people, because with gambling and drinking he had lost everything. Then, the Sufi saw a dream the same night that the handyman's face was turned into a fox and was snickering and smiling. The Sufi woke up and didn't understand what the dream meant. Then, he called the handyman, but he didn't answer. One call, two, three, many calls, no answer . . . Next day, next month, no answer from the handyman. The Sufi was worried about the handyman. He said to himself, "I hope he is OK. I don't care about the loan." Then, finally, he reached one of his friends. His friend said he left town and will not come back again. The Sufi said, "Alhamdulillah, he is OK."

IN PRACTICE

In Sufism, thinking good about people is the key even though the people may have bad traits. In the above story, it seems that the handyman intended to leave the town without paying the Sufi. Therefore, he seemed to trick the Sufi as shown within his dream interpretation. Although the Sufi might have understood the meaning of his dream, still he was worried about the handyman, not his money.

173. The Sufi and the Questions

There was a Sufi in the mosque. He used to answer everyone's questions. The people used to observe of him that depending on the person, he used to give different answers to each person. He was asked the reason. He said, "Everyone has a different understanding level. It is not what you say but how they understand it."

IN PRACTICE

The prophet[22] used to give short answers to desert travelers appropriate to their understanding. He used to implement the notion that everyone in practice has a different level. Recognizing this is important. Not everyone can be intellectuals. Not everyone can be devout but may want to know what is sufficient. Therefore, all the struggles are valuable to God.

---

22. Iyad, Qadi. 2006. *Ash-Shifa*. Madina Press.

174. The Funny Handyman and the Sufi

There was a funny handyman. He was making a joke that people always say Alhamdullillah (thank you God) but then complain. They say InshAllah (if God wills) but then they don't follow what they say. Sufi started smiling . . .

IN PRACTICE

Expressions have meanings. If the people don't follow what they say it is not the problem of expression but the problem of the person. "Alhamdullillah" (thanks be to God) is an expression to remind the person not to complain but to always be appreciative. When this is chanted it has an effect on the heart and mind. When the person says "InshAllah" it is a reminder that the real power is from God.

175. Sufi and the Deaf Man

There was a deaf person in the mosque. The Sufi was good friends with him. The Sufi knew sign language and talked to him. Everyone in the mosque used to feel bad for the deaf person that he couldn't hear or talk. The deaf person told the Sufi that he feels bad for these people. They waste their time, minds, and hearts in nonsense talk. The deaf person used to express gratitude to God that he can't talk. He was always in the peaceful state of silence.

IN PRACTICE

Silence is one of the desired states in the practice. A person who talks most of the time does not listen. He or she may think that the person understands, but not really. Real understanding and embodiment comes with experience, reflection, and personalization in the practice. Statistically speaking, a person who talks a lot can make more errors and can break more hearts than others. God knows the best, as Sufis avow.

176. Sufi Teacher and the Kids

There was a teacher in the mosque who used to teach the kids. After shouting at the kids, he used to give candies. Although the teacher seemed to be angry and shouting to an outsider, the kids seemed to love him. He used to smile also and explain the lecture well. Kids seemed to interpret the teacher's treatment not as abuse or hate, but as a method of teaching. The kids felt this genuine intention and feelings from the teacher. Sufi was watching this and said to herself, "Wow, this is similar to the relationship between the person and God."

IN PRACTICE

God does not get angry like humans. Anger in humans can be a deficient quality. God gives opportunities and learning experiences to people to excel in the path of perfecting their relationship with the Divine. It is up to the person to take heed from each experience as a self-learning opportunity to build a positive relationship with God.

177. Sufi and the Literalist

One day, the Sufi was sitting in the mosque. A literalist was teaching the knowledge of God to the children. Sufi was listening and impressed. He said to himself, "Wow, one should learn the initial knowledge of God without any interpretation from a literalist. Then, the person can learn the interpretation from the Sufis."

IN PRACTICE

In normative Sufism, it is very important to learn the religious laws as some people call them as literalist because they avoid interpretation. Legal laws or literal approach is the cloth and frame of the meanings. Without these pillars, the foundation can collapse. Therefore, a good Sufi in practice can be a good expert in legal or literal teachings of the religion.

178. Sufi and Different Languages

There was a Sufi who knew a few languages. He used to enjoy scriptures and saintly writings in their original language. He used to also look at different translations of the same text in different languages to get genuine, culturally embedded meanings. He was trying to understand and personalize the concepts in words in each language in order to reach their intended meanings.

IN PRACTICE

It is very critical and encouraged to chant and practice the divine phrases in their original language of revelation. Although the person may not be a native speaker of that language, the divine sounds have effects on the heart and mind without even understanding the meanings, according to the practice. When the person puts forth an effort to learn the meanings of the phrases, then the effects of spiritual engagement can increase.

179. Sufi and Her Book

One day a Sufi wrote a book. She was invited to teach people from her book. She was explaining and having the students write reflection papers on each chapter. Next class, she was listening to the students about what they understood. She was getting great pleasure from it.

IN PRACTICE

Similarly, one of the notions in the practice is that God created the universe to have the divine attributes and names to be known. The natural sciences and other sciences in our modern life can reflect the different names and attributes of God in practice. God is pleased when a person puts forth an effort to increase his or her knowledge of God. In other words, reading the book of the universe, the human self, and scriptures can increase one's knowledge in the path of God and God can be pleased about it.

180. Sufi and Phrases on the Tongue

There was a Sufi who used to memorize divine phrases and parts of the Quran in their original language of revelation. She was trying to understand the meanings but sometimes she did not understand the meanings, and yet still memorized it. One day, she was sleeping and woke up with one of the words that she had memorized, and found that she was repeating it involuntarily. She looked up the meaning of the word that she was repeating and said to herself, "Aha! That is the answer. Now everything makes sense."

IN PRACTICE

Divine phrases and verses from the scripture can embody different beings and can help the person in different parts of life difficulties. When the person appreciates God and all the divine phrases and the scripture from God, they can act like a superman to save the person in the times of need. It is kind of a payback time. When the person needs help, they come. This is a common belief across the tradition. Each phrase, chant, prayer, and recitation of the scripture can take different forms to help the person in this world and in the afterlife. There are narrations that the five times prayers of a person can come in the form of a human being after the person's death in the grave or on the judgment day and can comfort the person from all worries. When the person sees this unknown person the person asks, "Who are you?" and this unknown person replies, "I am your prayers that you used to pray. Now, it is my turn to help you."

181. Sufi and the Huffing and Puffing Handyman

There was a Sufi hiding in the mosque. He did not want people to know where he was in the mosque and he did not want to be bothered. He wanted to enjoy his readings, chanting, and coffee. One day, someone opened the door and Sufi was not looking. The man started praying and making a noise of huffing and puffing while he was praying. The Sufi said to himself, "It should be the old handyman" and it was.

IN PRACTICE

Huffing and puffing sounds of a person outside a prayer can mean complaints, negativity, or depression. When a person has these genuine sounds of huffing and puffing in a prayer this can mean charge and discharge or empty and fill effects, while one is re-establishing a connection with God. Therefore, when huffing and puffing sincerely and involuntarily comes in one's prayer, it can show a very high value of genuine connection of the person with God.

182. The Lucky Sufi

There was a Sufi who used to rent a house. His rich landlord loved him so much. One day, his landlord died and he left a will for the Sufi that the Sufi will inherit the house. When the Sufi heard this, he said, "Alhamdullillah, and this is exactly me and my Lord."

IN PRACTICE

The life is rented by God to the person. Then, God treats the person as if he/she owns her own life with free will and free choice. As a tenant of his or her house of body and soul, the person comes from nowhere as the owner of it and acts accordingly. Finally, the fake landlord sells the house to the Real Lord with a business transaction of recognition and appreciation of God. In the scripture, the Quran, this notion of business transaction between the person and God is mentioned in multiple places such as [57:11].

183. Black Magic

There was a Sufi who used to give lectures. One day there were a few new people who attended the lectures and made magic on the Sufi to see if she was really a genuine teacher. The Sufi understood this. She protected herself with the divine phrases from the effects of this evil attempt. She said to herself, "I feel bad for these people, instead of focusing on their own selves and benefiting from the lectures and group chants, they are trying to harm others."

IN PRACTICE

Black Magic has an effect on the people but it is considered lowly and a great sin to perform magic. Sufis learn the necessary tools, chants, and phrases to protect themselves from the evil talismanic effects. Ultimately, they firmly believe that the effect is created by God. By taking refuge in God, these attempts may have only temporary effects if any. On the other hand, the person involved in any type of evil, including magic, that person harms herself or himself before harming others. In the above story, although the people may have good intention to test the teacher's authenticity, it is considered evil to use magic to harm the Sufi. In other words, to achieve a good outcome or result, all the means to reach that goal should also be good. For example, one cannot steal money and help the poor. Stealing is evil and helping is good. Good and evil do not mix.

184. Milk, Pee, and the Sufi

There was a student who did not understand the concept of mixing good and bad in spiritual and ethical teachings on the path. He came to the Sufi and asked this question. The student used to like and drink fresh milk. The Sufi took a bottle of fresh organic milk and he took a drop of pee from the restroom and put it inside the bottle in front of the student. Then, the Sufi gave the bottle to the student and said, "Why don't you drink it? It's fresh milk." The student was disgusted and he was not able to drink it. The Sufi said, "Are you sure? It is all nice, organic fresh milk. There is just a tiny amount, less than 0.01% pee." The student smiled and said, "I understood."

IN PRACTICE

All the virtuous goals should be achieved by virtuous spiritual acts and intentions. A person cannot purposefully do evil and expect a good outcome. Even though the outcome may look good, God ultimately considers genuine intentions and efforts in connection with pure and sincere struggles. In the above story, the student did not drink the milk due to the impurity although it was a minuscule amount.

185. Rotation of the Days and the Sufi

There was a Sufi in the mosque. An old man came and said that his car was stolen. The Sufi was trying to help the person to call the police. The Sufi felt bad for the old man. Then, the Sufi went to his home. His wife said that her best friend's sister is dying due to pancreatic cancer. The Sufi was sad and prayed for her. Then, the Sufi got sick and was admitted to the emergency room. The Sufi thought about all these recent incidents and smiled to himself, "Rotation of the days."

IN PRACTICE

In Sufism, God rotates evil or good-looking days among people to reveal the real character of the people. Below is a passage from the Quran that alludes to this notion [3:149].

If an evil touched you
Then remember that
Evil touches others as well.

These are the days
We rotate among the people
Good and evil

So that the real characters
Of people are revealed
God knows it and
You become witness to it as well

Remember God does not like oppressors.

One of the states in practice is the station of patience. When an evil hits the person, if the person does not complain but still appreciates what comes from God, then the person can use this as an opportunity to excel spiritually. Although in practice, everyone asks for good and an easy life, if for some reason it does not happen, the notion of patience is practiced. In both good and evil-looking days, the person appreciates the relationship with God.

186. Sufi and Her Book

One day, a Sufi wrote a book about inner spiritual states and said to herself, "Wow, if a person reads this book they will be immersed in it." As the time passed and she observed the people, they did not give the proper attention to the book that the Sufi had originally expected. She now told herself, "Now, I understand. There is an original Book from God; people don't care and are heedless. If it is a human's book, it is normal."

IN PRACTICE

Heedlessness, or being in the state of "not caring" can be the attitude of many toward prophets, miracles, scriptures, and genuine writings of the spiritual path. It is most of the time not the fault of the text or messenger but the receiver or the audience. In physics, to decode the signals from a sender, the receiver should be able to decode the incoming wavelengths with the same frequency.

187. Sufi and Two Cases

There was a Sufi looking from the window. While looking at the window, she saw two people. One person was addicted to drugs and trying to terrorize people to get money. Another person was walking and seeing an old woman, wanting to help her with her stuff and carry her bags to the station. The Sufi was thinking to try to understand these two cases.

IN PRACTICE

In Sufism, external representations reflect internal states. In a human being, there is good, love, humbleness. At the same time, there are evil, anger, and arrogance. The person has a choice, free will, but is accountable for one's decision. The person has a goal on the path to excel in the betterment of oneself. If the person does not practice or exercise following a path, or rituals, then the person can be in duality in the inner self struggles, in choosing right or wrong.

A human's inner self is like a huge system of government. If the person has the systems or institutions to govern and implement with law enforcement through rituals, then a healthy government or society is constructed. This is called a self on the journey in practice. Therefore, in the above story, there are two different selves involved in making a decision and acting on it.

188. Third World Countries and the Sufi

There was a Sufi helping some refugees in the shelter house. While she was leaving the shelter house, an American friend of the Sufi approached her and told her, "I feel bad for these refugees. They come from third world countries, with raw conditions." The Sufi smiled and said, "I feel worse about the third world selves than the ones from the third world countries."

IN PRACTICE

There is the initial level of raw selves. This self is not trained, can enjoy the evil and prevent the good. The second level of self does recognize one's mistakes and feels sorry about it. The third level of self is the best, knows oneself and God, knows the good and the evil, acts on it, and intends to please God. The Sufi in the above story has categorized the self, according to the internal conditions of the person rather than the external ones.

189. Communication with the Unknowns and Unseen

There was a Sufi who used to engage with people in different religious traditions. She was really surprised when people were getting scared about the unknowns and unseen especially related to the ones after death. She really felt bad about them but was not able to do anything except give them some advice about believing in the Creator and practicing the rituals.

IN PRACTICE

Depending on the level of the person, there are really no unknowns and unseen. An advanced person on the path can experience God, angels, the good and evil doers, the authentic versus non-authentic, and all others with certainty. Death is a wrong word according to the Sufis. Death is only a removal of the barriers for the layman. For a Sufi, death is nothing newer than having temporary states becoming permanent stations. In the journey of ascension, the Prophet visited different dimensions of unseen and unknowns such as the various conditions and dwelling places of the people after death. One of the lowest states in spiritual advancement is the cognition of the condition of the people in the graveyard.

190. The Sufi and the Pancreatic Cancer

There was a Sufi. Her friend's sister became ill and diagnosed with pancreatic cancer. She was thirty-eight years old with a few kids and a crying husband. Everyone was visiting her in the hospital. A few days were left before her expected departure day from the world. Finally, she died and everyone was crying. The friends made some food for the family. The funeral ended and the deceased was sent to the cemetery. The Sufi visited her friend. She was still crying. The Sufi said: "We will meet them soon. They just left a little bit early before us."

In practice

Although death can look ugly, it ends the pains for the ones who are always missing God. In practice, tribulations and tests are given to the people to increase their spiritual level before meeting with God as long as there are no complaints in the relationship with the Divine. One can welcome the evil-looking incidents if one is constantly engaged in regular prayers, rituals, and reading the scripture. These daily practices are called wird or awrad, the daily spiritual regular practices.

191. Sufi and Her Teacher

There was a Sufi who did not see her teacher for a long time. She really missed her and left her home to drive eleven hours to visit her teacher. Her teacher always had guests visiting from different places. This time, it was not many but perhaps only sixty to seventy people. The teacher was giving a lecture. The Sufi sat down. The teacher from nowhere started explaining about the importance of using every second of time meaningfully and mindfully in the spiritual advancement in the relationship with the Divine. The teacher discussed spiritual arrogance and the difficulties on the path. The Sufi said to herself, "Alhamdullillah, I got what I needed. Thank you, Allah." Then, she left to drive another eleven hours to reach her home.

IN PRACTICE

The genuine teachers know and are aware of the students' need and accordingly they escort them on the spiritual path. It is not uncommon in practice for the people to visit a teacher for a short period of time after traveling hours and days, and then going back to their homes. A few minutes, an hour, a day can be sufficient to charge the person spiritually and then she or he can go back home. The presence of the teacher or the place can have an effect on the seeker depending on the sincere intention and the struggle of the person.

192. The Rich Sufi and His Teacher's Food

One day, there was a rich Sufi. He was not feeling well. He wanted to visit his teacher to be in his presence. He went and visited him. He felt better and was waiting for dinnertime to come in order to eat the food prepared in the Sufi center where his teacher resided. For dinner, as usual, there was soup and salad. The Sufi ate and felt much better and left the center.

IN PRACTICE

There is a blessing in eating from the food prepared in the place where the teacher resides. Due to a high level of spiritual presence, chants, and prayers, it is believed that the food has a curing effect of physical and spiritual diseases. In the above story, the Sufi was rich and he could have eaten a better food but he waited to eat a simpler but blessed food prepared at the Sufi center where his teacher resided.

193. The Teacher and Humbleness

One day, the Sufi visited her teacher. The teacher was giving a lecture and using some harsh words against herself to humiliate her own ego in front of the public. The Sufi was listening and trying to take a lesson from the lecture for her own self.

In practice

The teachers are humans. Although the teachers are spiritually blessed and the students revere them so much, they see and locate themselves at the lowest level in order to not be trapped with spiritual arrogance. Genuine humbleness and humility of the teacher is one of the character traits of a good teacher.

194. Sufi and the Hindu

There was a Sufi. He had a good friend who was a Hindu. They were discussing life after death. His Hindu friend mentioned their belief of reincarnation. The Sufi was thinking. He said, "When there are different species, if they mix, there may be abnormalities or exceptions. One may not base a general rule on exceptions or abnormalities." The Hindu friend was thinking... The Sufi continued: "In the scriptures such as the Bible, Torah, or Quran, God mentions explicitly about the Divine Self and about the unknowns after death." Sufi wanted to know the source of the afterlife belief in his friend's tradition and said: "Is reincarnation a logical deduction? Is it an interpretation from your scripture?" The Hindu was thinking.

IN PRACTICE

In Sufi practice, the logic should not contradict with the belief. Below is a methodology that the Sufis follow when learning from different sources of divine knowledge related to the known, the unknown, and the unseen:

1. The first source of knowledge is knowing God through God. In other words, how God explains the Divine Self in the scriptures.

2. Knowing God through the interpretations of the prophets and messengers of God.

3. Knowing God through the intellect (reason).

4. Knowing God through the interpretation of the saints.

5. Learning through conscience (sixth sense).

6. Having the experience at any stage during the learning process to confirm or triangulate the sources from one to five.

195. Sufi and the Safety

Sufi had a Christian friend. They were talking about the understanding of being saved in this world and the afterlife. His friend said, "If the person has correct belief, then the person can be saved." Then, the Sufi added, "I agree, that is a possibility but not a certainty until the person dies."

IN PRACTICE

If the person has the right belief and good action, the person can be saved from punishment and be rewarded. However, although this is all highly likely, it is not for sure. The notion is that the person does not really know the reality of his or her intention or sincerity in performing good actions. Therefore, there are a lot of stories in the tradition of people who were worshippers of God but thrown to hellfire as a result of showing off, or for trying to attract worldly gains and benefits. Conversely, there are stories about the people who were in external disobedience to God and died and were forgiven by God due to their internal sincere intention. Although there is a general rule in the scriptures that people who have the right belief and action can be saved, Sufism still maintains some uncertainty due to not fully knowing one's inner self. This notion of uncertainty always keeps the traveler spiritually alert and self-accountable in the relationship with humans and God.

196. Sufi and the Escort

One day a Sufi was looking at the window. He saw an escort truck carrying money from the bank. There were a few armed men protecting the truck. The Sufi saw this scene and in amazement said, "Wow, this is exactly the belief[23] of the person. It needs more escort."

IN PRACTICE

The right belief is very valuable and needs to be escorted. Therefore, when one is learning about God and the rules of the path, the originality and authenticity is vital. Choosing an authentic path, studying with a good and genuine teacher, and following these priceless guidelines are the key. Once the person starts the journey and builds up the core values of the relationship with the Divine, then this treasure and diamond should be escorted. This diamond cannot be put at risk by any inauthentic knowledge, teacher, or experience. The person should know the skills of letting in and blocking out so that the treasure can increase without being infected with the diseases.

23. Iman.

197. Firefighters, Roof Rats, and the Sufis

There were two Sufis. One was American and the other was from overseas. They were walking and they saw a fire truck that was going on a rescue mission. On the fire truck, it was written "roof rats." The Sufi from overseas asked the American Sufi why it was written "roof rats." The American Sufi said the firefighters praise that they can climb on the roof like a rat. The Sufi from overseas smiled and said, "If you call someone a rat in our country, it is a curse, not a praise."

IN PRACTICE

Sometimes, language has its contextual meanings depending on the culture. In the above story, a word at a wrong time and place can mean a curse or praise. In practice, it is essential to learn the etiquette of the spiritual behaviors in relation to the different contexts and people. This is called adab. It is especially important to learn the etiquette related to the teachers, lecturers, and other peers. It ultimately helps to establish a relationship with God with the notions of adab.

198. The Rich Sufi, Online Shopping, and the Poor Sufi

One day a poor Sufi visited the rich Sufi. She saw that her friend was shopping online although it was expensive. The poor Sufi said, "Why don't you shop in the store so that you can save some money and help the poor with what you saved?" The rich Sufi said, "I don't have time. My time is valuable. If I have some extra time, I would spend it in chanting and prayers rather than going to the store and shopping."

IN PRACTICE

Both approaches are acceptable as long as the person has the right intention. It is important not to assume or judge people externally but to always have good thoughts for other fellows.

199. Sufi and Temporary Things

One day, a Sufi missed his wife very much. He went home to see her but did not receive much attention from her. Then, he left his home. Next day, he missed his daughter and went home to see her. His daughter did not care that he came home and the Sufi was disappointed. Then, he left his home. Next day, he missed his friends that he used to hang around. He went to visit his friends. His friends were in their own world and the Sufi felt disconnected from them. Then, he left them. Finally, he decided to visit the places where he was born and where he had spent all of his childhood years. He went there and found that everything looked different and he felt so isolated and deeply in pain. At the end, he understood that he needs to travel to the internal house.

IN PRACTICE

In Sufi writings, the house generally symbolizes the heart where the person has a close relationship with God. In the above story, the Sufi was disappointed with the temporary friends. At the end, he turned to the permanent, real, appreciative, and understanding Friend—God. In practice, it is believed that everything can be a cause of pain except God. Everything can include all of one's loved ones, friends, and family members. A Sufi among loved ones can be lonely. A Sufi in prison can be happy, enjoying all pleasures.

200. Sufi Teacher and the Clock

One day a Sufi visited her teacher. There were twenty to thirty people sitting in a small room with the teacher. Everyone was sitting in this gathering in silence. There was only the chirping sound of the seconds of a clock in the room. This clock was an interesting one. In each second, a page was turning in this clock that looked like a book. The Sufi was thinking, and enjoying the silence and presence of the gathering and the teacher.

IN PRACTICE

In the above story, it is a common practice to sit in silence next to the teacher for a few minutes, maybe more. The effect of the presence of good and spiritual people has an effect on the person's heart and mind. Instead of a formal lecture, there was a silent lecture in the above story. The notion of presence of the teacher and the silent lecture is a term that is used in practice to emphasize the effect of being with good and genuinely spiritual people and teachers.[24] Also, a turning page in a book-looking clock can signify the importance of each second of time for advancement in the spiritual journey in relationship with the Divine. Some Sufis believe that if a second is equal to a passed second in the experience and knowledge of God, then that can be a loss.[25]

---

24. This is called tawajjuh of the teacher on the students. Tawajjuh are the inspirations of the teacher to the students in order to teach, elevate them spiritually, or protect them from evil.
25. The Prophet mentions that a believer is in loss if one's day is equal to a previous day in closeness to God and that there should be a constant advancement on the path.

201. Sufi and Perception

There was a Sufi who was not rich and not poor. She had a middle income. Each time she had a desire to eat from an expensive restaurant she said, "I mentally assume that I went to that restaurant. I ate a nice food and a nice dessert." After enjoying this mentally, she ate her normal, simple food at home and put the saved money in a box that she was planning to use to go to the restaurant. Later, she had an urge to buy an expensive car. She saved a good amount of money. Then, she bought a normal, simple car. Each time she was using her simple car she was assuming that her car was the most expensive car. She put the remaining money in a box that she was planning to use to buy the expensive car. Over the course of years, her savings accumulated and she used that money to build a mosque for the people to worship in and for the homeless to find shelter. The name of the mosque was called "Assumption."[26]

IN PRACTICE

In Sufi practice, the training of the self or ego is very important. The raw self is generally similar to a naughty child. He may ask a lot of things, beneficial or harmful. A parent does not give to the child exactly what he wants but gives in proportion with wisdom. If the child gets what he wants there may not be teaching or self-training or behavioral development. Similarly, a person should know one's self well and accordingly apply different treatment methods.

26. There is a real mosque in Istanbul, Turkey, with that name due to the story mentioned above.

202. Now I Understood! and the Sufi

There was a Sufi who did not understand why she was sometimes in spiritual pain and sometimes not. She was engaging in prayer, chanting, reading the scripture, going to mosque, and feeling good; but sometimes when she was not engaged she was feeling so much pain, detachment, and loneliness. One day, she was traveling on a plane. She was thinking again about the painful moments of detachment, disconnection, loneliness, and physical torture. During her trip, she was constantly engaged in chanting with her beads, reading her scripture, and learning from her sacred prophetic books. She was feeling so happy. She was looking down while walking and not looking around at the people and not engaging with her surroundings. As the moments of happiness continued, she said, "Alhamdulillah, now I have understood!"

IN PRACTICE

In the above story, the Sufi was in pain when she was detached from God and not engaged in any type of mental, verbal, or physical ritual. In one of the narrations from the Prophet, the highest ranked angel—Gabriel—comes, visits him, and teaches him that the highest level of spiritual pleasure, engagement, and happiness is removing yourself and your ego every time it blocks your spiritual progress and causes pain striving to always be in the state of Union.[27]

---

27. Ihsan.

203. The Level of Union and the Evil

As the Sufi was enjoying the station of union with the Divine, she went to visit some old friends. She took the bus, and then the train, and finally reached their home. She rang the bell three times but no one answered the door. They were supposed to be home. The Sufi did not get angry and left a small gift at their door with a note. She smiled and left to go to the bus station for her appointment. The application on her phone showed her that the bus was coming soon—in two minutes. Two minutes, three minutes, five minutes, ten minutes, there was no bus . . . She smiled and called the Uber and finally made it to her appointment.

IN PRACTICE

In the story above, the Sufi still experienced some type of annoying or evil-looking incidents but she did not perceive them as evil and she moved on. Her level of union with the Divine changed her perception, making her calm and peaceful when she encountered the evil.

204. The Uber Driver, Cursing, and the Coffee

As the Sufi was late to her appointment, she called Uber to get there instead of taking the bus. A nice Uber car came and picked up the Sufi. The driver was so nice and the Sufi was enjoying the ride. Then, there was a car which abruptly cut off the road in front of this Uber car. The Uber driver started cursing the other car and he became so disturbed. The Sufi was watching the scene and trying to get a meaning from it. They finally reached their destination. While the Sufi was leaving the car, she forgot her coffee in the car. The driver called the Sufi and said, "You forgot your coffee. That is the most important thing." The Sufi smiled and then said to herself, "This is the reason why the driver was so disturbed. There is no Union."

IN PRACTICE

A person's real spiritual state can reveal itself at the encounters of different evil-looking incidents. In the above story, although the driver seemed very nice in the beginning, he lost his temper in a very small evil-looking incident. When he mentioned that "the coffee is the most important thing," then the Sufi interpreted that the driver's short temperament is due to his engagement with temporal things such as coffee. A person in practice gets real empowerment from the permanent One, God, on the journey.

205. The Crying Boy and the Sufi

There was a Sufi. He saw a father and a son. The boy was crying for something futile. The father was looking at him and he was feeling bad for his son. The father did not give what the boy wanted. The boy was still crying and trying to get the attention of the father. At the end, the father taught a lesson to his son and gave him better than what he wanted and the son was so happy. The Sufi was looking at the scene and said, "SubhanAllah, that is the relation between Allah and a person."

IN PRACTICE

In Sufi practice, a person prays[28] constantly, cries, and asks. It may be that the person is asking for something futile, useless, or harmful. During the time of asking and crying through prayer, the person can feel pain and neglected. Sometimes, she may even think, "Why are my prayers not being accepted?" The One, who is always Active, Hearing, and Merciful appreciates the effort and sincere humbleness of the person in relationship with the Creator. At the end, due to these efforts, God can give the person better than what is asked for, although the person may not initially understand this.

---

28. Dua in Ar.

206. The Huffing and Puffing Man and the Sufi

There was a man who used to come to the mosque and pray. He used to constantly come and tell his problems to the Sufi. This man used to complain about his family members and other people, claiming that everyone was always unjust to him. If the Sufi wanted to give him some advice, he did not want to listen—only talk and blame others. One day, the Sufi was in the mosque studying. This man came and he was huffing and puffing. He saw the Sufi studying and did not want to disturb him. Sufi understood the case and prolonged his studying in order to not be disturbed. The man was pacing back and forth in the mosque, huffing and puffing, waiting and peering in on the Sufi to find out if he finished his studying so that he could talk to him as usual. Five minutes, ten minutes, half an hour, one hour . . . the Sufi was still studying. His head was in the book and the man was circulating within the mosque, huffing and puffing and checking if the Sufi had finished his studying. The Sufi smiled and said to himself, "I know you want to talk to me but I know I can't help you until you sit down and engage yourself with reading the scripture, engage in prayer and chanting, and do some self-reflection. Then your problems will be solved."

IN PRACTICE

Humans really don't solve any problems. Even their apathy and lack of concern about one's problem can add more pain to the person's suffering. The real helper, listener, and concerned is only One, God. Although the person may think that no one is hearing or talking back, the mystical answers from God can be revealed to the person whether the person understands or not.

207. Sufi, Cat, and the Natural Habitat

One day a Sufi visited a friend of hers in America. Her friend had an indoor cat. The Sufi was surprised that the cats were kept at home and they were not allowed to go outside. Each morning when the Sufi woke up, she saw that the cats were rushing to the window to look outside as her friend was opening the blinds. One day, the Sufi said to her friend, "Can I please take them into the backyard for a few minutes? I feel that it is their natural habitat. I feel bad for them as they rush every morning to look out the window." Her friend said, "Okay." The Sufi opened the glass door from the house to the backyard. The cats came to the edge of the door and they were scared to go outside and they didn't go. The Sufi was thinking . . . and finally she smiled and said, "This is exactly the relationship between the person and God. The cats need time."

In practice

In Sufism, it is the human's genuine nature[29] to establish a relationship with God. In a pure human self, a person can feel this desire and needs it fully. As the person grows, if the person moves away from his or her pure self, an artificial, trained self can replace that in the person. Then, abnormal can become normal. Unnatural can become natural. In the above story, since the cats were domesticated to stay at home, they felt that something was pulling them to their natural habitat. Therefore, they rushed every day to observe the sun, plants, and other beings from the window of the house. In this new self of the cats, when they were invited to go to their natural habitat they were scared. The Sufi said, "The cats need time" to indicate that to transform from unnatural to natural, it can take time but it is possible. One can always re-establish a natural relationship with one's own pure self and God but it can require time, sincere effort, and good teachers.

---

29. This is called fitrah.

208. Rain Drops and the Sufi

One day, there was a physicist Sufi. She was sitting under a tree and thinking about the gravitational force. Then, while she was in deep reflection, it started raining. The Sufi said to herself, "Wow, SubhanAllah! The raindrops are not touching each other and they are not falling with a fully accelerated speed that could make a hole in my head. It is all mercy and gratitude from God."

IN PRACTICE

Sufis often reflect upon nature, the natural phenomena, and about their inspirations in relation to the different names and attributes of God. In the above story, the physicist Sufi was amazed with each raindrop because they were repelling each other but not gushing as if they were pouring from a hose. She was also amazed with the fact that the raindrops fell with a final,[30] non-harmful speed upon the earth, as one normally can expect a huge speed due to the acceleration from the distance of thousands of feet.

---

30. This speed is called final velocity in physics.

209. Focused Eating and the Sufi

There was a rich Sufi who used to only eat one type of food in each meal and enjoyed it a lot. A friend of hers asked her what the reason was for her practice. She said: "When I have a variety of food on the table I cannot focus on the taste of each one. I may just take a bite from each to be respectful if someone brings or serves, but I generally focus on one type of food."

IN PRACTICE

In spiritual practices, it is important to focus on one path and become an expert, and then wander to taste others when there is an opportunity. In chanting, prayers, and meditation, the notion of repetition with one phrase can give the same approach of focus on taste through charge and discharge. The overall notion of believing in One Creator alludes to the notion that simplicity with focus is for everyone and that this approach is genuine, pure, and natural.

There are places to recognize complexity and there are places to recognize simplicity. Correct recognition in different contexts can help the spiritual traveler to benefit from it on the journey. Misplacements can distract and sometimes even take the person away from a genuine path.

210. The Nice Flower and the Evil Eye

One day, a Sufi brought a nice tulip flower to the mosque. She was enjoying it by looking at it while staying and praying in this temple. Every Friday, hundreds of people came to the mosque and prayed there. She used to take the tulip to her house in order to not show it to the hundreds of people. One day, she was traveling and forgot to take the tulip to her home. She came the next day and cried out, "My tulip, the evil eye." The Sufi was very sad.

IN PRACTICE

The effect of the eye on living things is an expected phenomenon. Therefore, if a person likes something or is astonished, one should say "MashAllah" to remove the effect of the evil eye. MashAllah can translate as "What a great creation of God." In the above story, there were a lot of people who came to the mosque and probably liked the tulip. Maybe they didn't say the word "MashAllah," and the tulip was affected by the eye and died.

211. The Marriage Problem and the Sufi

There was a man who used to have marital problems with his wife. He wanted to meet with the Sufi to get some advice. They went to a coffee shop. The man started talking for almost half an hour that his expectations were not fulfilled and that he was so disappointed with her. Finally, the man stopped talking. The Sufi said, "Are you done?" The man replied, "Yes." The Sufi said, "My only advice to you is: Don't make your expectations too high!" The man said, "Yes, you are right," and he kept saying, "I made my expectations too high . . . " and left the coffee shop repeating this phrase.

IN PRACTICE

In Sufi practice, humans are humans. They have their own limitations. If a person submits or surrenders to a human being instead of God, there will be frustrations and disappointments. If a husband sees his wife as perfect or vice versa, if a person views a friend as perfect, or if a child sees a parent as perfect, then they will definitely face frustrations. The only one to whom one can fully turn with full submission and surrender and with expectations of perfection is God. Most of the time, people's fake replacements of God with others puts people in jeopardy, stress, disappointment, and frustration. It is encouraged to always have positive and high expectations from God. If the person becomes frustrated in the relationship with God as well, then God is perfect. It is the person's own wrong perception and hasty, impatient expectations. If the person experiences frustrations from humans, then this could also be the same problematic perception of this person or possibly the imperfection and faults of these humans.

212. The Fried Chicken, the Mother, and the Sufi

There was a famous Sufi who was eating a nice fried chicken. He had a student next to him, eating hard, non-tasty bread. The mother of the poor student entered the room to check on her child. As she saw this scene, she got very angry and said:

"Shame on you, teacher! You are eating a nice fried chicken and my poor son is eating hard bread. Is this fair? Is this what you teach?" The teacher smiled and said to the chicken, "Kumbiiznillah, ... Be alive with the permission of God." The chicken became alive and the mother was shocked and scared. The teacher said, "When your son is at this level, he can eat whatever he wants."[31]

IN PRACTICE

The disciples sometimes can experience different conditions to discipline their eating, sleeping, and talking. The goal is to minimize them but it takes practice. Once one can gain the ability of controlling oneself, one can enjoy physical and spiritual joys in different modes in their full capacity and purpose.

---

31. This story is attributed to A. Jilani, a very famous eleventh century Sufi scholar and teacher.

213. Eating Meat and the Sufi

There was a Sufi who did not prefer to eat meat. One day, a Sufi friend of hers visited her and they started eating dinner together. There was a nice rotisserie chicken on the table. Her friend realized that she was not eating the chicken and she asked the reason. The Sufi smiled and said: "I don't know how and where this chicken spent its life . . . "

In practice

Eating meat, chicken, or fish is permissible. But some Sufis pursue a vegetarian approach for self-discipline as a personal preference. Some may only prefer to eat organic, clean, unprocessed, and especially spiritually blessed food. Therefore, they may not eat food unless they themselves raise, buy, or sometimes cook it. Some may not eat because they believe that the negativity or lack of spirituality of the person who cooked the meal can have a bad effect on the meal. Some Sufis believe that reciting "BismiAllah, with the name of God" can remove all of these negative effects and they can move on to eat whatever they are offered. So, it is a matter of personal preference.

214. Cat and the Garage Door

There was a Sufi who had a cat. This cat wanted to leave the house to go to the garage when the door was open. The Sufi did not want the cat to go to the garage because it was not a natural environment compared to the backyard. The cat was insistent every day. One day, the Sufi said to her cat, "Fine, you can go." The cat went to the garage. After a minute, the cat came back to the door meowing and asking her to open the door. The Sufi was busy and delayed in opening the door and the cat continued meowing and crying. At the end, after a few minutes, the Sufi opened the door and said to the cat, "I hope you learned your lesson. This happens exactly between people and God."

IN PRACTICE

Sometimes, a person may insist upon and want to do something that he or she may not realize is harmful. God may not give what the person is asking for due to its expected bad outcomes. But the person insists, even blames God, that God is not answering this person's prayer. Similarly, the cat in the above story insisted on something that the Sufi knew would be scary and bad for the cat. The cat insisted and the Sufi opened the door. After the cat's own experience, the cat went back to its home and knocked on the door with crying and meowing and the door was opened. When the person understands one's mistake, the door of repentance and going back and knocking at the door of mercy of God is always open. As long as the person is not in the state of arrogance and distractions, the person can re-establish beautiful connections with God.

215. The Sufi and Understanding His Wife

There was a Sufi. He was often upset that his wife was not spending much time with him as they grew older in their marriage. He was thinking about this. As he was reflecting on the marital problems of others, he realized that he had some similar problems. One night, he was disturbed by this and woke up in the middle of the night and prayed[32] in order to receive some guidance from God. At the end, he said, "Alhamdulillah, I got it. Men can become more sensitive as they grow older and expect more attention like a child. As men get older they don't feel that they have enough attention from their wives. Then, they can make a problem and even get divorced with different blames. Women can be more independent and still maintain the rationality compared to men. Therefore, I see a lot of men being taken care of by their wives in their old age. I think this is the root of my problem. Allah knows the best."

IN PRACTICE

It is important to correctly detect one's own problems and disturbances through self-reflection and focus. In Sufism, there is a lot of advice recommending to solve problems at night while people are sleeping through prayers and invocation to God. In the above story, the Sufi got guidance to rationalize the source of his problem. Therefore, he can now discipline his own perception in his marital relationship.

---

32. Night prayer is called tahajjud.

216. "Staying Out of Trouble" and the Sufi

There was a man who used to come to the mosque. He was very friendly and always seemed very happy. Each time the Sufi saw this man, he used to say, "I am trying to stay out of trouble." The Sufi used to smile and think about what he meant. One year passed, two years . . . and more. Each time the Sufi saw this man, he would say, "I am trying to stay out of trouble." One day, the Sufi had a car accident. He smiled and understood why the man kept repeating this phrase. The Sufi said to himself, "Having a day without any problem is a blessing and requires gratitude to God."

IN PRACTICE

Sometimes, a person may expect extraordinary things in life in order to be thankful to God on the journey. One can understand the value and happiness of the previous day when experiencing a difficulty or a problem in the present day. Therefore, a day without any evil or problem can elicit thankfulness and gratitude to God.

217. The Sufi, Child, and Disturbance

There was a Sufi in the mosque studying and praying. A child came with his father to the mosque. The boy was watching a cartoon on a smartphone and it was very loud. The Sufi was so disturbed. He was not able to focus and meditate. He was thinking about what he should do. He then pulled a small chocolate bar from his pocket and approached the boy and gave it to him and started praying next to him. The boy then muted the cartoon movie. The Sufi said, "Alhamdulillah . . . thanks and all gratitude is for God."

IN PRACTICE

It is very important not to break anyone's heart when correcting or advising. Therefore, it is more important to think about how to say something compared to what to say. It is very strongly believed that the virtual space formed by manners remains, not the content of the talk or advice in human communication.

218. The Sufi and the Floating Wood Log on the Sea

There was a physicist Sufi walking on the seashore with his friend. While enjoying their walk, they saw a wood log on the sea, floating nicely on the sea's surface. The physicist Sufi asked his friend, "Why do you think this log does not sink?" His friend thought the Sufi expected an answer from physics because he was a physicist and continued explaining all the laws of physics . . . Then, the Sufi physicist said, "Actually, the wood log does not sink because it does not panic." His friend smiled . . .

IN PRACTICE

There are always external and internal meanings to every minute detail of life. In the above story, although the wood log was very heavy, it did not sink and was nicely floating. The Sufi imagined a person's reasons, reactions, reasoning, feelings, and thoughts when they encounter something fearful and stressful and get trapped in it and die. One can consider a person who can die while swimming if there is panic or stress. Similarly, in spiritual endeavors, knowledge and practice help the person to not die in fear-provoking or evil-looking incidents. Actually, the person can enjoy this situation if the person knows how to submit and surrender instead of suffering and dying from it, similar to the case of the floating wood log in the story above. This spiritual level may take time, and practice, and one may need knowledge. It may not be easy to adopt it in the beginning of the journey.

219. The Sufi and the Cat in the Hood of the Car

One day a Sufi came to his home at night and parked his car in the garage. He did not see one of his cats at home. After a while his wife came and she was screaming, "Where is the cat? Did you run over the cat? I can hear her meowing and crying!" The Sufi was disturbed and immediately ran out and they found that the cat somehow went inside the hood from the wheel side and was stuck in there. Both the Sufi and his wife were panicking, felt very sad, and did not know what to do. They were calling the town for emergency animal rescue centers and friends. There was no help. Finally, they called the fire department and they came. After an hour, they were not able to get the cat out and suggested that the car should be torn down by a mechanic. They suggested that in the meantime, they should put some water and food next to the car in the garage, in case the cat comes out by herself to eat it. The Sufi and his wife were still very worried and panicking about the life of the cat. They continued calling multiple possible sources of help: AAA vehicle service, emergency mechanics, friends . . . They were on their way . . . While waiting for the help, the Sufi's wife opened the house door and screamed, "Mazza!" (the name of the cat). The cat was outside the door and she was OK. The wife started crying. The Sufi said, "Alhamdulillah, all thanks and gratitude is to God." In the meantime, he was also thinking . . . "Why my car? Why that cat . . ." He was trying to glean a meaning from this incident.

IN PRACTICE

Everything happens with a purpose, with a meaning, and a message for the person. In that sense, Sufis adopt a deterministic world approach. Therefore, some Sufis like the emerging theory of physics, the string theory. According to this theory, everything in the universe has a connection and effect on each other. For example, a butterfly's motion has an effect on the galaxies in the universe. Similarly, God sends different external messages to decode, guide, and connect with the Divine on the journey.

220. Final Stage of the Fireworks and the Sufi

There was a Sufi who was a giving a lecture. One of the students, who was in his seventies, asked a question. He revealed that he is having more spiritual experiences as he grows older in age and he asked the reason for this. The Sufi smiled and said, "In the fireworks show, there are more extensive displays as it approaches the end. Similarly, every journey has an end. As it gets close to the end, the signs may increase."

IN PRACTICE

As all journeys have an end, the spiritual journey also has an end according to the practice. The ending of the spiritual journey is bound to the external ending of the physical journey of life. In other words, when the person dies, the first part of the journey ends. As the person is coming closer to the final stage of the spiritual journey, the signs may increase. Similar to the fireworks mentioned in the story above, during the last stage of the show, more intense and colorful fireworks may appear.[33]

The moments of experience, life-changing incidents, the avenues of enlightenment . . . All these signs may come in abundance as the person grows older. Depending on the person's attitude, the person can realize and decode these signs, or move on and perhaps still not understand.

33. The verse alludes to this notion (Sa nurihimayatuna fi anfusihim and . . . hattayatabayannaannahulHaq).

221. The Sufi and the Oppression

There was a man and he had a daughter who was a Sufi. The father sometimes used to yell at his daughter and would not allow her to explain herself. One day, the father picked up his daughter from school and again started yelling at her and giving her some unsolicited advice. While they were driving, from out of nowhere, a car appeared next to their car and the father opened the window. The lady driver in the other car was angry and started cursing at the father and even said, "I will have my man find you and kill you." The father did not understand what was going on. He closed his window and kept moving. After a day, the Sufi daughter said to her dad, "Dad! I think yesterday, you didn't let me speak and you were yelling at me. Allah sent this lady from nowhere and she started cursing at you." The father regretfully said, "I think you are right. I am also thinking about that, too."

IN PRACTICE

Everything that happens to the person has a reason. Nothing is random. Nothing is chaos as long as the person knows the meanings. The person should follow the natural laws created by God as a means of respect to God. However, he or she should remember that in a limited human life everything is a sign to improve oneself on the journey and ultimately to better the relationship with Allah. Therefore, miracles are those incidents that break the natural laws to remind the person that everything is under the control of God. For a Sufi, if the person is attentive, mindful, conscientious, and sincere on the journey, then everything can continuously reveal itself with their miraculous real meanings.

222. Crying, Child, and the Sufi

A Sufi mother had a daughter and son. The daughter was older than the son. The daughter used to be mean and at time mentally abuse her younger brother. One day, the son wanted to take chips to school to share with his friends. The Sufi mother told her daughter to help her brother get the chips from the pantry. His sister did not let him and said, "He cannot get what he wants . . . " The younger brother started crying and tears were flowing down on his cheeks . . . The Sufi mother saw this and said to her daughter, "You shook the throne of God."

IN PRACTICE

Breaking someone's heart is similar to shaking the throne of God. In several sayings of the Prophet Muhammad, it is said that Allah is with the ones whose hearts are broken and who are oppressed. Therefore, the Prophet says, "Stay away from the prayer of the oppressed against you." In other words, if an oppressed person makes a prayer against another person, there is no hindrance for that prayer to be accepted.[34] In the above story, the mother alluded to those teachings for her daughter so that she could pay attention to her younger brother's needs.

---

34. Hanbal, Ahmad B. 2012. *Musnad Imam Ahmad Ibn Hanbal*. Dar-Us-Salam Publications. This is also one of the sayings of the Prophet.

223. The Sufi, Body, and Mindfulness

There was a Sufi who was trying to practice mindfulness with his body parts. Most of the time the taste faculty of the tongue in his mouth and his stomach were in conflict. Usually, his taste faculty in his mouth wanted to eat unhealthy, yet delicious food in abundant quantities. However, his stomach was telling him, "I don't want it. I will be the one who is going to suffer." The Sufi was using his mind and logic in decision-making when there was a conflict. Most of the time, he was deciding in favor of his stomach in his judgment, arrived at with his mind. One night, the Sufi was little bit depressed and upset, so he opened the fridge. The same dialogue started between his tongue and stomach. The Sufi's mind said, "I don't care about you, stomach. I will listen to the tongue this time." He started eating, and eating . . . Finally, he stopped. The Sufi suffered all night . . .

IN PRACTICE

Depending on the level of the person, it is important to have awareness about one's body parts. In other words, personalizing them, trying to understand each organ's needs and communicating with them through awareness is a level on the journey. This approach is also supported by the Quranic verse that the body parts would complain and witness against the person and talk on the Day of Accountability after death in front of God.[35]

---

35. In the chapter 41, verse 21.

224. Art of Living and the Sufi

One day the Sufi woke up to the sound of his wife screaming at the kids. She was trying to rush the kids to their extracurricular program. His wife didn't seem to be in a good mood. She finally left with the kids to drop them off, and then came back home around ten minutes later. The Sufi immediately woke up and said to himself, "Let me leave as soon as possible before I get hit by the storm!" (meaning his wife.)

He successfully left without bumping into his wife. On the way, while driving, he said to himself, "Alhamdulillah, thanks and all active gratitude is to God." A few minutes later, he received a long phone text from his wife. As soon as he saw the length of the phone text, he guessed the content of it, probably not something pleasant. Without looking at the message, the Sufi wrote, "Honey, I hope you are okay. I love you." A few hours later, he called his wife. Everything seemed normal and she was calm.

IN PRACTICE

It is an art to not be pulled into arguments. It is very important to avoid any environments and instances that can be unpleasant. It is a level to recognize the other's disturbances and spiritual states before engaging with them. In the above story, the Sufi was spiritually skilled to consider the possible evil outcome of the incident.

225. The Coffee Filter, the Wise-Fool ,and the Sufi

One day, the Sufi was sitting in the mosque. A person known as the wise-fool[36][xxviii] came to the mosque and wanted to make coffee. He took a paper towel and put it in the machine, instead of a filter, and made coffee. The Sufi said to himself, "What a weird wise-fool!" The Sufi was a little bit disgusted. A few months later, the Sufi wanted to make coffee. He looked for a filter but there were none left. The Sufi felt lazy and did not want to go and buy one. Then, he remembered what the wise-fool did, and the Sufi said to himself, "There is no other way; let me also try it." He used a paper towel as a filter and made coffee. After he drank the coffee, the Sufi said to himself, "Wow, not bad! I learned something from the wise-fool. I should not belittle anyone or anything in life."

IN PRACTICE

The feelings of superiority or judging or belittling others can put the person in the place of the one who is belittled or judged against. In the above story, the Sufi did not approve of the paper towel being used as a filter, but later on he himself used it and appreciated learning something new.

Discussion Questions

- ▶ What are the characteristics of wise-fool depictions?
- ▶ Can you give examples of wise-fool figures in history?
- ▶ How can one practice on oneself not to judge others?
- ▶ Is the wise-fool a nonconformist?

---

36. Wise-fool is a concept used for the friends of God who act foolishly and insanely so that people know that they are crazy or foolish so that people don't disturb them and praise them due to their piety. In original writings, wise-fool can be referred to majnun or majzub.

226. The Lonely Sufi

There was a Sufi who used to be afraid of breaking people's hearts. Therefore, he preferred solitude over socializing with people. People who knew this Sufi used to call him "the lonely guy." They used to feel bad about him but the Sufi in reality was perfectly happy keeping distance from people.

IN PRACTICE

It is suggested to be with people but at the same time being with God. Bastami, the Great Sufi says: "The true knower of God is the one who eats, drinks, jokes with you and sells to you, buys from you, while his heart is located in the kingdom of the Eternal Holiness.[19]" In other words, it is sometimes difficult to maintain a genuine relationship with God and at the same time with people because there is always a possibility of breaking people's hearts, upsetting them, or backbiting. Any potential harshness toward others or abuse can negatively affect one's genuine relationship with God. The Prophet mentions that the real believer is the person from whom others are safe from his or her hand and tongue.[20] As in the case of above the story, there are Sufis in practice who prefer solitude in order to minimize potentially negative engagements with others although this may not be the suggested norm.

Discussion Question

▶ What can be the balance between solitude and social engagements in practice?

227. Physicist Sufis and Driving

There were two physicist Sufis. One was living in Albany, New York, and the other was living in Buffalo, New York. The one in Albany wanted to visit her friend in Buffalo and left her home and reached Buffalo in six hours. When they met each other, her friend asked how the driving was. The Sufi replied: "It was enjoyable and calming. I took my time with silence, reflection, chanting, drinking my coffee, and enjoying my drive." The other Sufi smiled and wished that she had visited her friend in Albany instead of her friend coming to visit her.

IN PRACTICE

Every moment is very important and critical to use and increase the sweet relationship with God. A person is considered "unplugged" and disconnected from her or his surroundings while driving. Therefore, traveling is one of the means to refresh one's connection with God.

Discussion Question

▸ What are some different ways of "unplugging" oneself?

228. A Gift for an Orphan

One day, the Sufi went home to play with his children. He saw that one of their friends was there too. She was an orphan. The orphan loved the Sufi because the Sufi always gave her gifts each time he saw her. As usual, they all started playing with the Sufi: running, exercising, and playing. In each case, the Sufi's children were happy and proud of their father. They said constantly, "Our father is the best runner. Our father is so strong; he can do a lot of push-ups. Our father is the best football player." The Sufi thought about what to say to the orphan child after all these phrases so that the orphan would not feel bad or left out. He smiled and tapped her head and said, "Here is your gift." The Sufi gave a gift to the orphan so that she is not left out.

IN PRACTICE

Orphans have a special place for God and they should be handled gently. There are a lot of verses in the Quran admonishing against any harsh treatment of orphans. The Prophet reminds us of the great reward for a person comforting an orphan by tapping their head.[21] In the above story, the Sufi made a habit of giving a gift to the orphan so as not to take any risk of displeasing God and he also tapped the orphan's head.

Discussion Question

► Is the concept of the treatment of orphans lost in our contemporary society? Why?

229. Experiential Learning

One day, a Sufi attended a lecture. There was also a novice religious student who was angry present. He said: "I don't believe that a Sufi cannot be without stress." The Sufi tried to explain to him, but the student was very disturbed and angry about the problems in his life. The Sufi stopped talking, smiled, and observed silence.

IN PRACTICE

Most of the time, it is very difficult to explain the peaceful states of spirituality in the journey to God. Therefore, some of the experts of the path assert that these teachings cannot be taught in a lecture format but should be experienced and lived through practice and worship.[xxix][22]

Discussion Question

▶ Why is experience important along with knowledge and practice?

230. Spoiling the Honey

One day a Sufi attended a religious lecture. The people were angry, negative, and complaining about their problems, their relationship with God, and their religion. The food served in that gathering was excellent but the conversation was not. The Sufi tried to enjoy the food but she was disturbed by something and she was not able to detect its source. After she left, she understood that the negativity and unappreciative attitudes for God were what disturbed her spiritual honey.

IN PRACTICE

The relationship with God is like honey on the spiritual path.[xxx] A person on the path is required to guard this valuable more than their money and wealth because this is the real source of hope that makes the person move positively on the spiritual path. Although the physical entertainment (the food) in that gathering was excellent, the Sufi was disturbed due to the spoiling of her spiritual state.[23]

Discussion Questions
- How can the relationship with God be like "honey"?
- Why is it important to guard spiritual valuables?

231. Accepting Everyone at Their Level

There was a Sufi who used to be angry with her children when they pestered her. Afterward, the Sufi calmed down and engaged with herself in self-dialogue: "Why did I yell at them? They are kids. It is normal. Why did I lose myself again? Shame on me!"

IN PRACTICE

Recognizing everyone in their own positions, age, gender, and culture is very important. Misplacing or not recognizing this can make a person unjust in humane dealings. In the above story, the Sufi was trying to apply this concept. Similar to the above case of the Sufi, it is always valuable to take account of oneself in order to improve spiritually and truly accept everyone at their level.

Discussion Question

▶ Is self-accountability a positive or negative practice in tradition? Why?

232. The Heavy Rain and Darkness

One day, it was raining very heavily. Darkness covered the sky. Although the Sufi was enjoying the rain, he did not want to take a chance and went to the mosque to pray.

IN PRACTICE

Rain can be a blessing or a problem. Some of the oppressive people were punished with heavy rain or some other systems from the sky by God. The Prophet Muhammad used to enjoy rain, and used to like walking in rainy weather to receive blessings[20]. At the same time, the Prophet used to run to the mosque in any type of dark weather with heavy rain to ask forgiveness for all humanity from God in case it was an indication of punishment. Therefore, the Sufi implemented the way of the Prophet in the above story and he did not take any chance.

Discussion Question

▶ How can one understand something as a blessing or evil?

233. The Drunk Man, the Sufi, and the Sufi's Wife

One day, the Sufi was sitting in the mosque. A drunk man came to the mosque crying and said that he was a loser in life and did not want to use alcohol anymore. He was advised by AA[37] that he should follow a spiritual path in order to stop this addiction. After going back and forth to mosque a few times, this man decided to be a Muslim and became good friends with the Sufi. One day, this man called the Sufi, crying on the phone, and said, "I am drunk again. I can't help myself." The Sufi went to the drunk man's home where he found him lying on the floor unconscious. The Sufi carried him on his back and took him to his home. The man slept in Sufi's peaceful home until the next day. The man woke up embarrassed in the morning about his situation but he was happy that he had a real friend now when he was in need. On the other hand, the Sufi's wife was not so happy that the Sufi brought a drunk man to their home.

IN PRACTICE

It is important to help people who are in need. Sometimes, a person can be in uncomfortable situations while helping others. Therefore, the intention and humility are the key to keep up the levels of piety. In the above story, the Sufi could have said, "I prefer worshipping God to helping this man," because Sufis take enormous pleasure in their engagements with God. But, in this judgment call, the Sufi decided to take this man to his home in order to help him, despite his wife's displeasure.

Discussion Question

► How can helping others sometimes be a problem?

---

37. AA: Alcoholics Anonymous is an initiative to stop the addiction of alcohol.

234. The Prostitutes

There was a Sufi who used to see drunk prostitutes, standing at the corners of the streets in the middle of the night, selling their body for food on the street. While the Sufi was coming from the mosque to his home, he used to tell them to follow him to his home where they could have a nice meal with his wife. The Sufi's wife used to feed them, give them new clothes and some advice. The Sufi and his wife wanted to help these women change their lives, but the people in town did not know the reality of what was happening. His wife used to tell the Sufi, "I am afraid that when you die no one will attend to your funeral due to your bad reputation in town with prostitutes following you home." The Sufi used to smile and reply, "Don't worry, the sultan will come and attend my funeral." One day, he died, and no one wanted to attend his funeral due to his bad reputation.

During those times, the sultan used to disguise himself to walk the streets in order to check on his subjects. As he was walking that day, he heard that there was a funeral and no one wanted to attend. He knocked at the door of the Sufi's house to learn more and found the wife crying. She explained the situation and said that the Sufi used to say, "Don't worry, the sultan will attend my funeral." As soon as the sultan heard this, he wept for the sincere piety of the Sufi and revealed his identity to the wife.[xxxi]

IN PRACTICE

It is very important to disengage oneself with any type of doubtful actions. In the above story, as an exception, the Sufi was dealing with the prostitutes to help them. In practice, it is important to know that ultimately, the real judgment call will be made by God for the real intention of the person. Accordingly, the person will be rewarded or questioned about their actions overwritten by these intentions.

Discussion Questions

▶ Why is important to reveal intentions to people if you only care about God?

235. Contemplating about Life and Death and the Prayer

One day, the Sufi was thinking about life and death, and how life was busy and death was approaching. She felt helpless. Then she remembered that death is not an end but the beginning of another life. Although she didn't know much about the details of the afterlife, something unseen or unknown, she prayed to God that she would be safe from all the trials of death and afterlife.[24]

IN PRACTICE

Engagements and conversations with God through prayer are very critical. In changing moments of life, prayer can uphold a person and take him or her from the darkness of hopelessness and fears to the light of hope and happiness. In the above story, the Sufi was in a self-critical engagement with herself about life and death. As soon as she felt the unease of unknowns, she immediately engaged herself in prayer.

Discussion Questions

▶ How are the trials of death?
▶ How can one be safe from the trials of death?

236. The Evil Haircut

One day, the Sufi had a haircut. When his wife saw him, she said: "You look like the evil characters with your new haircut." The Sufi replied, "You are watching too many Hollywood movies." The Sufi smiled and moved on.

IN PRACTICE

There is no evil-looking person or being. Our constructions of evil through watching television, depicted images in newspapers, and even events like Halloween can establish an artificial understanding of our surroundings.[25] In this perspective, the practice constantly urges spiritual cleaning through reflection and chants such as *La ilaha illa Allah* that there is nothing to attach to except God. Or, one can chant *astaghfirullah* which means, "Oh God, forgive me for all my insincere and artificial physical and spiritual engagements."

Discussion Question

▶ What is the importance of physical appearance in practice?

237. The Children and the One-Eyed Pirate

One day, the Sufi was taking a walk with her kids. There was a man who seemed to be recovering from eye surgery, wearing an eye patch, walking on the other side of the street. As the kids saw the man, they told each other, "Look, there is a pirate!" The Sufi was embarrassed and said to her children, "He is not a pirate. He had surgery on his eye. Therefore, one of his eyes is closed."

IN PRACTICE

It is important to deconstruct the impeded fabrications through childhood and adulthood about others and God. A wrong construction about people and God can trace its remnants to an undesired state of judgment for people as well as alienation from God. The children's judgment of the man as a bad character due to their exposure through television, cartoons, or books made them assume bad things about others.[25] A person's wrong construction of God as a male or a female with gender with human qualities can alienate people from God because of their negative experiences with humans.[26]

Discussion Questions

► How can one's incorrect opinions or ideas about God alienate the person establishing a positive relationship with God?
► What are some of the alienating images of God in the discipline of religious studies?

238. The Lost Phone

One day, the Sufi was packing for travel and couldn't find her phone. She checked her car. She checked her handbag. She couldn't find it. Although she couldn't imagine traveling without her cell phone and felt uneasy about it, she also thought about how nice travel could be without being bothered by the phone. She remembered that the only person that called her was her husband and he was already traveling with her. In the meantime, the Sufi was also trying to understand the possible wisdom behind the evil-seeming incident of losing her phone. Using her husband's cell phone, she texted her own phone. "If you find this phone please text me." A day later, a person texted that she found her phone. After coming back from her trip, the Sufi went and picked up the phone. The person who found the phone was an artist. The Sufi gave her a nice gift to thank her about returning the phone. The artist had an interest in Sufi themes reflecting them in her artwork. Then, the Sufi now understood the wisdom of losing her phone: a possible long-term friendship between the Sufi and the artist.

IN PRACTICE

It is important to interpret the evil-seeming incidents with a possible positive outcome graced from God. Sometimes, people's immediate negative response to evil-appearing incidents can ruin their entire life. The notions of patience, wisdom, and reflection should be practiced in all encounters of life.[27]

Discussion Questions

▶ Why is it important to interpret everything with their other meanings in practice?

▶ How is randomness or chaos understood in practice? Why?

239. Religious People

One day, the Sufi was sitting in the mosque. He was sitting and observing the representations of the religious affairs in the mosque. As he looked around, he saw a few men who were proud of being the administrators of the mosque, and they were backbiting and gossiping about people. The Sufi experienced some type of disgust and said, "*Alhamdulillah,* thanks to God, I did not learn the religion from these people."

IN PRACTICE

It is very important to genuinely live what you practice. The purpose of prayer, charity, fasting, and all other worship activities are to clean one's heart from spiritual diseases. If the person is becoming arrogant with religious affiliations, then this person is using the religion for his personal spiritual destruction.

Discussion Question

▶ What should be the ideal relationship between piety and religious affiliation?

240. Smoked Salmon

There was a Sufi who liked smoked salmon a lot. Each time she ate it, she used to get a headache and she did not understand the reason. Again, one day, she knew that salmon is good for you, and reasoned that she should eat salmon, and ate a good amount of smoked salmon. The next day, she had a migraine. She did not understand why she had the migraine and asked a doctor. The doctor informed her that yes, the salmon is good, but there is too much unnecessary salt in the smoked salmon, raising her blood pressure. The Sufi finally understood the reason.

IN PRACTICE

It is very important to understand the general rules along with their applications in different circumstances. There can be a general rule related with a food item or a spiritual practice. Its application may differ from person to person with their benefits and harms. In the above story, the smoked salmon is beneficial but only if taken in small quantities. Too much of it can be a problem due to its salt content. Similarly, the balance in spiritual practice, the applications depending on the context, time and person are critical content.[22]

Discussion Question

► How do Sufi teachers use the notion about the application of spiritual needs depending on the context, time, and the person?

241. Intentions for Food and Fun

One day, the Sufi was thinking, "I eat every day. I want to have fun every day. How can I make these times valuable for God as well as similar to my prayers and worship?" She kept thinking and thinking until finally she exclaimed, "*Alhamdulillah*, thanks to God, it is my intention."

IN PRACTICE

Intention is the key for everything.[28] There are permissible things in religion such as eating and having fun. A person can turn those permissible things into worship if she or he makes an intention saying, "I am eating so that I can worship better. I am giving break to worship or prayer by having some fun so that I can concentrate and focus on my prayer once I come back." According to the tradition, the time and effort spent by this person on these regular actions then can transform into worship and something pleasing to God with his or her intention.

Discussion Question

▶ Why is intention more important than the action in practice?

242. Fears and Stress

One day, the Sufi was thinking about an interesting dream that was a little bit scary. There were rich representations inside her dream. She thought about how she should interpret it. She said to herself, "There is no other way to interpret it but in a good way."

IN PRACTICE

It is important to find people who would positively interpret one's dreams. In one of the sayings of the Prophet Muhammad [28], God says "I will treat My servant in the way he or she expects Me to be." Therefore, it is always important to have a good opinion of God. Similarly, if there is a bad dream it is important not to say and publicize it and ask protection from God from the evils in the dream. God can do anything. Even if there is a bad destiny written for the person due to the signs in a dream, God can change an expected bad outcome into a positive one with the divine power.

Discussion Questions

- ▸ What is the significance of dreams in practice?
- ▸ What are the guidelines of dream interpretation?

243. Yesterday and Today

One day, the Sufi was thinking about what she did the previous day. Then thought about what she had done today thus far. She said to herself, "*Alhamdulillah*, thanks to God, I learned something new today to increase my closeness to God."

IN PRACTICE

It is very important not to live stagnantly, having a similar or same day without positive change in one's relationship with God. The Prophet says[29] "The person is not from us, if he or she has the same day consecutively." In other words, every day is an opportunity to increase one's knowledge, practice, and closeness to God. Other people do not need to know about it and may think that this person is having the same simple life every day. However, one should be able to assess his or her positive self-progress every day in one's relationship with the divine.

Discussion Questions

▶ How do people evaluate the progress in their daily encounters?
▶ How can one evaluate one's positive or negative change with aging?

244. Cutting the Grass

There was a Sufi who used to cut the grass in her backyard. As she was cutting the grass with the noisy lawnmower, she used to see bugs jumping frantically around. She used to feel so bad for the bugs she decided to not cut the grass again.

IN PRACTICE

It is very important to respect all of creation. The size of it does not matter. The life is given by God. One of the attributes of God is Alive[38] and gives life. This is one of the attributes of God that God only manifests but the creation cannot manifest it truly. In other words, God gives life and people observe things that are moving. If God made something alive and observable by the person, then he or she is expected to respect this moving creation's freedom of life unless it harms the person.

Discussion Question

►   How can one make a balance between respecting creation and fulfilling the needs of life?

---

38. Al-Hayy.

245. The Wound

One day, the Sufi was in the restroom. He saw a wound on his body. He did not understand how and from whence it came. He left the restroom, thinking back, when he found the reason for the wound. He immediately prayed, cried, and asked forgiveness from God. Then, the Sufi sought medical help.

IN PRACTICE

Whatever happens has a reason. Nothing is random without any cause. There are external and internal meanings for everything. Some people may call this as destiny.[39] In the above story, before seeking medical help, the Sufi immediately looked at an internal possible reason for the wound that appeared on his body. After his contemplation, he correlated the reason for the wound with something that he did that was possibly harmful for his relationship with God. Therefore, he prayed and asked forgiveness from God, Real Cause [30]. After this initial step, the Sufi went to the hospital to ask for medical assistance.

Discussion Question

▶ How can one always look for internal and external reasons in different encounters of life?

---

39. Qaza and qadar.

246. Cancer and the Unknown

One day, the Sufi was thinking of cancer. He said to himself, "Why do people say that there is no cure for cancer? Why do people not know the reason? Why?" As he was thinking all the negative connotations about cancer, he then smiled and said "I understand. The realities, the unknowns, and God."

In practice

One of the attributes of God is the Real Cause. God makes the means such as diseases or cancer to remind a person of their limits and the need for being dependent upon God. Humans often appear to be more self-confident and independent with the advance of scientific medical research and solutions to diseases. The emergence of cancer-type diseases can be a new way of reminding and challenging the people about their need for God.

Discussion Question

▶ What is the understanding of God in practice in the encounters of evil-seeming incidents?

247. The Cell Phone App and the Happy Old Man

One day, there was an old man sitting in the mosque. The Sufi observed this man. The old man pulled out his cell phone and used the digital counter on his cell phone app to chant. He seemed to be quite happy with his app. He looked around himself to show how much he was proud of the type of advanced technology that he was using, the digital counter! The old man did not realize that a digital counter on a cell phone is an old application but he just found out about it. The Sufi smiled and said to himself, "This is exactly the same in the spiritual path. Everyone thinks that they have the highest level."

IN PRACTICE

At a certain spiritual state, one can think that he or she is at the highest state. But others above him or her can look at this person and can smile like the Sufi in the above story. Therefore, one should always know the possibilities of being in a lower spiritual state than others.

Discussion Question

► How should one ideally view oneself compared to others in practice?

248. The Harsh Voice

There was a Sufi in Nisantas, Istanbul, Turkey. When he used to talk to his children, they felt that their father was harsh with them. After realizing this after many years, he started communicating with his children by writing on paper and with sign language. His children thought that their father was "cool" and they started talking about him to their friends. The father was happy because now his children loved him and they listened to their dad.

IN PRACTICE

It is very important to tune one's voice in communication. It is very important to be in a soft and calm tone with the people of regular interaction like family members and friends. It is very important to maintain a serious tone in interactions of public life, especially in business. The teaching of tuning down one's voice in communication is often mentioned in the verses of the Quran,[xxxii]in the practices of the Prophet, and the lives of the saints of God.[31] One can see the habit of tuning down one's voice as an imitative way of reaching to the genuine way of practicing calmness, softness, mercy, and caring for the entire creation of God.

Discussion Question

► What is the long-term expectation of practicing tuning down one's voice?

249. Oppression and Friends

One day, the Sufi visited her friends late at night. She was very excited to see them. They chanted nicely, ate Sufi treats, and had a great time. The Sufi started talking about her achievements since she did not see her friends for some time. After a while, the Sufi left and went home. She was not able to sleep. Next day, something was bothering her deeply, and she tried to figure out what it was. Finally, she said to herself, "My oppression."

IN PRACTICE

All the good achievements are given by God to a person. All the evil comes due to the call of the person and thus evil is created. This is a very fine notion to understand, theodicy, the concept of evil in practice. Therefore, the person should be in enormous gratitude to God by saying, "*Alhamdulillah*, thank you God" due to being chosen as a simple means for any type of good. If the person claims any ownership of this achievement, then the person in reality lies and oppresses him or herself. Every lie spoils and dirties the sweet relationship with God. This can make the person disturbed, uneasy and can take the person to a spiritual darkness and misguidance. Therefore, the pronouns "I" or "my" are dangerous pronouns which can take the person to oppression, lying, and arrogance. The statements of "my work," "I achieved," or similar ones are clearly minefields that can backfire upon the person spiritually due to bragging.

Discussion Question

► How can one be selective in using pronouns in daily conversations?

250. Late Night and Evil

There was a Sufi who used to sleep late at night. After having a nice time during most of his time in the day and night, his sleep was much disturbed about the engagements that he did right before he slept. He thought about the reason and solution for this. Then he said to himself, "My dealings late at night!"

IN PRACTICE

It is important not to involve conversations or any engagements after the last prayer.[40] During these times, there are possibilities of engaging in evil stipulations due to human hormonal changes and existence of other unseen beings released on earth as the Prophet Muhammad mentions in his sayings. There are narrations that mention that the Prophet did not sleep before praying the last prayer and he did not engage in conversations after praying the last prayer[28][20].

Discussion Question

▶ Did you experience a similar case of a bad outcome in a night engagement? How?

---

40. Isha prayer.

251. Candies, the Dirty Guy, and the Sufi

There was a dirty guy who used to come to the mosque. He smelled bad and no one wanted to stay next to him while praying. One day, he came to the Sufi and said, "Here is a bag of candies for your kids." The Sufi did not want to offend him and took the candies from him with thanks. The Sufi thought to himself, "It is probably very old and smelly candies; I won't even open the bag." The Sufi took the bag to his car and kept it there for a few days, afraid to open the bag. One day, he wanted to reward his kids. While he was thinking what to give to them, the Sufi remembered the candies and said, "Let me open the bag to see what it is inside." The Sufi opened the bag and surprisingly, he saw the most expensive brand of candies and chocolates inside. The Sufi reprimanded himself, "My bad thoughts about others. Shame on me!"

IN PRACTICE

It is very important not to judge people according to how they look. There are a lot of sayings in practice that the shabby looking people can be very high in their spiritual levels with God.[20] It is also very important to have good thoughts about others.

Discussion Question

▶ How can one avoid coming to a false conclusion about others?

252. The Fly Catcher

Once there was a big mosque with big glass windows without any openings. Flies used to enter the mosque through the door but got trapped inside, flying against the windowpanes trying to escape. Just before sunset, the Sufi would collect the flies with a paper towel without hurting them and put them outside. She used to take a great pleasure and satisfaction as she saw each of them flying outside freely. She used to say for each freed fly, thirty-three times, "*Alhumdulillah*, thank you God" to appreciate doing a good deed that God gave her the ability to do.

IN PRACTICE

All of living creation is precious and respected due to the Creator who gives life. Therefore, it is very important to save a life, as the Sufi above was so happy to save the lives of flies. It is important to recognize that the ability of doing a good deed is from God. Perhaps the Sufi preferred to do this good deed before sunset because this time is very critical in the practice in increasing one's good deeds. Every day angels present God the person's daytime deeds before sunset and night deeds after sunrise.[28] Therefore, the Sufi preferred this time for saving the lives of the flies.

Discussion Questions

- ▶ What is the significance of change in practice?
- ▶ What does sunset and sunrise signify in one's relationship with God?

253. Two Prayers

It was the time of the annual festival prayer.[41] People were in dispute about the date of the annual prayer due to disagreements about the lunar calendar. Everyone asked each other in which mosque they followed to pray. If the answer was the questioner's mosque, then they felt happy, but if it wasn't they wanted to argue why their mosque and their date was the right one. The Sufi was watching all these and smiling to herself and saying "*Alhamdulillah*, thanks to God that there is a difference about the date of the annual prayers, so that I can go both days to a different mosque to pray the annual prayer instead of praying only in one mosque. I wish everyday there was an annual festival prayer in every mosque."

IN PRACTICE

The legal ruling for the annual prayer is praying one time in one mosque once a year. However, in practice, praying to God is not a burden but a sweet desired engagement with God. If the person finds different opportunities similar to the Sufi in the above story, he or she can increase those means to derive sweetness in one's relationship with God.

Discussion Question

▶ Do the people establish a relationship with God due to spiritual pleasures or for other reasons?

41. Eid prayer.

254. The Meat-Eater and the Vegetarian

There was a pious Sufi who used to be a farmer in his country and enjoyed eating meat a lot. Then he migrated to America and became an intellectual writer, spending most of his time at a desk in his chair. He still liked eating meat but found himself getting sick often in his new home country with his new occupation. His other Sufi friend was vegetarian and was worried about his friend's health. He always thought that his friend used to get sick because of eating excessive meat. One day, the Sufi who liked meat a lot experienced severe diarrhea and rashes on his skin. His friend advised him, "You really need to change your eating habits. You are not anymore the active farmer Sufi but the one sitting on the chair all the time, so know who you are and adjust your diet accordingly!"

IN PRACTICE

It is important to know who you are and watch what you need and eat. As one's lifestyle changes, a person needs to adapt their eating habits accordingly. Especially in Sufi encounters, a person may need to eat better, worship, and to excel spiritually. If this is not serving the purpose, then this can be a problem.

Discussion Question

▶ What is the importance of food in one's practice?

255. French Fries and Soda

There was a Sufi who use to attend some Sufi gatherings. At one of these gatherings, some Sufis would eat burgers and French fries with excessive mustard and ketchup washed down with high-fructose sodas. As the Sufi was looking at them, he smiled and wondered to himself, "How can one eat artificial and unhealthy food and still be a Sufi?" Sometime later, one day the Sufi was very hungry, but didn't have any food in his home. A friend happened to stop by and brought some French fries with soda and unhealthy cookies. The Sufi said to himself, "I am so hungry, I will eat." He ate. He felt guilty of breaking his healthy food eating habits but at least he now had some sympathy for the other Sufis at the gathering eating junk food.

IN PRACTICE

It is recommended to eat healthy in order to maintain a healthy bodily and spiritual relationship with God. It is sometimes acceptable to break the rules to conform with a group if one does not make a big deal of it. This is especially true if a person is invited as a guest—then one is expected to eat whatever is served without acting weird or overly pious.[19]

Discussion Question

▶ What are the etiquettes of being a guest and host?

256. The Angry and Sad Men

It was the day of the year for Muslims for an annual religious festival.[42] The Sufi attended the mosque for prayers. Everyone seemed to be very happy, smiling and greeting each other. Although the Sufi always preferred loneliness and not to socialize, she attended the festival nonetheless. She greeted everyone the same as others. As she was walking out of the building she saw a mother and daughter walking, but they seemed very upset. She saw some angry and sad men as well. The Sufi wanted to greet them but she was scared. She really did not understand and said to herself, "It is really the practice of the Prophet Muhammad not to make others uncomfortable but smile." However, she did not have a good feeling from these people and went home without greeting them. Later she returned to the mosque and though the festival was over, there were still many people there for a funeral. The same people who had looked upset and sad were there: the deceased was their father. The Sufi now understood the reason for their looking unhappy during the festival and felt sad, blaming herself for her quick judgment about others.

IN PRACTICE

There could be exceptions to all general rules and teachings. Having a funeral on a festival day of joy and happiness can be an exception for some people not to be happy and joyful. Having a genuine empathy for their pain is a virtue and God rewards the people who have sympathy for the ones with broken hearts due to hardships.

Discussion Question

   ▶   Is it expected to decrease or increase the number of prayers or the amount of worship at the times of holiday, feasts, and festivals? Why?

---

42. Eid.

257. The Young Disciples

There was a Sufi who used to be quite annoyed with her own children. She thought to herself, "How should I change my perspective about them so that I don't get annoyed with my own kids?" Then, she said to herself, "If I see them as students to be trained on the path, then I will expect everything to be normal."

IN PRACTICE

It is important to raise one's children on a spiritual path. Most of the Sufi teachers raise and train their own children as their own disciples.[32] It is a negligence and mistake if one becomes a teacher for others but not for their immediate kinship groups. The best way of teaching is being a role model and increasing the presence with the disciples. The children become like disciples.

Discussion Questions

- ▶ What are the traditional methods of raising one's own children in practice?
- ▶ How can a person balance the roles of being parents and spiritual masters for one's own children?

258. Spiritual States and Baklava

There was a Sufi who used to love baklava, a sweet treat. As she was excelling in her spiritual states, self-discipline, awareness, and mindfulness journey, she appreciated that while she was eating baklava it tasted very good. Later, she was suffering psychologically upon realizing that baklava was mostly unhealthy. It is high in calories with sugary carbohydrates. The Sufi said to herself, "I need to find treats that are healthy and tasty."

IN PRACTICE

It is really important to be aware and mindful of what one eats.[33] It is not only eating a blessed food but eating healthy and pure food that is important. Keeping the body healthy can make the person more sustainable in one's relationship with God in quality and quantity measures. Therefore, although one may desire to die and meet with God, it is also important to have the intention and goal of having a long, healthy life in this world in order to prolong the sweetness of worship and relationship with God.

Discussion Question

▶   What is the relationship between food and worship?

259. The Sufi Teacher and Baklava

Once there was a Sufi teacher. When she was served baklava, she would take one of the delicious pastries, then put it back on the plate without eating it, only licking her fingers. Her disciples watched her to learn practical self-discipline techniques to train the self or ego.

IN PRACTICE

It is important to observe and learn from the teachers. Most of the learning happens when the students or disciples spend time with the teachers in their normal affairs.[34] The genuine teacher lives what she or he teaches. In the above story, the teacher was self-disciplining herself by pretending as if she ate the high-calorie and not fully healthy traditional treat, baklava. She did not totally shun the sweet even though she knew that her ego wanted it. Instead, she let her ego taste it by licking her fingers. Recognizing one's desires and needs of the self or ego is the key and training it accordingly in steps using wisdom makes the person achieve their self-training and spiritual goals.

Discussion Question

▶ What are the other methods of disciplining one's ego?

260. The Radiologist

There was a radiologist who often brought his work home with him. His wife was a Sufi, and due to her husband's work, she used to see at home some of her husband's patients' different internal organs: liver, kidneys, gallbladder, and so forth. She got surprised, sometimes disgusted, and sometimes had feelings of awe. One day, she thought to herself, "Why are people physically attracted to each other? Their internal organs are all the same . . ."

IN PRACTICE

It is important to recognize that externalities do not mean anything. Although God created all humans perfect and beautiful in their external appearances, what matters in the spiritual journey is the internal piety of love, respect, and appreciation of God. This notion is called *taqwa*. This concept is much emphasized in both the scriptures and the sayings of the Prophet. The Prophet says "God does not value your physical appearances but values what is in your hearts and actions.[20]" The verse of the Quran mentions that God created different ethnicities and genders to know each other and to maximize *taqwa* with diverse interactions. vixxxiii

Discussion Question

▶ What is the relationship between the internal and external in practice?

261. Dark Monday

The Sufi woke up Monday morning. It was dark. When she looked outside from the window, she immediately felt pain and longing for travel to another place. But she could not do it because she needed to go to work the next day. She said to herself, "Fasting! I know it will be a little bit painful but the result will be good for sure."

In practice

One of the ways to change one's perspective in life is through fasting. Fasting is from sunrise to sunset without intake of any food or drink. Fasting, as recommended by the Prophet on Mondays and Thursdays, helps the person to discipline her or his ego and self. Accordingly, the person can have a better perspective in mind, body, and life. If the person performs fasting only for God as a ritual, God rewards the person in this world and the afterlife according to the Prophetic narration.[28][20] All the genuine struggles to train one's raw ego is awarded by God if it is done correctly.

Discussion Question

► How does fasting help change one's perspective?

262. Store Closing, the Sufi, and the Deal

One day, while the Sufi was driving her car, she saw a store that was closing. She went into the store and bought a few items. An item usually worth $100 was sold for $1. She bought a few items and thought that she got a great deal. She planned to share the deal she got with her friends and family. Then for a minute she stopped and started thinking about the owner of the store. She felt sad about the owner and how possibly the owner was going through bankruptcy. She said to herself, "I wish I bought it for its normal price and did not feel so bad for the owner. It is so sad. I now understand the Real Owner gives much without losing."

IN PRACTICE

It is very important to have sympathy for others for their losses. If someone is losing and others are benefiting from that loss and gaining, then it is not a real gain. The sincerity of a person should dictate asking, praying, and desiring good for everyone. God as the Real Owner can give very expensive and precious goods in this life and in the afterlife for a very cheap price if the person makes a simple effort to buy it.

Discussion Question

▸ What is the concept of spiritual bankruptcy?

263. On the Floor of the Mosque

One day the Sufi lied on the floor on the carpet in the mosque. He was tired, and felt as though he fell asleep, but was at the same time awake. He was aware of noises around him, but when he tried to get up, he was unable to. He gave orders to his body, but his body was not listening to him. He thought, "Now I understand what death is like. The body dies but not the soul."

IN PRACTICE

It is important to understand what death is. When a person dies, his or her physical body dies but this person's soul does not die. The frame of the body is not under the command chain of the soul anymore. There are narrations from the Prophet that buried dead people can hear the people around them from the grave.[20] In the Quran, it is mentioned that sleeping is similar to death as well.[viixxxiv] In the above story, the Sufi was in the state of half sleep and half awake. There is a special name for this state.[43] The Sufi in this state rationalized the relationship between the soul and body through his own experience.

Discussion Question

▶ What is the relationship between sleep and death?

---

43. *Yaqaza* means the mixed state of sleep and awareness.

264. Difficult People

There was a Sufi who used to lose his temper when dealing with difficult people. After each time he lost his temper, he regretted it and said to himself, "I wish I was patient; I wish I didn't say that, I wish I didn't talk too much . . . I wish. I wish . . ."

IN PRACTICE

It is important to control oneself through trial and error, repentance, and asking forgiveness from God. The Prophet once asked who was the most powerful person in a patriarchal society. Everyone present in the gathering answered that it was the muscular person who could knock down his enemies in a fight. The Prophet replied, "No, it is the person who can control his or her anger."[28]

Discussion Question

► How can one compare anger management techniques with the teachings of Islam?

265. Enemy Advice

There was a woman who wrote her first book. Everyone gave her advice on how to make the book better. Her Sufi friend gave her advice also on how to improve the book. The author thought that everyone was jealous of her, therefore they were criticizing her book. The Sufi said to her, "Look! If everyone is saying the same thing about your book, then you should really stop seeing them as your enemy and appreciate what they say and improve it."

IN PRACTICE

It is important not to see people as enemies, haters, or jealousy banks when they give advice. Creating imaginary adversaries only increases one's own arrogance due to not accepting any criticism. It is important to improve oneself even though others may not have a sincere intention when giving advice. Jealousy is always possible and real in practice. There are litanies and prayers to be protected from the evil eye.

Discussion Question

▶ Why it is difficult to accept criticism from others about oneself?

266. Crooked Advice

One day, the Sufi asked advice of his friend about helping a person in need. His friend suggested some ways of helping but they did not seem ethical and honest. The Sufi felt uneasy at the idea of the crooked suggestions. His friend kept insisting that there is nothing wrong if the end result is good, and that it is OK to cheat. The Sufi kept saying that was not right. The communication went back and forth without any result.

IN PRACTICE

It is important to reach a virtuous act through virtuous and ethical steps. A person gains power and strength from being honest and just in all his or her affairs. Doing everything ethically with consciousness of God can reward the person in this world and in the afterlife. There are a lot of cases that a true, honest person may not be appreciated by one's peers, friends, or family members but only truly appreciated by God.

Discussion Question

► How do you explain the above statement "reaching a virtuous act through virtuous and ethical steps"?

267. The Kids and Candies

There was a Sufi whose wife bought boxes of candy snacks for their children to take to school. The snacks were healthy organic ones, but expensive. His wife used to put the candies in the fridge and pantry, accessible to the kids. Quite often the Sufi would hear his wife chiding the kids for finishing the snacks at home leaving nothing for the next day's lunch bags. The Sufi listened to her, smiled and said to himself, "If the candies are accessible then it is normal to finish."

IN PRACTICE

Spiritual candies are given by God as an encouragement for the traveler on the journey.[35] If a person has the choice of getting the candies, then the candies will not survive and finish. Therefore, one should know that all the spiritual candies[44] or miracles are given and controlled by God. The person does not have any control over them unless the person is enabled or empowered by God. This is even true for the prophets. The prophets can show miracles or spiritual candies as long as God empowers them and gives them the ability to do so. Therefore no one can claim ability of divinity except God. In one of the chapters of the Quran, the Prophet mentions his humanness, and that if he knew what would be in the future, then he would increase his good deeds. No one knows the future except God.

Discussion Question

▶ How do you interpret the concept of "spiritual candies" in your personal life encounters?

---

44. *Karamahs* in Arabic are spiritual candies as a terminology in Sufism.

268. Going to the Bathroom before Sleep

There was a Sufi who used to go to the bathroom before going to sleep. He felt that if he didn't, then his body's organs would complain and ruin all of the homeostasis he worked for. Some nights he did not want to go to the bathroom but he did anyway out of habit. One night, he was so tired he slept without going to the bathroom first. The next day when he woke up he did not feel well. He said to himself, "Now, I will hear all day the internal complaints."

IN PRACTICE

The body parts can complain in this life and the afterlife. In the Quran,[viiixxxv] it is mentioned that some of the body parts of a person will talk and witness against the person. In the above story, the Sufi considered each of his body parts as a separate individual and tried to fulfill their needs.

Discussion Question

▶ How can one identify oneself if his or her organs take a position against this person? In other words, how do you define "self"?

269. The Low Voice

There was a Sufi who used to think that most of her problems with her family and friends were due to her loud, intimating voice. Therefore, before talking she used to make an effort to lower and dim the tone of her voice. As soon as she did that, she realized people were much nicer, warmer, and more gentle to her. One day, she forgot to do it while she was in conversation with her friend. She looked at her friend's face and saw that she got really irritated and annoyed. Immediately, she changed her voice to the low and dim tone. Her friend started smiling and shaking her head in agreement about their discussion.

IN PRACTICE

It is important to control one's voice tone while speaking with others, especially if it is other fellow spiritual travelers, teachers, or parents. There is a teaching in the Quran[lxxxvilxxxvii] about this manner and etiquette when talking to the Prophet in a lower and softer voice.

Discussion Questions

► How do you interpret the concept of voice tone, low or high pitch?

► How is one's voice tone related to one's spiritual disposition?

270. Self-Struggle, the Goal, and the Sufi

One morning as the Sufi woke up, she was thinking: "What should I eat or drink so that it does not bother me later in the day so that I can still nicely worship God today? How should I not lose my temper with my kids as they are preparing for the school yelling and screaming so that I can still nicely worship God today? How should I text and e-mail my colleague about work so that it does not bother me later and I can still nicely worship God today?"

IN PRACTICE

This is the goal: self–struggle.[45] The goal is not struggling and fighting with others but struggling and controlling oneself for betterment in the journey to God. In the Quran, it mentions for the Prophet Abraham that he meets God in the state of calm heart, free from the spiritual diseases.[46] The Prophet reminds his companions that when they come from a self–defense physical fight that this was a minor struggle compared to the one when a person struggles with him or herself.[28][20]

Discussion Questions

- ► How do you interpret the concept of self-struggle?
- ► Do you think that it is more difficult to deal with oneself compared to others? Why?

---

45. *Jihad.*
46. Qalbun Saliim.

271. The Worried Sufi

There was a Sufi who used to be worried about the unknowns of the day when she used to wake up. She used to be very uncomfortable and wondering what to do. Then she said to herself, "I will do everything as best as I can ethically and pleasing to God and then I will show reliance in God. I won't lie. I will be honest. I won't oppress anyone or myself. I won't break anyone's heart. I won't waste my time and will use as much as I can for worshipping God." After making those promises, she felt good and said to herself "*Alhamdulillah*, at least I made the intention *inshAllah*."

IN PRACTICE

Every day is a new opportunity with unknowns, possibly with evil and good-looking incidents. There are daily prayers of the Prophet Muhammad to be performed before sunrise and sunset because each new day starts with sunset in the lunar calendar. These prayers are performed especially thanking God after immediately before or after sunset and sunrise, asking protection from all the evils and asking blessings for that day. Intention is the key in all the actions. If someone makes the intention, as the Sufi in the above story, then intention itself is the biggest prayer to God. Lastly, when everyone does in his or her capacity the struggles as the promises of the Sufi in the above story, then the people should not take much more burden on themselves but truly and fully rely on God. This concept is known as *tawakkul* in practice which means doing as best as you can then, having reliance on God.[36]

Discussion Questions

- ► How can one apply the concept of "tawakkul" in daily regular engagements?
- ► Do you consider that starting the day with a prayer is important? Why?

272. The Intellectuals

One day a Sufi attended an intellectual religious gathering where people discussed various issues. The Sufi said, "The religious sciences cannot be discussed as normal social sciences. One should have a holistic approach of respect, and humility in attitude and in language even when one is expressing different opinions on an issue." The people seemed to be offended with the Sufi's logic. They said, "We are intellectuals. We can discuss in a modern and in an unlimited way so that religious sciences can flourish like other sciences. That is the reason why religion is backwards! It does not apply the modern ways!" The Sufi smiled and left the gathering.

IN PRACTICE

It is important to distinguish the religious sciences from others. Especially if the Divine knowledge is the topic of discussion, then one should adapt the proper etiquettes of words, thoughts, and movements. This helps a person learn, apply, and improve. Sufis' silent moments are filled with deep satisfactory and respectable reflection of God. Their words are the statements of pearls deeply penetrating to the hearts. It is not being a good speaker that is important, but having the proper etiquette with God.

Discussion Questions

- ▶ How do you define the concept of "intellectuals" in the story?
- ▶ Do the spiritual followers use the term "intellectuals" for their experts in the field? Why?

273. The Cool Car

The Sufi mom had a cheap car. Her kids always thought that their mother had the coolest car. They said to her, "Mom! You have such a nice car. My friends think that either you have a Ferrari, Porsche, or Tesla. But it's even cooler than those!" The Sufi smiled to herself, "If they knew the value of this car compared to the ones that they are talking about, they would be disappointed!"

IN PRACTICE

In one's relationship with God, people may have very high opinion about a person. They may see this person as a saint or friend of God. In essence, the person knows himself or herself. Putting false clothes on oneself without realizing it can lead to lies and arrogance. Therefore, there is the prayer of the Prophet "Oh God! Please elevate my status in the eyes of people and lower my status in my own eyes.[37]" The Prophet asks elevated status in people's eyes because he wants people to respect and listen to his message from God. However, he teaches us to look upon our own selves with lower value not to be arrogant. The Prophet asked God to embody this understanding in himself and taught others to follow the same path.

Discussion Question

▶ Why do we have a tendency to be proud of our children or our group identities?

274. Texting and Driving

There was a Sufi who was driving. He saw a driver in the next lane who was texting on her phone while driving. After a few seconds, the woman did not see the car stopping in front of her. She almost hit the car in front of her but finally stopped just before doing so. The Sufi looked at her face. She looked fearful, stressed, and pale after being saved from an accident. The Sufi smiled and said to himself, "I don't understand these people. In this stressful life, these people put more unnecessary stress on themselves by texting and driving. Instead of enjoying the road, the trees, and different scenes while driving and being with God, they want to put more stress on themselves. I don't understand!"

IN PRACTICE

It is important to use every opportunity to benefit in one's relationship with God. Focused driving while enjoying the nature, silence, and making chants are some of the ways some Sufis discharge themselves from the fears, stress, and anxieties of the day. In the above story, the Sufi witnessed an opposite case by another driver. She put stress upon herself by texting on her phone while driving. The Sufi did not find this texting practice logical.

Discussion Questions

- ▶ How can one make driving enjoyable?
- ▶ Why are some of the activities considered distracting in driving compared to others?
- ▶ How do you interpret the concept of self-reflection, silence, and chanting while driving?

275. The Stingy Sufi and the Ice Cream

There was a stingy Sufi who took her kids and her friend out for ice cream. Her friend was delayed for the ice cream party. She said to herself, "Let me buy the ice cream before my friend comes. If she comes later she can pay for her own ice cream." She bought the ice cream for her kids and started eating with them. After a few minutes, her friend arrived. The Sufi was embarrassed and said to her friend, "Let me buy your ice cream too as I promised." Her friend ordered her ice cream. The Sufi was about to pay for the ice cream when the owner of the store said, "She is on me. You don't need to pay for her." The Sufi thanked the owner and felt embarrassed about her thoughts.

IN PRACTICE

It is important to be generous. God gives much to people and does not ask anything in return except the recognition and appreciation of the One and only God. In the above story, the Sufi had a spiritual sickness of being stingy and fear of spending on others. God sent her a sign, then she felt bad and embarrassed about this issue.

Discussion Question

▶ Why is generosity considered as virtuous compared to being stingy?

276. Teachers and Gratefulness

One day, the Sufi was upset and disturbed about the ungratefulness of people about their teachers. She had a friend who was complaining about her teacher who did a lot for her. She said to herself, "I don't understand. You benefited a lot from your teacher. Now, you see something you don't like and you don't agree as if your teacher did not do anything for you." The Sufi was very sad about the ungratefulness of people for their teachers.

IN PRACTICE

The people that we benefit from have rights on us. The first gratefulness is expected for God, then for parents, then for teachers. It is not ethical or fair to act ungrateful, as when the person does not recognize and appreciate the benefits that one receives from one's teacher.

Discussion Question

- Why is being ungrateful not a noble trait?

277. The Bald Head and the Ponytail

There was a Sufi who used to always shave his head. He preferred to have a bald head because he liked having short hair. The Sufi also did not have time and effort to take care of long hair. He knew that if he had long hair it would be a mess all the time. He never understood how a man could have a ponytail and used to talk badly about them. One day, he looked at the mirror. He realized that he was losing his hair and some part of his head had already become bald. He was sad despite always shaving his hair. He decided to not cut nor shave his hair anymore because soon enough his head would be naturally bald due to the hair loss. After a year, his hair grew long and now he had a ponytail. He looked at the mirror. He did not like the look of himself with the ponytail, but he did not want to cut it because soon he would lose all his hair. Now, the Sufi was preserving his ponytail although he did not like it.

IN PRACTICE

It is important to appreciate all the favors from God before we lose them. The first favor is existence with good health. Another favor is knowing God and having the ability to pray to God. Another favor is having strength to walk, to eat, to breath, to sleep, to think, and so forth. When we get sick or when we lose some of those abilities we tend to look at people with the abilities and to be envious of them. Another important point in the above story is the situations, responsibilities, or people that we don't like much. Once we come to know that we can lose them we start grasping or holding them tight. Therefore, the spiritual state of appreciation is very important in practice. God especially gives the Prophet Muhammad a high status due to his constant mode of appreciation for God. Therefore, the word or title "Muhammad" means the one who always appreciates and thanks God.

Discussion Question

▶ Why do we tend to attach value to things once we realize that we will soon lose them?

278. The Headache

One day, the Sufi woke up with a severe headache. She was in much pain and wondered about the possible reasons for the headache. She avoided taking any medicine until she performed some spiritual healing and talismanic practice. She went to the bathroom to make ablutions,[47] washed up herself with sacred teachings. Then she started praying. She felt a little better but the headache was still there. She started reading some talismanic verses from the last three chapters of the Quran. After reading thrice, she blew on her hands and wiped her body with her hands as the Prophet suggested.[38] She felt even better but still she had some traces of the headache. As she wondered what type of painkilling pills she should take, or if she would just bear the pain, she decided upon doing some Prophetic suggested prayers for illness. Then, she fell asleep and after a while woke up feeling much better. She said, "*Alhamdulillah,* thanks to God, I didn't need the medicine."

IN PRACTICE

It is important to consult God in any issue or problem before seeking assistance from other means. Other means can help as long as God empowers them. In the above story, painkiller pills can be considered as "other means" for headache. One can take it but should remember that the cure is still given by God. The Sufi did not need to consult to other means and she only used the talismanic readings from the Quran[39] and litanies of the Prophet to ask help from God. If they did not work out she could have taken the medicine and ask God to make the pills sufficient or remedy for her headache.

Discussion Question

▶ What should be the disposition of a person when he or she first expresses their need to God?

---

47. *Wudhu.*

279. The Mosque's Wooden Table

There was a small wooden table in the mosque. People in the mosque used to put the garbage can on this table. One day, the Sufi was looking for a table to put the Quran on and to read from it. There were no tables in the mosque except the plastic ones. As the Sufi always preferred natural pieces, she did not want to put the Quran on a plastic table. As she searched, she saw the wooden table with a garbage can on top of it. The Sufi smiled and said to herself, "Now, your status will be elevated and noble, *inshAllah*, with the will of God." She cleared, cleaned, and perfumed the table. Then she put the Quran on it to read it. After a few months, this wooden table became the most wanted and preferred table in the mosque for reading the Quran. No one wanted to use the plastic ones. One day, the Sufi entered the mosque, two people were fighting for this table. The Sufi looked at the scene and said, "Garbage history, nobility and fame, and the elevation of God."

IN PRACTICE

Sometimes we don't realize or take into consideration a person's past when we criticize them. On the spiritual path especially, everyone has a garbage history. Even the selected people of God, the messengers or prophets, were guided to a better spiritual state after receiving revelation from God. When a person is elevated by God to a noble level the person should always be humble, thankful, and appreciative of God's favors and remember his or her past. It is known in the Muslim history that Arabs were desert and tribal people with unhuman renderings and dealings. It is much of the appreciation of early Muslims[48] to always remember their past and appreciate God's guidance to humanity and civility with the advent of Islam. This appreciation made them advance rapidly in the early Islamic period compared to later periods in the history when people received or inherited the religion from their parents as a culture.

Discussion Question

▶ Who or what determines the value of things?

---

48. *Sahabah.*

280. The Long-Haired Brother and the Bald Brother

There was a Sufi who had a bald friend. People used to refer to him as the "brother with bald hair." This man used to get annoyed with this description until finally he got some surgical hair implants. After a few years, his hair grew long and people started calling him the "brother with long hair." He was now happy and confident about his new nickname. The Sufi observed this change in his friend's approach and smiled and said to himself, "What others think; does it matter?"

IN PRACTICE

It is important not to worry about others' opinion especially if it is related to the externalities. Looks or bodily appearances are one of the traps that people fall in without understanding the essence of the existence of a person. Therefore, there may be some Sufis who may not care what others think. There may be other Sufis who can try to fit into the similar outlook of their culture so that they look normal and ordinary like others.

Discussion Question

▶   What are different positions in one's outlook in practice?

281. Seeking Guidance

Over many years, the Sufi was wondering, "Why do some people have guidance and know about God?" One day, he visited one of her friends who was very rich. He was a new Sufi. The new Sufi was so humble that he even saw children as her teachers. The older Sufi said, "I found the answer: Humility!"

In practice

God can inspire an answer to a question after many years if the person has a genuine struggle and intention of learning. It is not unusual to see Sufi stories about a Sufi master struggling with his or herself about a dilemma and years later, the answer can be given by God. The concept of guidance in practice appears often with the traits of humbleness and humility. There may be people who can know orthodoxy, the right or authentic path but due to the identity, group ownerships, arrogance or other reasons they may not have orthopraxy, the right practice. Similarly, Satan was very intelligent as mentioned in various scriptures but he always lost due to his lack of humility.

Discussion Question

▶ Why do you think humility is one of the important keys for guidance?

282. The Lazy Sufi

There was a Sufi who used to read her protection prayers and litanies in the morning and night. One day, she was lazy and was not able to wake up in the morning to read and perform her prayers before she left home for work. She had a very bad day. At the end of day, she was realized the reason for having such a bad day. She said to herself, "My laziness about my protection prayers."

IN PRACTICE

It is very important not to start and enter the day and night before one engages, reads, and protects themselves with prayers.[40] If someone misses them, it is normal and expected for an evil to happen in that person's day. It is expected to have reliance on God regularly through prayers for protection from evil and bad outcomes.[41]

Discussion Question

▶ Why are the protection prayers or litanies very critical?

283. One Hand, One Leg, One Eye

There was a Sufi who used to practice having one hand, one leg, or one eye for part of each month. She would put one of her hands in a cast for a week and use only one of her hands. The next month, she used crutches to walk and to do her work and daily needs with one leg. The following month she put a cover on one of her eyes in order to only use one of her eyes for her daily needs and at work. The Sufi did not tell anyone this secret. She was pretending as if an accident or something happened to her. Except one day, a friend deduced the Sufi's secret practice, and asked for the Sufi's reason. The Sufi said, "I will tell you the reason only because you probably think I am crazy. I want to appreciate what God gave me. Sometimes, I see people around and they don't appreciate what God gives them and God tests them with difficulties. I want to truly feel this appreciation for God before any trial or evil hits me. You may still think that I am crazy but it doesn't matter."

IN PRACTICE

It is really important to be in constant appreciation and in constant gratitude for the favors of God. Most of the time, people value what they lose. People are envious of what they don't have. In the above story, the Sufi was trying to instruct and train her own ego for this true sense of appreciation of God.

Discussion Question

▶ Why do people tend to look at others and notice what the others have but they don't have?

284. The Dirty Coffee Machine

One day, the Sufi wanted to make coffee. She started pouring water from another container into the coffee water tank in order to fill it. As she was pouring, the container's cap fell on the ground. The Sufi pondered the message of the falling cap. After she finished pouring the water, she looked into the container and saw dirt in the bottom of the container. Then, she smiled and said to herself, "This is the message." She dumped the water, cleaned the tank, and filled it with a clean container.

IN PRACTICE

There is a meaning and sign in every minute detail of life. Everything happens with an external and internal reason. If a person does not ignore these signs, then he or she can use everything and every moment for their advantage. Then life's incidents become more purposeful with awareness. These positive signs can come from God as long as the person has the intention and struggle to regularly maintain the prayers to God.[39]

Discussion Question

▶   Can there be a meaning for every simple incident in one's life?

285. Remembering Role Models

One day, the Sufi was feeling uneasy. She did not act in a way that her teacher wanted her to act. She was remembering the days that she spent with her teacher. Her teacher was a true role model. She was gentle, nice, and patient. She did not rush to correct people's mistakes. She used wisdom in her style of communication. The Sufi considered all of these and she was ashamed of herself for her inadequacies, and said to herself, "It is difficult, but I guess this is the struggle and self-improvement."

IN PRACTICE

It is very important to try to better oneself. Realization of mistakes is the first step to change. One should not give up the struggle because it is difficult. Teachers as role models are present to show to their students that it can be done and there are other humans who can achieve some results at the end of self-struggle. In all stages of life, one should always humbly ask assistance and guidance from God in different types of self-struggle.

Discussion Questions

- ▶ What is the place of good teachers?
- ▶ What are the signs of a good teacher?

286. Weakness and Power

Lately the Sufi was feeling weak and old although she was still in good health and young. She wondered if it was related to the type of food that she had been eating or she was missing taking some of her vitamins. Then she thought about some of the Sufis who were eighty or ninety years old but were still active like young people. They were involved with good groups and social work and spent a good amount of their time worshipping and praying to God. Then she smiled and said to herself, "Maybe that is the reason: they pray and ask from God constantly to be active and to have energy for the good deeds and worship."

IN PRACTICE

One of the prayers that is recited after each prayer is asking God to help the person worship and pray to God in an easy and enjoyable manner. [42] This prayer is one of the famous prayers of the Prophet Muhammad. As the person faces different challenges in life with age, health, and different life-related conditions, the energy or the zeal for worship and doing good may not be at the desired level all the time. Therefore, it is very important to ask God to enable the person to be involved with the good actions and worship until one dies.

Discussion Question

▶ What is the importance of prayers or asking one's needs constantly from God?

287. The Disconnected Traveler

One day, a Sufi teacher was teaching about the importance of disconnection. One student was chanting the Divine phrases and praying. He became disconnected from his surrounding and was set to begin spiritual travel. Then after a while he reconnected with his surroundings after the chanting was over. The teacher explained charge and discharge in chanting, and how one should focus on himself rather than the noises, lights, temperature, or anything in the physical environment.

IN PRACTICE

It is very important to focus while performing the chants. One of the famous chants is *La ilaha illa Allah*. The person tries to take everything out of his or her mind and heart and focus only on the One and Only Creator, Allah. By doing so, the person discharges themselves from all worries, stresses, anxieties, and fears.[22]

Discussion Question

▶ Is it possible to disconnect from one's surroundings in a crowded environment where there are a lot of distractions? Why?

288. The Loud Greeter

There was a man who used to greet everyone very loudly in the mosque. When this man approached the Sufi, the Sufi pretended that he was doing his prayers in order not to be disturbed. After a while, everyone in the mosque started greeting each other loudly. The Sufi smiled and said to himself, "Even though I don't like it, I think this man started something good as a practice. At least people are greeting each other and not grumbling."

IN PRACTICE

It is important to greet each other and smile. The Prophet recommends one of the rights of a person over another is greeting each other nicely when they see each other[20]. However, some Sufis, as in the above story, prefer silence and solitude. The Sufi avoided socializing but when he saw that the loud greeter encouraged others to increase the practice of greeting, he critiqued and disagreed with his own self and applauded the achievement of the man for starting something good.

Discussion Questions

- What is the effect of greeting in social life?
- What is the effect of greeting in spiritual life?

289. The Professor

There was a Sufi who used to teach at a college. She felt that some of the students were treating her in a disrespectful way. She said to herself, "I need to be patient." As the semester was getting close to the end, the Sufi gained empathy for these students and made good friends with them. After the semester was over, one of the students wrote a reflection about the Sufi's class that it was his best class in the college. When the Sufi read this she said to herself, "After every difficulty there is an ease."

IN PRACTICE

It is important to be patient in all different walks of life. Husband–wife relationships, student–teacher relationships, parent–children relationships, and friend relationships: all require patience to be successful and to have long life effects. In the above story, the Sufi had empathy for her students' not respectful behaviors which helped her actualize and apply patience in her relationship with them. After this self-struggle, as God mentions in the Quran[x] after each difficulty there is an ease that rewards the person's self-struggle in the form of patience both in this world with positive results and in the afterlife if the person had a right and good intention.

Discussion Question

► What is the wisdom of having a difficulty after an ease and having an ease after a difficulty in circular days destined by God?

290. Tea for the Traveler

One day, a stranger who was mentally ill visited the mosque. Everyone was fasting but the stranger did not know about it. He made tea and wanted to show his generosity and gave a cup of tea to the Sufi. The Sufi said that he was fasting. The stranger insisted that the Sufi needed to take the tea cup from him. The Sufi did not want to argue and took it from him and put it to the side. The Sufi thought to himself, "What is the message?" After a while, a traveler who was not fasting came to the mosque looking tired. The Sufi said to himself, "Now, I get the message." He gave the tea to the traveler. The traveler was happy and the Sufi smiled.

IN PRACTICE

There is a meaning in everything. Nothing is haphazard if a person can understand it. Travelers, the sick, and mentally ill are all exempt from fasting. In the above story, the Sufi did not want to argue with the stranger who was mentally ill because there was no use. On the other hand, the Sufi did not understand why this happened until the traveler came to the mosque. Then, the Sufi found a meaning in this small incident.

Discussion Questions

- ▶ Is it possible to understand the real reason behind every evil or good seeming incident if one is patient?
- ▶ How can one define the notion of "the real reason" behind every incident?

291. Breaking the Fast

There was a Sufi who used to have a difficult time with fasting. When she went without any food and drink she often got headaches. Breaking the fast was enjoyable for her, however; it was a spiritual achievement. With this dilemma of pain and joy, she always had a hard time deciding if she should fast or not. She said to herself, "I can do anything but I can't do without coffee." As the sunset time came, she used to forget all the pain that she went through the day due to fasting. She used to say "*Alhamdulillah*, thanks to God for another achievement." She grew confident, happy, and focused after fasting.

IN PRACTICE

One of the difficult practices that can be a good way of disciplining the self or ego is fasting. The ritual of fasting is having no food, drink, and spousal intimate relationship from sunrise to sunset. In tradition, all the spiritual efforts are rewarded by God. In the sayings of the Prophet, God rewards the fasting person in a special manner compared to the other forms of worship in practice. The Prophet says, "The fasting person has two rewards: one at the time of breaking the fast and the other is in the afterlife, amazed with enormous awards from God.[28][20]" The Sufi in the above story experienced the utmost pleasure and happiness at the time of breaking the fast as the initial reward mentioned by the Prophet. She felt good, focused, confident, and happy after this spiritual achievement.

Discussion Question

► How does fasting help the person to focus and collect one's spiritual messiness?

292. Children, Patience, and Prayer

There was a Sufi who used to get easily annoyed with his children. He used to yell and scream at them, especially when they used to make a mess in the house. After a while, he used to feel bad and said to himself, "I wish I was patient and could be nicer to my kids." Every day, it was the same scenario: first, yelling and screaming, then feeling bad about his treatment of his kids. One day, he said to himself, "I am making myself miserable with this situation. I need to do something." Then, he said to himself, "Let me pray." He prayed and asked help from God for his situation. After a while, he smiled and said, "*Alhamdulillah*, I know what to do now. I need to practice my patience but I can't be patient unless I am strong. But I can't be strong unless I make my relationship with God stronger through more prayers."

In practice

Patience is not a virtual concept.[43] This trait solidifies in one's character with constant and regular prayers. Therefore, a minimum of five times prayer exists. Depending on the need and the situation of the person, one can increase these daily engagements to be more spiritually strong. In the above story, the Sufi needed to embody the notion of patience. He realized his shortcomings. He was constantly doing self-struggle and blaming his own ego and self. One of the praiseworthy steps in spiritual journey is the state of the self or ego when it realizes its mistakes and puts blame on it instead of blaming others. The next step comes after the diagnosis of the spiritual disease, and its treatment is reached through knowledge and practice. The Sufi realized that one of the ways in the practice is to embody patience through prayers.

Discussion Questions

▶ How can daily regular prayers embody patience in one's spiritual strength?
▶ What are the levels of self or ego in practice?

293. Hugging at the Airport

There was a Sufi who came from overseas to visit his friend. Many years had passed since they had last seen each other. His friend was waiting outside the airport to pick up the Sufi. As soon as the Sufi came out from the airport, he saw the Sufi. Both the Sufi and his friend were very happy to see each other and they had a few tears in both of their eyes. The overseas Sufi greeted his friend and gave him a hug but the local Sufi was not comfortable and said to his friend, "In this country, if two men hug each other it may have some other meanings." His Sufi friend from overseas asked what he meant, and his friend replied, "I will explain it later."

IN PRACTICE

When people greet each other, some hug regardless of gender. Same-sex hugging or holding hands walking on the streets does not mean that they have sexual relationships. These are the ways of showing their close friendships as practiced in some of the Sufi cultures. It is also common to cry among men when they see a friend who was absent for a long time. The reason for crying is to express happiness or joy for reunion.

Discussion Question

▶   How can one interpret the famous relationship between Rumi and his teacher Shams?

294. The Serious Sufi and the Smiling Sufi

There were two Sufi friends. One was always serious and the other was always funny and making jokes. One day, the serious Sufi asked the funny Sufi, "Why do you always make jokes although what we deal with is very serious? The afterlife, death, accountability, prayer, etc. . . ." The smiling Sufi smiled and said, "My exterior may be funny but inside I am burning serious."

IN PRACTICE

It is important not to make people uncomfortable even though the spiritual journey is very important and serious. Most of the time, the separation between the pious and non-pious can be due to their external interactions. In practice, all the internal interactions which is the essence of the spiritual journey is only undertaken for God and to please God. The Prophet used to say: "If you knew what I knew, then you would laugh less but cry a lot.[28][20]" Yet the Prophet used to sit with people and listen to their jokes and smile. Sometimes, he also used to make jokes with the contents of wisdom and truth. The Prophet did not make people feel uncomfortable or cold. The Quran praises this quality of the Prophet and mentions that if the Prophet was harsh, then the people would not be around him as much, as they loved to be around him.[xixxxviii]

Discussion Questions

- ▶ How can one balance between the real self and external self?
- ▶ Can one consider external self as fake if it does not match with internal self? Why?
- ▶ Why do people often tend not to like serious people?

295. The Sleeping Stranger

There was once a man who had been sleeping at nights in the mosque for a few weeks. This was a man that people in the mosque did not know much about, and they were uncomfortable with this stranger. One day, while there was only the Sufi and the stranger, the Sufi approached him and asked if he was the son of a woman who had passed away two weeks ago. The man said, "yes." The Sufi said to himself, "Now, everything makes sense." The next day, the man was sleeping in the mosque again. One of the administrators of the mosque was a harsh man and reprimanded the stranger, saying, "This is a mosque. You cannot sleep at night here." The Sufi witnessed this and felt bad for the stranger. After the prayer finished in the mosque, the Sufi took a courageous step and made an announcement in the mosque. He introduced the stranger to everyone and explained why he was sleeping in the mosque.

IN PRACTICE

It is very important to have empathy for people. The Sufi with Divine guidance understood this sleeping man's situation and guessed that he was the son of the lady who passed away recently. It is common that people need more help and support at the time of loss. Therefore, one can find many instances where people sleep and spend more time in the mosques and temples when they are spiritually troubled and in need. In this story, the Sufi handled the case with wisdom without confronting the harsh administrator directly, but addressed the problem to the general audience. This was one of the ways the Prophet used to solve any problem and issue among people. The Prophet did not target any specific person and accuse them of their mistakes but tried to teach them with the habit of introducing general guidelines for everyone.[38]

Discussion Question

▶ Why do people tend to have increased quality and quantity of spirituality at the time of loss?

296. Warm Water in the Morning

There was a Sufi who liked coffee a lot; however, she started her day by drinking warm water rather than drinking coffee. One night, a friend of hers stayed overnight with the Sufi. Her friend knew that the Sufi loved coffee. She wanted to surprise her with a nice brewed pot of coffee in the morning when they woke up. The Sufi realized this and mindful of her friend's feelings she said, "I really love coffee but I need to train my body, stomach, and organs about what will come later in the day. Therefore, I start with warm water in the beginning then increase its strength by adding small amounts of coffee as time passes during the day."

IN PRACTICE

It is important to realize the stages of training and learning. The spiritual journey requires self-struggle constantly. The spiritual achievements come with self-increments. In the above story, the Sufi was implementing this notion in her everyday affairs even in her habit of drinking coffee.

Discussion Questions

- ▸ Can you give examples from the spiritual trainings of teachers for their disciples who implement the notion of incremental progress in the spiritual journey?
- ▸ How one can relate this concept with the early followers of Prophet Muhammad in Makkah compared to Madinah?
- ▸ How can one implement the notion of incremental progress in their spiritual journey?

297. Imbibing Patience

There was a Sufi who used to lose her temper. Each time she lost her temper she used to regret and blame herself about not being patient. She suffered pain after each incident of impatience. One day, she said to herself, "I don't know what to do." Then she started reading the Quran and reviewed all the verses about patience. After, she was once again convinced logically that she should not lose her temper. Then, she felt better and promised to herself that she would be more mindful in applying patience.

IN PRACTICE

To imbibe patience is very important. It is a continuous struggle to embody the true meaning of patience. One of the ways to implement patience is with prayer. Another way is constantly being mindful that seemingly evil occurrences can be a gain if one is patient. This notion is constantly advised in the Quran. God is with the one who is patient. God is the supporter of the patient one. A person should always rely on God in the instances that require patience. Patience can be applied when facing evils. Patience can be applied for being on the right path. Patience can be applied for the struggles against one's own self if it encourages the person to do evil. If a person starts complaining and blames others, then at this stage there is no patience.[20] This is the stage where the blame comes in the relationship with God. The relationship becomes shaky and unfruitful. Therefore, the Sufis practice chanting *Alhamdullilah* to appreciate God. In the instances where utmost patience is needed they chant, *hasbiyallah*, God is sufficient for me.

Discussion Questions

▶ Is it difficult to implement the notion of patience?
▶ Why is patience a virtue in many spiritual and religious traditions?

298. The Pain and the Pleasure

Each time after a painful ritual such as fasting, the Sufi used to feel good and strong for at least a week. However, before each optional fasting, she was always hesitant if she should fast that day or not. If for any reason she did not fast that day she did not feel well and got a headache. If she fasted she sometimes got a headache and she thought that her headache was related to her fasting.

IN PRACTICE

Fasting is one of the practices that focuses a person's mind and heart. It is also one of the ways of removing depression, stress, and anxiety. It is recommended to fast three days per month or one day per week as an optional practice. Mondays and Thursdays or the mid three days of the month are especially chosen for fasting as practiced by the Prophet.[20] In the story above, the Sufi received the benefit of fasting for at least a week although it was difficult for her.

Discussion Questions

- ► How can or cannot fasting trigger headaches?
- ► Why is fasting medically recommended if fasting can trigger headaches?
- ► What was the wisdom of the Prophet about getting headaches? Can headaches be related to fasting or other reasons?

299. The Focused Sufi

One day, the Sufi was in the mosque. Two people started arguing about a religious matter. The Sufi said to himself "I won't get involved." He tried to focus on his prayer. Finally, the arguing people left. The Sufi said, "*Alhamdulillah*, thanks to God." A few minutes later, a crazy man came to the mosque. He started shaking people's hands and disturbing people while they were praying. The Sufi said to himself, "Maybe, this is a sign. Let me go to my car and finish my prayer and meditation over there." He went to his car and continued his meditation. After a while, he went to back into the mosque. Everything looked and felt peaceful and calm once again. Then, the Sufi serenely finished his meditation and said "*Alhamdulillah*, thanks to God."

IN PRACTICE

Full focus during the prayer and meditation is very important. These are valuable times for a person to discharge and charge oneself spiritually. Sometimes, if the conditions are not amenable it is important to find other possible places to focus. Most of the time, mosques are places in which people can find tranquility, calmness, and peace for prayers. But there are always exceptions to the general rule. When there is the possibility of disturbance or evil outcomes, a person can leave the mosque until the negativity is gone then he or she can go back.

Discussion Question

▶ How can the spiritual medium of a place change in the case of argumentation or dispute among people?

300. An Argument at the Mosque

One day, there were two people arguing in the mosque. One was an Arab and the other was an Indian. The Arab said, "We should follow the Prophet." The Indian said, "No, that is *sunnah muakkadah*." The Sufi looked at them both, smiling, and said to himself, "They are both saying the same thing but using different language of terminology. That is the main problem in our world."

IN PRACTICE

It is really important to have wisdom of understanding of people with their cultural, ethnic, and gender background. In the above story, two people from the same religion are arguing about a religious matter. They mean the same but because they use different words they think they disagree and argue. In the case of the Arab fellow in the story, he feels that he is qualified to directly access the primary sources related to the practice of the Prophet[49] by quoting the Prophet on a religious matter. Whereas the fellow from India follows his teacher and uses a technical term from his school of thought.[50] The Arab fellow does not know this technical term, and thinks the other one doesn't know anything. The Indian fellow does not know the source of the quote from the Prophet quoted by the other fellow, and thinks the other one equally ignorant.

Discussion Question

▶ Is it common to witness people arguing about an issue but they really mean something similar or the same? Why?

---

49. Hadith.
50. Hanifi school of Islamic legal system.

301. The Sufi, the Semi-Buddhist Sufi, and the Teachers

One day, there was a Sufi and semi-Buddhist Sufi and they were good friends. The semi-Buddhist Sufi also had teachers from the Buddhist tradition. They argued about whose teacher was better than the others.

IN PRACTICE

A wise Sufi tries to avoid religious arguments about the superiority of one's teachers over another. It is always important to respect other traditions if someone is identifying or viewing themselves as "semi" as in the story above. Semi is a term borrowed from physics when the nomenclature is used for example for semi-conductors, half or partial conducting metals. Semi in this case can mean a person following half of the teachings of one path and following the rest from another spiritual path. The arguments of identity chaining the person to specific teachers or schools is not new, unfortunately, along the history of practice. Genuine Sufis are not trapped in these futile arguments although one can view her or his teacher as the best and the most valuable. As one Sufi teacher said, "One can claim that his or her teacher or school is the best but one cannot claim that theirs is the only way."

Discussion Questions

- ▶ How can one define the concept of "semi" in one's life?
- ▶ Do you encounter people often who see or define themselves as "semi"?
- ▶ What is the advantage and disadvantage of being "semi"?

302. The MP3 Player and the Corpse

Once there was a Sufi alone in the mosque, enjoying reading the Quran, praying, and reflecting on the verses. After some time, a group of people entered the mosque with a dead body for funeral preparations for the next day. The Sufi still tried to enjoy his reading of the Quran and praying but at the same heard some crying of the family members in the back bemoaning their loss. After half an hour, the family members left the body with a Quran MP3 player in the washroom next to the prayer area. There was no one in the mosque again except the Sufi and the dead body in the washroom with the Quran playing in the background. After the Sufi finished his prayer, he smiled and said to himself, "This is life. If I don't read the Quran when I am alive, then what is the benefit of listening to it from MP3 when I am dead? The people leave and once again you are with the Beloved."

IN PRACTICE

Death is reality but not a bad one if the person internalizes it through practice and worship before it happens. In the above story, the Sufi underlines the real connection with the Quran when one is alive. An unnatural or weak connection can be made when one is dead as well but not as much. People read the Quran to the deceased for comforting and easing the travel from our life to the next.[44]

Discussion Questions

- ▶ How does recitation of the Quran or divine phrases affect the death or the soul of the deceased?
- ▶ What are the common practices of prayers or recitations when one visits a grave? Why?

303. The Patient Sufi

One Friday the Sufi was in the mosque enjoying his praying and reading the Quran. There were also three talkative men in the mosque. Others in the mosque treated them poorly, but the Sufi treated them gently and kindly. They knew and liked the Sufi and wished to consult him, but they also knew that they should not disturb him while he was reading the Quran or during prayers. One of the men needed the Sufi's attention and sat next to the Sufi. In general, the Sufi would not let himself be distracted while reading the Quran, but on this day he responded patiently. The man happily returned to his spot in the mosque. When the other two saw how the Sufi responded, they were encouraged as well and went next to the Sufi one by one. The Sufi responded kindly, thinking to himself, "Today is a special day, Friday. I am practicing patience."

In practice

If a person is enjoying a nice sweet dessert, he or she may not want to be disturbed.[45] For some senior Sufis, one's relationship with God in the prayers and reading the Quran can have the same sweet taste. In the above story, the Sufi had that experience with the prayers and reading the Quran; however, he understood the desire for the three man to talk to him and entertained their conversations. The Sufi also realized that he should still continue his engagement with the prayer and reading the scripture after the disturbance by practicing genuine patience.

Discussion Questions

▶ Is it considered inconsiderate if one does not respond to one's need due to the person's sweet engagement in prayer or worship of God? Why?

▶ Is it difficult to achieve the level of taking pleasure or sweetness from one's prayers?

304. The Sunset, the Nice Breeze, and the Sufi

One day, the Sufi was sitting in the mosque. She was enjoying the sunset, the prayer, and the nice breeze from outside. She looked back upon some old memories from when she was a child. She felt that she had wasted all her life without Allah and said to herself, "I wish I knew then what I know now."

IN PRACTICE

One of the ways to test the upward spiritual journey is that the person does not desire to go back to the living conditions of the past. In other words, the person constantly learns and increases one's knowledge in their relationship with God. Every next day is better in that relationship than the one before. In that perspective, a person ideally is expected not to miss the past due to climbing upward spiritually. However, it is normal to miss old friends, places, and good experiences.[46]

Discussion Question

▶ How can one use the negative effect of past feelings positively in the present?

305. Submission, Decision, and the Sufis

There were two Sufis: husband and wife. They were trying to decide which teacher they should send their children to for their self and spiritual training. The wife said, "Let's decide and get it over with." The husband said, "I am not sure really which one is better." They discussed and talked without reaching a solution and until both were tired. After a few hours, the wife received a text from one of the potential teachers of the child saying, "I am sick; please don't send your child." The husband said, "*Alhamdulillah*, the decision is made."

IN PRACTICE

In choosing what they want for themselves, for their families, and others, there are times when people use logic and their minds to make the best life decisions. One of the main concepts in practice is the concept of positive and active submission and surrender to God. One may call this as reliance or *tawakkul*. It is a positive submission and surrender to God because the person does not see the relationship between God and oneself as something negative and passive submission to an authority. The One Who is Caring, Merciful, and at the same time the Most Powerful and Wise can do anything for the person if the person submits and surrenders. This notion takes all the burden of worries, stress, and unnecessary load from the spiritual shoulders of a person. The above story is a small example of this in practice. The concept of submission or reliance can reveal itself explicitly as in the above case. In other cases, it may be implicit, so a person should know the etiquettes of the path to reach this level and apply it with patience in different parts of life.

Discussion Questions

- Why is it so difficult to make decisions for some people?
- What is the balance between indecisiveness and decisiveness in an ideal spiritual path?

306. Blessing the Coffee

There was once a class with a Sufi and his teacher who was also a famous coffee maker. The teacher often made coffee for the students before class. The Sufi asked if the teacher could teach the Sufi how to make the coffee. The teacher said, "OK, first you say 'bismillah', with the name of God, then put in the filter and water with your right hand. It is important to use a natural filter and make the coffee light. Put seven small spoonfuls of coffee in the filter while saying *bismillah*. Enjoy its aroma while it brews, and serve it as soon as it is done so that it doesn't get bitter. This is the recipe of my famous coffee."

IN PRACTICE

It is important to chant on the food and drink to get a blessing from God. The chanting is the recognition of the blessing of God.[47] According to some Sufis, it tastes better when chanted on. It is the practice of the Prophet to use odd numbers such as 1, 3, 5, or as mentioned 7 for the number of spoonfuls of coffee. Sufis are careful to choose an organic coffee filter and use natural and organic ingredients[51] as suggested by the Quran. There is actually an entire market for the practice of herbal and healthy and prophetic food habits and medicine.

Sufis adjust their qualities and tones to benefit everyone without leaving people out of the circle. Strong coffee only appeals to the specialized drinker. Therefore, making the coffee light can increase its accessibility to even those not commonly coffee drinkers. It is important to maximize the tastes as the teacher suggests by drinking as soon as it's brewed, and savoring the smell of the coffee while brewing and before drinking it. This notion alludes to the practice of mindfulness and awareness while being engaged in chants or other everyday affairs.

Discussion Question

- ▶ How does one's chanting over a food possibly affect the taste of it?

---

51. Tayyib.

307. Accountability, Children, and the Sufi

One day, the wife of the Sufi listed all the bad things that their children did. The children were not listening to their mother. The mother felt helpless. The Sufi said to himself, "If I discipline them, I would be seen as harsh. I won't do anything and will just be silent and watch what happens." Days passed, and the mother became uneasy about the children's abuse, and started to lose control of herself. The house was becoming a chaotic environment. The Sufi said to himself, "I think I need to do something. Let me act firmly." The Sufi called the children and listed all the blames that were reported by the mother. There was silence from the children. The Sufi declared, "One of you needs to sleep upstairs and the other downstairs. You will not sleep in your beds tonight because of what has been happening lately." One went upstairs and the other went downstairs and both children burst out crying. The mother was uneasy, her heart broken. She tried to talk to their father into removing the punishment. The Sufi remained firm, thinking, "*SubhanAllah*, this is similar to people and their relationship with God."

IN PRACTICE

It is important to realize that there is an accountability in this world and afterlife. People are at different levels in their ethics and spirituality. Some people may not do evil because they are afraid of its consequence. Others may not do evil because it is not right for them ethically or spiritually. The accountability in the afterlife is necessary for both the affairs of spiritual and worldly engagements. Most elect the spiritual path of performing good actions to avoid evils as classified by God in order to not displease God. They avoid evil because they love God. On the other hand, the lower level travelers, with no blame to them, can perform good and avoid evil due to fear of accountability and the desire for reward. All are good and fine.[22]

Discussion Question

▶ What can be the problems of humanization of the Divine realities in the above case?

308. Terminology of Jealousy

The Sufi one day went to an interfaith meeting. There were Christians and Muslims, and they were talking about God. The Christian fellow said, "We believe that our God is jealous." The Muslim fellow said, "Allah does not want anyone to be worshipped except Allah." They continued debating. The Sufi looked and smiled and said to himself, "Our Creator is the same. They both say the same thing but in different words and terminologies."

IN PRACTICE

It is very important to worship only God. It is very important to keep proper etiquette and respectful attitude toward God[52] when one is expressing words and even thinking about God. This may be called *adab* with God. Therefore, although what is implied with "jealous" is understood when one is using this word about God, but it can also be alienating due to popular human use of this word in negative contexts. [26] One of the parts that Sufis focus upon in their practice is to change terminologies for people in order to approximate them with what they mean all the while with a consideration of keeping the attitude of respect, appreciation, and a humble attitude toward God.

Discussion Questions

- Why do we have different classifications of relationships with others depending on the people and context such as professional, socia, and family relations?
- How does one expect an appropriate relationship with God similar to the case of different classifications of relationships in a person's life? Why?

---

52. Adab.

309. The Overflowing Cup

One day, the Sufi poured coffee into a small cup, trying to get in as much as possible. It spilled on his hand, scalding him. He said to himself, "I was greedy. I wanted to get more than I can handle. I got burned."

IN PRACTICE

God gives people what they can handle or what they can bear with tests, trials, and spiritual achievements. When a person wants to achieve more, sometimes it could be difficult and can possibly backfire upon him or herself. Therefore, the person should be always in the mode of appreciation of God for the all of life's encounters.

Discussion Question

► Is having limits as humans a blessing or not? Why?

310. Advising Patience, Real Patience, and the Sufi

There was a nice Sufi who used to advise people to be patient. One day, he heard such shocking news about himself that it changed his life. He said to himself, "I now understand it is not easy to be patient." He smiled sadly and felt the pain of the deep change in his life.

IN PRACTICE

It is really not easy to implement the teachings. "Easier said than done" is a good expression to show the notion of the embodiment of patience. When a person loses their loved ones, job, or other things to which the person is attached, it is difficult to implement the notion of patience. The trials and tests attack the person from their attachments. The constant expression of *"La ilaha illa Allah"* removes the attachments from a person's heart and mind.[22]

Discussion Questions

► Why is it difficult to implement patience?
► Is the trait of patience earned or given at birth? Why?

311. Life Vests

One day, the Sufi witnessed an evil-seeming incident. The pain of the evil remained with her for days. The Sufi constantly asked the question to herself, "Why, why, why . . ." At the same, the Sufi asked God to make it easy during this painful period of grief. She said to herself, "It is a dead end. I need to move on."

IN PRACTICE

Sometimes endless reasoning self-conversations can drown a person in pessimism. It is important to ask God to ease the pain of a person during times of evil. The person should continue their day-to-day practices. These practices can act as life vests to save a person from pain. Therefore, the person can activate the belief of destiny with submission and surrender and move on as mentioned in the above story.

Discussion Question

► What should be the balance between self-accountability and excessive questioning of oneself leading to pessimism?

312. Bad News

The Sufi was living her life regularly with not much change. She enjoyed the prayers and reading the signs of God every day in nature and in the Quran. One day, she got news of a loss that she expected would affect her entire life. She felt pain, but then she thought about similar experiences in her life. After each change, there was something good and even better than before, but she needed to be patient. She said, "OK, I know: I plan and Allah plans. I just need to submit and surrender myself and ask for the good outcome of this change from Allah." She also realized that she was becoming older and remembered death and said to herself, "*Alhamdullillah*, I will meet with Allah soon. I hope all the changes are good that will ultimately benefit me *inshAllah* in this meeting."

IN PRACTICE

Expect the unexpected. Initially it can be painful, but ultimately a person can treat their pain with prayer, reading the Quran and understanding and personalizing it. In these unknowns and the unexpected, one should always try the easy and natural way: submission and surrender and trust in God, Allah. On the other hand, complaining, not submitting or surrendering will produce friction as in the laws of conservation of energy in physics. It will cause the person to lose energy unnecessarily. Another powerful way of coping with any type of grief is embracing the concept of death. When a person knows that this life is short and they will meet with the Lover—God—soon with all the struggles on the Divine path, then the person can also feel relief from grief as well.

Discussion Questions

► Why are unexpected news often not welcomed?
► What makes a news expected or unexpected?
► Can a person develop a skill to cope with the concept of dealing with different types of news? How can this be related to one's relationship with God?

313. Circular Days

There was a Sufi who tried to understand the meanings in people's lives. She realized that sometimes people are hit with evil and become sad. Sometimes, they are so happy because of their achievements. Sometimes, they seem neutral. The Sufi said to herself: "This is like a circle. It goes and comes back again."

IN PRACTICE

Understand that God changes the conditions of people throughout life. The Quran uses an expression as "rotating the days among people." In this perspective, a possible piece of wisdom in the change of the conditions of people is to evaluate whether they will maintain the state of appreciation of God in good, evil, and neutral times. Therefore, one of the goals in the spiritual journey is not to change the level of positive appreciation for God in all conditions: adversity, joy, and neutrality.[48]

Discussion Question

▶ How can a person welcome and appreciate an evil-seeming incident?

314. The Religious Laws, the Spiritual Discoveries, and the Sufi

One day, the Sufi was thinking about the benefits of fasting. Then, she deduced from her spiritual discovery that Monday fasting prevents sicknesses and Thursday fasting prevents evils in one's life. The Sufi used to be sick on Mondays when she did not fast and she used to get bad news on Thursdays when she did not fast. One day, the Sufi fasted on a Monday but still got sick and she said to herself, "Either my discovery has an exception or it is wrong."

IN PRACTICE

Religious laws are there for everyone. They put the boundaries of limits with logic and they should be objective. If a person does not follow a religious guideline or a religious law, then he or she will be held responsible in front of God.[48] Conversely, spiritual discoveries can be sometimes right or wrong as well as personal and subjective. There is no requirement for it, but if a person follows these discoveries, they may receive spiritual "cookies" in this world and afterlife. Although there is always wisdom in following religious laws or guidelines, a person does it or performs it because God says so. This wisdom can be sometimes known or unknown to the person. The person intends not to do it due to its benefits but to please God. Alternatively, the Sufis also try to practice with this intention. In addition, they tap into the possible wisdom of a practice and extend it to their lives with some personal embodiment of these rituals.

Discussion Questions

- ▶ What makes religious laws more dependable than religious personal experiences?
- ▶ Why are clear and simple religious and spiritual guidelines important?

315. The Hailstorm

There once was a Sufi who had a very special relationship with God. One day, she got hit in her life with something evil. She thought about what she should do. First, she prayed to God. Second, she wondered what the next step she should take should be. Although the effect of the evil was painful for her, she tried to be patient. She said to herself, "OK, I need to ask the opinion of at least three people who love me and are willing to help me in dealing with this evil." She opened up to her first friend, but while she spoke she felt uncomfortable about it and immediately a hail shower started outside. She contemplated the meaning of the hail as she went to her second friend to discuss her problem. She started the topic and again felt pained sharing her problem with a person other than God. Again, a hail shower started outside and she thought about the meaning of the hail. She started praying and afterward smiled and said to herself, "Hail means God does not want me to open my problem to anyone. God is sufficient for me! What a nice Friend! What a nice Supporter!"

In practice

There are different levels in one's relationship with God. In normative practice, it is encouraged to discuss one's problems with the experts of the field who have concern for others. But for some high level elect mystics and Sufis, opening one's problem to someone other than God is a disrespectful attitude to God. In other words, God is the Best Supporter and Friend for the person. In the above story, the Sufi interpreted the hard hail shower from nowhere in each instance as a sign that her close relationship with God required only taking God as the real and the Best Friend and Supporter in all types of evil encounters of life. As the teaching of the Prophet Muhammad, one of the expressions chanted every day seven times in the morning and at night is the expression of "Hasbiya Allah La ilaha illa Hu Alayhi Tawwakaltu wa Huwa Rabbul Arshil Azim," which means God is Sufficient for me, there is no deity except God, I rely on God and God is the Most Exalted High Holder of Authority and Dominance.[42]

Discussion Question

▶ How can a person develop secrecy and privacy[xlixxxix] with God?

316. The Daily Deception

As the Sufi woke up every day, she felt energetic, powerful, and hopeful. When she went to bed, she felt very pessimistic, fearful, and weak. One day, she thought during the time of midday: What is the balance? What is real? What is deception? Then, she heard that someone died and there would be a funeral in the mosque. She said to herself: "Now I understand; this is the reality."

IN PRACTICE

Life is limited. Every day, hope is good to keep a person going as long as it is balanced with the reality of death. In other words, one of the spiritual diseases that most people fall into is the notion or deception of living as if the person is not going to die. The reality of death gives the person the checks and balances for this life and the afterlife. On the other hand, a person who is in self-deception of not dying can be hit hard with death or an evil, leading to death if she or he does not actualize this reality. Some Sufi scholars think that most of the painful detachments of life are due to this disease of lack of considering and reflection on death and dying.[53]

Discussion Questions

▶ Can thinking about death make a person depressive and pessimistic? Why?
▶ Why is it suggested to think about the reality of death?

---

53. This disease is called "*tulu-amal*" in Sufi terminology.

317. Joking in Company

One day, the Sufi attended an interfaith gathering. There were some discussions about teachers and their level of piety as they are the role models for humans. One of the attendees started explaining one of the teachers' parents' ethical behavior and how parents affect their children. The Sufi made a joke about the story, and everyone started laughing. The Sufi paused for a minute, horrified. He said to himself, "What did I do? Shame on me!"

IN PRACTICE

Respect beliefs, values, elders, and teachers. Although we are living in a society of jokes, the Sufis believe that jokes have limits and should not touch upon sacred items. According to the Sufis, the religion, the belief, and the practice is all attitude, *adab*. In other words, the state of being with God and friendship with God requires maintenance of proper respect and *adab*. Most of the time, people lose their good friends due to overstepping boundaries. In this case, having respectful boundaries with the sacred—scriptures, teachers, and God—is the key for successful and a regular spiritual journey until one dies.

Discussion Questions

▶ What should be the balance among the topics selected for joking or fun?

▶ Can religious topics be risky as topics of making jokes or fun? Why?

318. Learning, Questions, and Patience

One day, the Sufi was teaching the importance of patience in asking questions while learning. She did not talk to the students and maintained silence. The students were trying to ask questions. The Sufi smiled and continued reading her book. After a while, the students kept reading their books as well when they saw that their teacher was reading. The Sufi then said to herself, "Most of the time, if we learn patience before asking questions, the answers will be given in a sweet way."

IN PRACTICE

It is important to wait for the answer to a question until there is a good time and place for it. A wrong question at a wrong time and place can make the person deduce wrong meanings. This can alienate the person from genuine learning. One of the genuine ways of learning is to be with a teacher and learn and observe natural discourse, occurring events, and deduce meaning. There are a lot of times that a teacher can formally answer people's questions for them to learn as well.

Discussion Questions

▶ How do you understand the above teaching about asking questions especially at our times of encouragement for inquiry?

▶ Do you learn better when you ask a question, or when you observe and deduce the answers by reflection and spiritual experience?

319. Memories, Pain, the Reality of Missing, and the Sufi

The Sufi used to think about all her past nice memories. She felt much pain longing for them: her old friends, mother, father, brothers, sisters, and cherished places. One day, the Sufi again remembered all these nice memories. But now she did not feel pain of longing. She thought and said to herself: "Everything that I miss is temporary. I give them a value as if they are permanent and can benefit me. I think I just miss God who is my Friend regardless of time and place."

IN PRACTICE

It is normal to be saddened by memories, especially of missed good teachers, parents, and friends. But all memories and created beings have limits. Putting too much value on them can be painful and result in not giving the full due to the One who deserves to be missed limitlessly. Compared to all other missed items, God knows and appreciates a person's missing and burning feelings for union with God.[49] These emotions, feelings, thoughts, instances, minutes, or days can elevate the person in front of God vertically. This person can be rewarded immensely in this world and in the afterlife by God.

Discussion Question

▶ How can one minimize the effects of pain due to the detachment from loved ones?

320. The Difficulty of Being Human

One day, the Sufi was thinking about how difficult it was to be a human. The Sufi thought to herself: "I should not break anyone's heart. I should be nice. I should be fair. I should not be angry. I should not be jealous. I should truly appreciate God." As she was thinking about all of that she said to herself "*Alhamdulillah*, I am trying *inshAllah*."

IN PRACTICE

It is difficult to be a true human being. Everyone can claim that they possess human qualities, but in practice that is not always the case. The statements by the Sufi are some of the expected traits of a person on the path: not breaking people's hearts because God is with the broken hearts; being fair even if it is against your own interests; using anger to fight injustice not for oppression. The most difficult part is not truly appreciating God. But, in the end, God appreciates all the efforts but not the results. Therefore, the Sufi says, "*Alhamdullilah*, all thanks and gratitude belongs to God for I am trying."

Discussion Question

- ► Why is trying or struggle one of the most important notions in practice?

321. Fears, Belief, and the Sufi

One day, the Sufi was thinking about why she was fearful every day: afraid of people, afraid of the unknown, fearful of death, and so forth. She chanted the divine phrases but she was still fearful. She said to herself, "I should pray to God to embody these phrases in my life."

IN PRACTICE

Life and practice are a struggle. The person is expected only to take refuge in Allah in all the circumstances of fearful instances. Although one may still have the traces of fear from others, it is important to aim to remove this fear with practice, prayer, and through struggle. Although the Sufi was practicing the divine phrases and chanting them, she still carried the feeling of fear in daily discourses and encounters. She concluded that she needs to embody the removal of fear from everything except God, through "*La ilaha illa Allah.*" There is nothing to be fearful of except not taking refuge in God.

Discussion Questions

▶ What makes humans different than the angels in practice?
▶ How can one relate the schmooze of Satan with Adam in Heaven in the context of manipulating Adam to be perfect like the angels?54

---

54. One can review the Quran [7:20–21] about this incident.

322. Flies, Friends, and Life

One day, the Sufi was reading a book on a cold day in the mosque. There was no one except a small fly flying around the Sufi. The Sufi said to the fly "*SubhanAllah*, on a cold winter day, it is amazing to see a fly. Everything outside is dead because of the snow. How beautiful is life! How beautiful is *Al-Hayy*! How beautiful is my friend, the fly!"

IN PRACTICE

Anything with life reminds one of God. Anything with life is a sign from God. One of the names of God is *Al-Hayy*, the Source and the Creator of Life. Some people chant this phrase in times of depression and anxiety in order to relax and to receive positive energy from God. There are a lot of Sufi stories about being friends with animals. It is not common in the history of this genuine practice that people have been imprisoned by others when they preached all inclusive, loving, and respect requesting motifs for God. Therefore, it is not uncommon to encounter stories of imprisoned Sufi where the Sufis are friends even with some of the disliked animals for most humans such as flies, snakes, or mice. The Sufis view them as not something to be disliked but as holders of life, reminding of their Creator, *Al-Hayy*. They are signs from God if one can understand their meaning and purpose.

Discussion Question

▶ Why do people tend to be happy when they see a living being in a deserted area even though this living being can be something or someone disliked in normal conditions?

323. The Unemployed Sufi and Reliance to God

There was a Sufi who had a very personal and close relationship with God. Whatever she asked from God, God gave her exactly what she wanted. One day, she lost her job. She was afraid that if she asked God, God would give her what she exactly wanted. Then, she said to herself "I will make *tawakkul* and show reliance to God and pray for whatever God chooses to give for me. I am happy as long as God is pleased with me. "

IN PRACTICE

It is important to reach the level of reliance, *tawakkul* in practice. Most of the time when evil happens we tend to blame people or God and ruin our relationships. In the above story, the Sufi had a very close relationship with God through constant prayer and appreciation. Therefore, God gave her always what she wanted in life. The Sufi reached one of the highest levels of reliance called *tawakkul*. In this stage, all the evil or good-looking incidents are the same for the person as long as God is pleased with that person.

Discussion Question

▶   Is it easy or difficult to make reliance or tawakkul? Why?

324. Benefit of the Doubt for the Deaf Man

There was a deaf man for whom the Sufi felt much compassion. He asked what he could do as work in order to help him. The deaf man mentioned that he could do some cleaning for the Sufi, and the Sufi accepted. The deaf person did not show up on the promised day. They agreed for another day. He did not show up again. They agreed again for a third time. The deaf man did not show up again. The Sufi thought to himself, "I am not going to think that he did not fulfill his promise. I will still make a good excuse for him."

IN PRACTICE

God knows the inside and out of all things. As humans, we try to help people with our best intention. In the above story, the Sufi did not want to think badly of the deaf man. It is important to make or generate good excuses in one's mind in order not to blame people for their faults. This is called *husnu zann*, thinking always good about others. The opposite of this is called *su-i zann*, thinking and assuming always bad about others. The person is always encouraged to practice *husnu zann* and not the opposite.

Discussion Question

▶ What is the benefit of thinking always good about others?

325. Emotions, Mind, Disputes, and the Sufi

One morning, the Sufi was in dispute with his wife. He said to himself, "If I use my mind, I will not burst out with my anger and not discharge myself. I will be better later but not now. If I use my emotions, I will explode and discharge myself. I will feel good now but will regret and feel terrible later. What should I do?" He was unable to help himself and used his emotions and burst out with his anger, but by midday regretted his choice and said to himself, "I wish I had used my mind."

IN PRACTICE

It is important to use one's mind when emotions and mind are in conflict. Emotions are not always called heart or conscience. The true emotions or inspirations coming from the heart or conscience do not conflict with the mind, logic, and reason. If they are conflicting, then these emotions can be self- or Satan-generated sources that can lead to evil. At times of conflict, disputes, and anger, these emotions or thoughts can overpower a person's mind, heart, and conscience. One should make their best effort not to be trapped in these temptations in order not to say "I wish" later.

Discussion Questions

► Why do we tend to follow our emotions although we know that it is wrong to do so?

► In which cases are there benefits or harms of saying "I wish"?

326. Disputes, the Sufi, and Moving On

One day, the Sufi was in conflict with her husband, and for a few days afterwards her husband was still angry with her. He took the dispute personally and carried his anger. The Sufi thought, "I should not take it personally but move on." A few days later, everything seemed normal. The Sufi said: "*Alhamdulillah*, thanks and all appreciation belongs to Allah SWT."

IN PRACTICE

It is important not to take things personally and expand the conflict more among people, especially between spouses. This notion is much embedded in the Quran as a suggested way of "moving on with peace": not taking things too personally in disputes. There are many stories about rulers in Islamic history whose spouses used to freely criticize and yell at them. These rulers wisely observed silence and patience, especially in family relations.

Discussion Question

▶ In which cases are there benefits or harms from taking things personally?

327. The Cancer of Arrogance

There was a man who used to always criticize the concept of surrender and submission. He used to always try to rationalize everything. The Sufi used to try to explain to him the importance of submission and surrender to God as well as the importance of reason. The man got offended and used to say, "This is why we need enlightenment. Religion always puts us in darkness. We need to rationalize everything." One day, this person got sick. His illness continued for a month, a year, and then two years. Doctors finally diagnosed him with a rare type of cancer. The Sufi was saddened by the news. The devastated man came to the Sufi and said, "Now, I know what you mean. I need to pray to God and submit myself to the All Powerful One."

IN PRACTICE

Belief is an attitude, and an attitude of humility can elevate a person. Sometimes different life experiences can make a person angry with everything and even alienate them from God due to frustration and anger. It is important to always remind oneself of the weaknesses, needs, and fragility of humans. Constant prayers and chants with their meanings charge the person with power by connecting him or herself to the source of All Power, God.

Discussion Questions

► How can one understand the concept of submission in one's relation with other humans?

► How can one understand the concept of submission in one's relation with God?

► What is the relationship between submission and arrogance?

328. Distractions and Focus

One day the Sufi was thinking about the purpose of life, its distractions, and the peace found with focusing on Allah. Then, he remembered two names of Allah, *Al-Wahid* and *Al-Ahad*. He said to himself, "This is the key: being with Allah everywhere at all times of distraction is *Al-Wahid* and being with Allah when you are alone and focusing on Allah which is *Al-Ahad*. This is the purpose. This is the trial. This is the difficulty."

IN PRACTICE

It is important to be with God always in one's virtual space of tranquility and calmness. *Al Wahid* means accepting Allah, the One, through all many creations. *Al-Ahad* is knowing Allah, the One and the Unique by focusing on one creation. Sometimes the distractions in life can make one heedless about God. With constant effort and struggle, it is important to connect the name of *Al-Wahid* to God.

Discussion Question

▶ How can one develop the habit of forming a virtual space of tranquility and calmness?

329. The Bored Sufi and the Virtual Space

329. The Bored Sufi and the Virtual Space

One day, the Sufi attended a meeting at her work. She was not interested much in the topic discussed but she was still trying to pay attention in order not to be disrespectful. She kept thinking what she should do in order to collect herself spiritually, not be bored, and how to enjoy her time and presence in that space. She said to herself "*dhikr.*" After a few minutes, she felt much better.

IN PRACTICE

It is important to recognize people's spiritual needs. Just as one may need to leave a meeting for a few minutes to go to a restroom, sometimes spiritual urges can come at different times so that a person may need a few minutes of break. In that respect, prayers regularly during the day five times can help a person minimize and structure these spiritual urges as they may pop up at any time and place. As in the case of the above story, a person sometimes may not need to leave the room or the physical space of presence. Rather, the person in a boring meeting can transform their state to a virtual space of peace and tranquility by reorienting and assuming himself or herself through a few seconds of remembrance of God ("*dhikr*"). In this transformation, one can change any undesirable physical condition to a state of peace and ease through chants, prayer, and spiritual re-orientation.

Discussion Question

▸ How can one's spiritual engagements affect the productivity of a person at a workplace?

330. Salawat, Remembering Teachers, and the Sufi

One day, the Sufi woke up feeling anxious and did not feel good. She asked herself what she should do. Then, she started making *salawat* and *tahiyyat* and immediately felt better.

IN PRACTICE

It is very critical to remember all the teachers, especially the main one, the Prophet. There are a lot of practices of chanting to remember the Prophet in different forms called *salawat* and *tahiyyat*. In some Sufi cultures the tradition is to get together, to sing, and to chant these phrases collectively. It is also customary to recite these chants daily in times of difficulty and sickness. The remembrance in the form of chants can bring blessings and ease in one's life.

Discussion Question

▶ How can remembering teachers and chanting on them (such as salawat) bring easiness and tranquility in one's spiritual state?

331. The Barber, the Beard, and the Accident

Once there was a Sufi who was very proud of his nice, long beard. He used to hold it when he was stressed. He used to look at the mirror and smile, proud that he was following the ways of the prophets by having a nice, long beard. One day, he went to a barber to trim some extra hair on his neck. This particular barber was a Sufi, always engaged with chanting and remembrance of the Divine phrases. During one of these moments, as he was trimming hairs on the Sufi's neck, he closed his eyes in his trance. By accident, he cut the beard of the Sufi. The Sufi screamed and cried, "My beard!" The barber jumped. He did not know what was happening. The Sufi who lost his beard smiled and said to himself, "My attachment to my beard."

IN PRACTICE

It is *Sunnah*, encouraged, and rewarding to follow the ways of the role models such as prophets. However, one should remember that doing so can cause arrogance and unhealthy attachment, and negate humility. In the above case, although the Sufi was proud of his beard, he understood that any attachment can be a test on the path of God if it is not seen as a means to please God. In other words, the only attachment one should have is to God.

Discussion Question

► How can a person practice the religious guidelines and still see them as means but not the goal?

332. Learning with the Children

One day, the Sufi was studying with her children. She gave some studying materials to them. At first, the kids whined about the work. As they continued studying, they got excited about learning and discovering on their own the unknown realities. The Sufi as a teacher knew all the answers of the questions that she was trying to teach. As the lessons continued, she was amazed about the reaction of the kids and their self-satisfaction due to learning by struggle. The Sufi said to herself ,"If I gave the answers from the beginning they would not learn this well, and would not enjoy and appreciate the knowledge." The Sufi said to herself "*SubhanAllah*, this is similar to the tests, trials, and struggles to self-witness of one's actions and come closer to God until one dies."

IN PRACTICE

It is important to realize that Allah knows everything, future and the past. One of the secrets of life is that Allah creates humans to self-witness their own journey in their relationship with God. Thus, humans cannot claim otherwise in front of God after death.

Discussion Question

▶ Why do people tend to appreciate their own effort of self-discoveries compared to outcomes or achievements given without much effort?

333. The Sufi's To-Do List

One morning, the Sufi woke up and was excited to start her prayers, read the scriptures, and reflect on them. Then she remembered all the things that she needed to do that day, and she grew a little depressed, unhappy, and stressed. But she finished the nicest part of her day: the prayers and reading. Then, as she started the second part of her day, she said to herself, "I just need to do what needs to be done. If the things do not go in the way that I wanted, at least I tried within the reasons and means."

IN PRACTICE

It is important to follow the reasons and means through the faculties of the mind although one's heart or spiritual faculties may not feel engaged about it. These are the times where the mind should dominate the heart. When a person is used to being in a secluded life of prayers without socializing with people, they can feel secure due to the lack of human disturbances. Once a person starts interacting with others there are always possibilities of stress, broken hearts, oppression, and evil. Therefore, some Sufis prefer living in mountains in seclusion. But most Sufis find that this is not the way to go. It is better to live a social life and be with people, being patient to their vulgar treatments with the intention of teaching them while at the same time living in a virtual space of union with God through prayers, chants, and reading the Divine scriptures.

Discussion Question

▶ Is it possible to earn a peaceful state of mind and heart in both worldly and spiritual matters? Why?

334. The Bugs, the Belief, and the Sufi

One day, there was food at the kitchen table. The mother put a cover on the food to protect it from the bugs. The Sufi saw it and said to himself, "Wow, this is similar to protecting one's *iman* (belief) from bugs when interacting with others."

IN PRACTICE

It is important to choose people of genuine knowledge and practice with whom to surround oneself. Once a person is with them the person should benefit through all means: presence, observation, and asking questions. If a person is with unauthentic people of knowledge and practice, one should be trained how to filter, what to learn, and what to block.

Discussion Question

▶   Why is it so emphasized to protect one's spiritual valuables?

335. Wishing for Coffee

One day, the Sufi was thinking of making a nice coffee for herself to enjoy. She started to think to herself, "I need to get up, put water in the coffee machine, put in the coffee and then I need to wait until it brews. It is too much work. I wish it just happened as I thought about it."

IN PRACTICE

According to the teachings in practice, patience and struggle are needed to achieve the worldly pleasures in this life. For example, if someone wants to travel for vacation, they take the challenge of difficulties of traveling and they need to be patient until they reach their destination. Therefore, if the person acquires the traits of being patient and applying self-struggle and uses it for noble purposes for this life and the afterlife, then God promises in Heaven the pleasures without any self-struggle or patience. The pleasures in Heaven will appear in front of the person as the person thinks about them.

Discussion Question

► Why are the worldly or spiritual achievements or results linked to struggles?

336. Trials & Tests

One day, the Sufi's best friend -the lamp- was again hijacked by the jealous ones. The Sufi was so upset and disturbed that he said to himself, "This is the third time! They are showing a childish attitude by removing my lamp again! I don't understand these people. They come to pray and look so pious, and yet, they do evil in the mosque." The Sufi said, "I will leave it to Allah SWT and I am afraid the retribution may not be so pleasant."

IN PRACTICE

One should expect trials and tests although one should constantly pray to God for protection against them. Although a person may not do any harm to others, there will be people who will try to bother, harm, and sometimes abuse that person anyway. In these circumstances, opening yourself to God and then taking the necessary measures is important. Sometimes, it is important to be patient and not do anything. Sometimes, the person may need to take some measures with wisdom. Everything depends on the context.

Discussion Questions

▶ Discuss a time when you witnessed a conflict situation work itself out better without your interference. This may be because you intentionally restrained your emotional reaction or it may be because of circumstances beyond your control, but the important thing is that, afterwards, you acknowledged to yourself that your interference would have complicated the issue.

▶ Discuss a time when you accidentally made a situation worse by interfering, even with good intentions. What caused you to take action? Was it fear, anger, or another emotion? A desire to control the situation, or something else?

▶ What is the value of exercising patience and wisdom in the appropriate context regarding improving one's relationships with other people?

▶ What is the value of exercising patience and wisdom regarding improving one's personal relationship with God?

337. The Downtrodden

There was a man in the mosque who used to come and pray. Everyone saw him as evil, nasty, and treated him badly and did not want to engage with him except for the Sufi. The Sufi liked to engage with the people who were seen as outcasts, or poor as was suggested by the Prophet.

IN PRACTICE

It is important to engage with the people who have low class status in the society especially due to their economic and social status levels. The Prophet preferred to sit in the company of the poor and disadvantaged. He preferred to eat on the floor as the slaves at the time were eating on the floor and he mentioned that, "I am the slave of God so I sit to eat on the floor." [1]

338. Knowledge and its Use

One day, the Sufi was thinking about knowledge. She said to herself, "There are a lot of things to learn in life. Life is short. What should I learn? My life is not long enough to learn all knowledge." Then, she said, "Okay, I should learn the knowledge that is useful for me in this world and in the afterlife so that I can apply that knowledge in my life now."

IN PRACTICE

Unused or not-purposeful learning or knowledge can be distraction. The person does not learn for the sake of learning. First, make the intention and set a goal for acquiring knowledge with its application. The most important knowledge is understanding one's purpose with scriptures as well as understanding the universe within this framework. As the person learns, everything can now make more sense and the person can increase his or her quality and quantity relationship with God. This type of knowledge and engagement benefits the person both in this world and after death.

Discussion Questions

- What kind of knowledge is useful to you in your life?
- What knowledge do you personally find to be without purpose in your life?

339. Ant and the Prayer

One day, the Sufi was about to start her daily protection, *"A'uzu bi kalimatillahi tammati min sharri ma khalaq"* and an ant appeared in her hand. The Sufi said, "Wow! this is the power of the prayer!"

IN PRACTICE

Prayers are the weapons of the person [50]. God protects the person when he or she takes a full refuge in God with the correct prayers as instructed by the Prophet. In the above story, the Sufi started reading her daily protection prayer as taught by the Prophet[xl]. As soon as the Sufi started the prayer, she saw an ant on her body that she did not realize was there before and she immediately took it away from her body. The above prayer means: "I take refuge in the full and perfect words of God from the evil of God's creation."

340. Displeasing God

One day, the Sufi saw a religious scholar and they started chatting. During the conversation, the Sufi said a word about himself that could imply some self-praise. After the conversation was over, the Sufi was thinking to himself, "I hope I did not displease or upset God. I don't care what this guy thinks of me but I care if I displeased God."

IN PRACTICE

It is an attainable spiritual level to do everything only, but only, for God. Although it is difficult to reach this level in its truest sense, one can always try to attain it and set it as a goal in one's intentions and dealings. With the Grace of God, hopefully, one can reach this stage of spiritual development.

Discussion Questions

- What are some of your spiritual goals?
- What are some ways to develop the habit of examining one's intentions?
- How does seeking only to not displease God help one develop integrity in dealings with the world?

341. Without Pain

One day, the Sufi was thinking about the wisdom of having nails that need to be cut constantly. He said to himself, "We could have been created without this need. There should be a wisdom behind it." Then, one day, while he was cutting his nails he said to himself, "If I cut any part of my body I will scream, but not my nails." Then, he said, "This is the wisdom. If Allah SWT wants, he can make anything without pain in the same system; although everything can be painful in the same system!"

IN PRACTICE

It is important to understand that God can do anything beyond and reverse of the laws of science. Sometimes, exceptions in a system are present to remind us of this reality. Sometimes, we get so much used to the routine practices that we lose the main purpose and cannot see the bigger picture. In practice, it is important to have this mindset of learning and getting a meaning from everything in relation to its true creation purpose by God.

342. Achievements and Balance

One day, the Sufi received news of an achievement that she had earned. She was expecting the results and she had been preparing herself so that when she got the news of achievement, she wouldn't care. The most important thing for her was the relationship with Allah SWT. Yet, as soon as she got the good news, something again entered her heart. She said to herself, "Again, and again! I cannot get rid of this disgusting feeling of arrogance and all lies although I was preparing myself before it happened. Again, the pain of cleaning these feelings starts....."

IN PRACTICE

All of the spiritual or worldly achievements or victories can give birth to the people of losers. In other words, the points in life when we receive good news of our achievements regardless of if they are spiritual or worldly, can make the person arrogant with self-induced lies of pampering, if the person does not embody the reality that everything good is given by God. Therefore, all goodness and all achievements are all due to the Mercy and Grace of God given to the person. Yet, although the person knows this, if the person still gets those feelings he or she must immediately engage oneself with *astagfirullah*, forgiveness and *SubhanAllah wa bihamdihi*, remembrance of God in order to restore balance and remove these false, smelly lies.

343. Best Husband Ever!

One day, the Sufi was taking a walk. He saw a man cutting the grass and caring for his lawn in front of his house. The man wore a shirt on which was written "Best Husband Ever!" The Sufi approached the man, smiled and said, "Nice shirt! Where did you buy it?" The man said, "My wife bought it for me! Look at me! (showing the lawnmower) don't I deserve it!"

IN PRACTICE

It can be easy to make people happy. Especially, in spousal relationships, something that is minor can be a major for the other person. It is interesting to analyze the life of the Prophet in his family relations. Everyone was so happy with him. It is narrated that the Prophet used to be very relaxed with his family members in order to make them comfortable. He was always in a pleasant mood, smiling and asking the need of others. Yet, he was taking care of his own personal needs such as stitching his clothes, cleaning, etc. but not asking people's help.

Discussion Questions

▶ How do you make people happy? What thoughtful things do you say and do?

▶ How do people make you happy?

▶ What can you do extra to make others happy that you haven't been doing?

344. Meeting After Years

There was a lamp which did not work for years. The Sufi was hopeful that one day the lamp would work and give its light as in the old days. One day, the Sufi was reading the Qur'an and thinking about the meanings and possible interpretations. At that time, she really needed more light to focus. She touched the switch of the lamp and the lamp gave its light. The Sufi started laughing, "You know when to work!"

IN PRACTICE

Everything is controlled by God. The living and non-living things can be a misleading classification in Sufi terms. The so-called non-living things such as rocks or stones also glorify God according to the teachings of the practice. Some people even witness their chants. In the above story, perhaps, the lamp did not want to miss the opportunity of giving and sharing its light while the Sufi was engaged with the Noble Book of God, the Qur'an.

Discussion Questions

► Have you ever had a friend arrive after many years of darkness and light up your life with the love of God?

345. Thanking-Gratitude?

One day, the Sufi was thinking about how to not to be arrogant when God sends constant bounties upon the person. Then, she said, "Perhaps, it is in gratitude or thanking God with *Alhamdulillah*." Then, she said, "But there are a lot of people who may say Alhamdulillah yet still have arrogance." Then, after some time, she said to herself, "True gratitude comes with the self-denial that these blessings are not from or due to the virtue of the person but from God."

IN PRACTICE

It is very critical but difficult to embody the simple-looking notions such as gratitude, thanking God with the expression *Alhamdulillah*. Saying these phrases is only the starting point. There is a lot of work to be done. Constant self-struggle against the feelings of arrogance combined with embodying thankfulness to God can be two balancing factors in this struggle. The Prophet was truly called and received the title with this name of "Muhammad" who truly showed gratitude to God because of his embodiment of these teachings in his life.

346. Cat and the Sufi

One day, the Sufi went home. Her husband was yelling to the cat to leave the house. The cat was an outdoor cat living in the backyard. The husband started chasing the cat but was not successful to get it out. Then, he left. The Sufi was doing her work at home. Then, she saw the cat. She tried to take the cat out. Finally, she was successful but she felt bad. She said to herself, "What if I upset the cat?" Then, she went into the backyard and started looking around for the cat. The cat was not there. The Sufi looked for hours, but the cat was still not there. Normally, the cat did not leave the backyard. The Sufi felt so bad and prayed to God asking forgiveness about the cat.

IN PRACTICE

It is always possible that the engagements of breaking people's hearts, oppressing a person or an animal can displease God. Therefore, the person should not take it easy about anything or take for granted any engagement, but should always be God-conscious and vigilant. Sometimes a word can make an effect of a bullet in people's hearts. Consequently, this can cause the person to be punished after death.

347. Definition of Tea

One day, two friends- one from Egypt and the other from Turkey- went to visit another friend who was from Egypt. The host said, "What do you want to drink"?" The Egyptian guest said, "Thank you. Nothing. I don't want to trouble you." The Turkish guest said, "If you have some hot water and pour it on a tea bag, I can have that." The Egyptian guest screamed and said, "That is what is called tea in Egypt!" The Turkish guest said, "There is a certain way of making tea in Turkey. When we make tea it takes at least 15-30 minutes."

IN PRACTICE

What we commonly refer to can have different definitions depending on the person, culture, and time. Sometimes a pious person may not be pious according to another person. Similarly, the real value and definition of everything reveal themselves when they are related to God. In other words, definitions can change. Yet, when one wants unchanging or permanent or absolute effect, then he or she should link themselves to the One Who is Permanent, God.

348. Balash and Coffee in Egypt

There was an American married to an Egyptian girl. After getting married, they went to Egypt to visit her family. The girl had some relatives who had a coffee shop in an apartment building where the relatives used to live on the upper floor. After they arrived, the Egyptian wife said to her American husband, "Why don't you hang around with my cousins in the coffee shop and I will go upstairs to see my aunt." The husband was very happy because he liked coffee so much. The cousins hugged the American husband of their relative and treated him with nice cappuccino. After he finished they asked if he wanted another cup. The husband said to himself, "I may as well try something else." Then, he wanted mocha. After he drank, out of politeness, they asked if he wanted another one. This continued until the seventh cup. The Egyptian barista got tired and said, "*Balash!*" The husband understood the case and said, "I really appreciate your hospitality."

IN PRACTICE

Everything is *balash* given by God. *Balash* means free of charge, given without any price. God gives so many things daily- air, health, the ability to see, hear, digest, and even excrete. Yet, we seem to not even recognize them but be ungrateful. Out of all these simple-looking but critical bounties, God only wants recognition from people of the true, only, one and unique Creator Who constantly showers blessings on people.

Discussion Questions

- ▶ What are some ways you practice mindfulness in your daily life?
- ▶ What activity do you take time to slow down & really appreciate in your day?
- ▶ How does practicing gratitude help your relationship with God?

349. Harvard vs SubhanAllah

There was a Sufi who used to study at Harvard. When she met her friends during the winter break, everyone was talking about this Sufi and how she was going to the prestigious and top school, Harvard! Each time they used to say 'Harvard' the Sufi used to say '*Astagfirullah*' in her heart and mind. Then, the Sufi said to herself, "Each time they pronounce the word 'Harvard', it is as if the juice of satisfaction is coming from their mouths. I wish they would say '*SubhanAllah*' for the juice of embodiment of perfection of Allah SWT in their hearts."

IN PRACTICE

It is important to realize how we embody the words. For example, when a person says the word *Harvard* if certain feelings are coming to a person's mind and heart, then this can be called a true embodiment whether it is something right or wrong. Similarly, in spiritual endeavors, the full connection should be there when we say *SubhanAllah* to fulfill all of our cells with the embodiment of 'perfection of God', *Alhamdulillah* 'showing full and true gratitude only to God', *Astagfirullah* 'cleansing oneself from all the dirty and filthy feelings of arrogance and praise of oneself and asking forgiveness from God for these false emotions'. The Sufi wished that the people would embody the beneficial divine phrases in their relationship with God instead of the artificial human-made phrases such as *Harvard*. The Sufi was saying the phrase *Astagfirullah* in order to remove from herself any possible filth of arrogance as the people admired the Sufi because she was studying at Harvard.

350. The Snake and Ungratefulness

One day, the Sufi attended a gathering at the park. At the gathering, there were some ungrateful and disrespectful conversations about sacred items such as the divine scriptures. The Sufi felt uncomfortable being at that gathering. While she was thinking, she saw a garden snake approaching her. The Sufi said to herself, "This is a sign that I should leave this gathering quickly."

IN PRACTICE

One of the valuables of a person is their relationship with God with the true *iman* or *tawhid* which can be translated as the core of the authentic and true belief. In this case, the person should be more overprotective of this valuable-their *iman*- than of their children or family members, wealth, and other entities that the person is expected to protect. If the person's *iman* is tainted, then the value of the other mentioned things will be tainted. When people have attitudes of ungratefulness, disrespect, and degradation towards the sacred items related with Allah, one should leave that gathering as the Sufi did and even she got a sign in order to hasten to leave.

Discussion Questions

▸ Have you ever found yourself in a situation where you became uncomfortable with the disrespectful behavior happening in the environment? How did it make you feel?

▸ How does that feeling compare with when you are in a gathering of people who respect each other and God?

▸ Why do you think it makes a difference?

351. The True Reliance-*Tawakkul*

One day, the Sufi was thinking to herself, "Whatever I asked, God gave me from the worldly seeming affairs. I hope they don't come after death and bite me. I should from now on, ask whatever is good[xli] in worldly seeming matters and keep asking for the highest levels similar to the prayers of the Prophet." Then, after a while, the Sufi was experiencing changes in her life that she did not ask for. She still liked and was pleased with these changes that God gave to her. While she was thinking one day, she said to herself, "Before, I used to ask and God gave to me. Now, God gives me opportunities without my asking for them. I should always be pleased with God for both evil and good-seeming incidents destined for me. I hope that God is also pleased with me."

IN PRACTICE

The notion of reliance or *tawakkul* has different levels. One of the highest levels of this station is to melt your own desires in the pleasure of God. This is similar to a small ice cube melting in the ocean. In other words, when the person is pleased with God in all the encounters of good and evil seeming incidents, then it can be said that the person is walking on the path of reliance, *tawakkul*. The expression that the Sufi uses in the above story "*I hope they don't come after death and bite me*" alludes to the notion that we will be accountable in front of God after death about the intentional engagements of our preferences in this life.

Discussion Questions

- ► Why is it so hard to give up self-will?
- ► How can I help myself to find the beautiful parts of bad-seeming things that happen in my life?
- ► How can I help myself to trust God's will enough to surrender my will to God's will in all my affairs?
- ► How would relying on God entirely affect my relationship with God?

352. The Professor & Four-Year Colleges

There was a professor who was a Sufi. One day, he was thinking about his students. Every four years, new students were coming and the other ones were graduating. He said to himself, "This is the life exactly: freshman is the birth of the person; sophomore is the teenage & youth years; junior is the adulthood; and senior year is the elder age; being ready to graduate and ready to die to meet with God in order to face the outcome of all life efforts and get the diploma or not."

IN PRACTICE

Life is changing. A generation comes and replaces another one constantly and silently. Each generation can be similar to the referrals in college terms as the class of 1976, 2019, or 2063, for example. Therefore, the person should normalize and realize this temporality in one's life although he or she may want to live one thousand years and not die.

353. Maintaining the Marriage

One day, the Sufi was giving advice to his kids. He said, "Maintaining the marriage is the most difficult task. There are times when people are effortlessly happy. Then there are times when couples are upset. These are the times when you must not act with your ego, arrogance, and shows of power that say 'I don't need you'. Humans are humans. Shaytan likes to break the bonds between people. What Shaytan enjoys most is seeing broken families."

In practice

It is important to realize what is expected and then take precautions accordingly. As our moods, spiritual states, and manners constantly change with age, gender, culture and with different social dynamics, it is important to first realize this and then prepare some preventative measures. If one expects a perfect marriage without any problems, this is a lie and fictitious. The reality is that those times will be there but most important is to train ourselves to still act positively and constructively with wisdom in these situations. The current discourses focus on aftermath events such as abuse, validity of prenuptial agreements, or legal rights, etc. There are few or none emphasizing spiritual trainings with wisdom in these marital relationships. There are few or none who give advice to married couples with genuine wisdom. Most advice assumes and finds the counseled to be abused and oppressed, and accordingly, they give advice to combat, fight, and save the person. The counseling language seems to be devoid of all these positive approaches.

354. Worms and their Purpose

One day, the Sufi was putting the garbage can out at the roadside. It was garbage day. While she was pulling the garbage can, a bag fell from the can onto the ground and lots of grain-size worms fell from the bag out onto the ground. They were moving all over the place. The Sufi was disgusted so much. She said to herself, "What should be the wisdom of creation of them for spiritual journeys?"

IN PRACTICE

Any feelings of disgust can be related to one's unappreciative and ungrateful attitude towards the Creator, God. This is called *kufr* in terminology. Any engagements of *kufr* can be similar to the worms attacking one's *iman*, which is defined as one's sweet and honey-based appreciative and grateful relationship with the Creator, God. If there is no *iman* in a person, then the person can be soaked in *kufr*. He or she may not even realize these spiritual worms because this person can be considered as being drenched in the swamp of worms.

Discussion Questions

▶ What is an important spiritual practice to do immediately when encountering feelings of disgust in order to start cleansing the heart?

355. The Man Being Fed with a Hose into his Body

One day, the Sufi did not feel good and went to the mosque. Another Sufi saw him in the mosque and came over next to him and said, "I just came from visiting a friend of mine. He is at home and sick. He cannot eat or drink. They are feeding him with a hose going to his stomach. His kids are doctors and very successful people. Yet, they cannot help their father." Then, the other Sufi stopped talking and left. The Sufi said to himself, "*Alhamdulillah,* thank you God."

IN PRACTICE

Sometimes, we forget to be grateful to Allah although we may think that we are pious. Each occurrence of feelings or emotions of being down can be a sign of this ungrateful disposition to God. In the above story, when the other Sufi realized this internal struggle in his friend, he rushed to his help by sharing a real experience of his as a reminder. In practice, the real friends help each other especially when they are down and they need spiritual help.

356. Time Travel

One day, the Sufi visited his friends. There were a few people in a small room. After chatting with them, there was a silence. The Sufi was working on his computer. He looked at the others. Everyone was either on their computer or cellphones. The Sufi said, "If people from 50 years ago came to our time, they would consider us weird."

IN PRACTICE

Change is good and appreciated as long as it is good and serving to increase one's relation with God. If it is the opposite, then it is a bad change. One should ask God for help and use one's willpower not to be dragged into the flow of distractions.

Discussion Questions

- How can I manage my screen time to help myself focus on my real life?
- In what ways has technology helped me as I continue to develop my relationship with God?

357. The Intentions & the Relations with the Children

There was a Sufi who used to do her best to please her children. She was excellent to them in order not to be the 'bad' guy but the best person as a 'friend' with love. There was another Sufi who used to please God and accordingly treat her children. She used to sometimes be the 'bad' guy unlike the prior Sufi. After a few years, both of their children grew. The children who were treated in the best way with the intention of pleasing them did not turn out with gratitude toward their mother as compared to the other children's attitude toward their parent. The frustrated and mistreated mother said to herself, "What did I do wrong? I did everything to please them."

IN PRACTICE

It is important to make the intention to please God before pleasing people. God can change the hearts of people, can give them love and appreciation for their hearts. If it is done with this intention, then the same close people or engagements can transform as a source of test or trial for us.

358. Adab the Core

One day, the Sufi was thinking about why Satan lost and angels won. Then, she said to herself, "It is the core, the *adab!*"

IN PRACTICE

Adab is the embodiment of always having a good opinion of God. The people without *adab* can even seem to be religious but if they don't have this understanding, then this disease sooner or later will reveal itself and make them lose all their efforts. Satan is a prime example of this. Angels are the opposite. Humans are mixed between the angelic and satanic levels.

Satan did not understand and lost the *adab* by questioning without *adab*, and showing displeasure to the Divine Will of Allah SWT about the creation of humans. Angels kept their *adab* by trying to understand the wisdom about the creation of humans and fully submitted to the Divine Will of Allah SWT. Humans were the trial and test for both, and humans adapted by going between two extremes. The Prophet has the highest pole of submission to the Divine Will of Allah SWT even surpassing the angels. Conversely, there are humans at the lowest poles due to having no *adab* and even they surpassed Satan.

359. Heart & the Recognition

Lately, the Sufi was avoiding all the social gatherings in order not to be recognized. One day, the Sufi's husband desperately asked and insisted that she go with him to a social gathering. The Sufi accepted and said to herself, "I know I will suffer later." She attended the gathering. She was trying to monitor her heart. She realized that there were still remnants of the desire for being recognized. The Sufi felt very uncomfortable with herself. After she went to her seclusion place, she made *istigfar*[55].

IN PRACTICE

It is very important to constantly struggle and tackle the intrinsic diseases of the heart. One of these diseases is the sickness of being recognized and applauded by people. The ego wants titles, fame, and self-admiration. Yet, these can be spiritual filths similar, maybe, worse than urine and other impurities. The person should be in a constant struggle of transforming one's ego[56] to different classifications of the true and happy self[57].

---

55. asking forgiveness from Allah

56. Nafs-Ammarah, raw ego.

57. Nafs lawwamah (blaming self), nafs mutmainnah (satisfied self), and nafs radiyyah (fully pleased and happy self).

360. Fair Weather Friends

There were a number of dogs who used to be fed with nice food every day by their owner. Among them was a dog called Kelb. All the dogs were very happy and proud of their owner including Kelb. They held their owner in high esteem. After years of a nice, grateful, and loyal relationship between the dogs and their owner, there were rumors among the dogs in town that the owner was putting some poison in their food. All the dogs started talking about this rumor. Not long after, some of the dogs fed by the owner started talking bad about their owner. This was shocking for Kelb. The dogs started leaving their owner. Some of them still stayed with their owner. Kelb said to herself, "It is shameful of my friends who left. How can you be fed food all these years and survive, and then, leave your owner due to some rumors?"

In practice

We learn from our teachers as they are also humans. The attitude of gratefulness, appreciation, and loyalty towards our teachers should prevail more when our teachers need us even if they do mistakes as humans. Even if they do not make mistakes, it is not uncommon to witness rumors and oppression towards genuine teachers in the past and today. Yet, one can observe the prime projection of this attitude between the person and God. God gives this person so much. One day, an unpleasant or evil-seeming incident touches this person. Then, this person stops his or her relationship with God. What a loss on the person's part!

361. Rewards & End Results

There was a Sufi who had children. Each time they would read Qur'an they would come to their father and mention how much they read and then expect a reward from the Sufi. The Sufi would then buy them some toys. There was also a wise-fool who used to come to the mosque and read the Qur'an. Each time he read the Qur'an, he also used to come to the Sufi and mention how much he read and expected a reward from the Sufi. The Sufi then used to give him a few dollars. The Sufi then thought of both cases, and said to himself, "The importance of rewards, encouragement, and necessity for Heaven in the afterlife…"

IN PRACTICE

It is important to do everything to please Allah. Each person is different in their relationship with Allah. It is normal to be encouraged and motivated by the end result. This end result can be a toy, a few dollars or an eternal life in Heaven. Yet, the highest and noblest of these end results is the Pleasure of God.

362. The Love of the Prophet

One day, the Sufi attended a lecture about the love of the Prophet. He was glad that he attended to experience the immense love of the speaker for the Prophet. Then, the Sufi said to himself, "I hope we can embody the true love for the Prophet but it is not fake."

IN PRACTICE

The Prophet Muhammad is the utmost pearl and diamond of all humans in all his engagements and character traits. When one studies in detail the life of the Prophet saw, one can realize the utmost example of caring, kindness, gentleness, and calmness. Yet, at the same time his model of controlling his anger and of a just, fair personality exemplifies one who lived a perfect life as a human. The humanness of this perfect role model sets a practical example for the followers about the applicability of the Divine Teachings in the lives of all humans.

Discussion Questions

▶ What in particular do you love about the Prophet Muhammad, or any of the prophets?
▶ In what ways do you try to mode the behaviors and attitudes of Muhammad and the other prophets in your life?

363. Realities, Definitions and Dresses

There was a Sufi who used to study psychology. She was thinking about the definitions and the efforts at understanding different human psychological states. There were a lot of technical and convoluted terms as is to be expected in each discipline. Yet, the Sufi said to herself, "Our definitions and terms in each discipline are similar to the dresses that we wear. Although the dress may seem to fit on the person, that dress may not exactly represent the person."

IN PRACTICE

In our understandings of ourselves, there are different disciplines and approaches like in psychology. Yet, sometimes a technical term in a discipline for the classification of a person derived after a long struggle may not truly represent the inner mind and emotional renderings of a person in its true reality and purpose. In some cases, these terms can be a distraction to separate the person from their own real self. Therefore, for the people of heart (ahlullah), mere knowledge through mind is invalid unless verified by experience with the guidelines of the Qur'an and *sunnah*[58].

Practices and applications of teachings of the Quran by the Prophet Muhammad

---

58. Practices and applications of teachings of the Quran by the Prophet Muhammad.

364. Love On the Way

There were two Sufis- a husband and a wife. One day, the Sufi husband got a cut on his limb. The Sufi wife gave him a long lecture about how he does not take care of himself well. About a week later, the Sufi wife got a cut on her limb in exactly the same spot as her Sufi husband. The Sufi wife said, "Maybe…my not so nice thoughts about my husband."

IN PRACTICE

When people are close to God, sometimes God can send small warnings with love, kindness, and caring so that they can correct themselves. These nice warnings, like in the above story, are expected to encourage a person to engage in self-reflection.

Discussion Questions

- ▶ Have you ever noticed a loving reminder being sent when your attitude or behavior needed adjustment?
- ▶ Are you grateful and receptive when you receive correction?
- ▶ How can we become more grateful for correction from others, and use it to improve ourselves, our relationships, and our lives?
- ▶ How can we learn to take criticism from others in stride, and not have a negative reaction to it, internally nor externally?
- ▶ How can we learn to be less critical of others?

365. External Evil Revisited

The Sufi was traveling. She again felt the existence of evil that visited her before. She said to herself, "I thought I was finished with this evil. It came again. She immediately rushed to her protection litany of prayers."

IN PRACTICE

As we live in the world of evil and good, there will always be the swing between the evil and good. This evil can come from internally, from within one's own self. It can also come from outside. Regardless, the person should always be prepared to respond to evil-looking incidents by taking refuge in God with the litany of prayers.

366. Owner's Manual

One day, the Sufi bought a new machine from Amazon. He was so happy and was working to assemble it by meticulously going through its manual. As he was working diligently and carefully, he was also thinking about the concept of a manual for humans. Then, he said to himself, "Yes, it is the Qur'an and other scriptures sent by God."

IN PRACTICE

Allah SWT teaches us our own realities with the Qur'an. In popular language, the Qur'an is the manual of a human being. They read the Qur'an in order to understand this machine-looking being with more complicated faculties of emotions, experiences, memories, concerns, worries, attachments, and reasonings. If a person takes a simple machine in order to understand its proper usage, without its manual, he or she may spend hours and still may not figure out fully its usage. On the other hand, if there is a person who makes a little bit of effort in reading the manual, that person can slowly but surely make the incremental steps of understanding and utilizing this machine. If there are any issues one can constantly go back to the manual to figure out the problems with their solutions. Similarly, the Qur'an, the scriptures, and all the prophetic teachings[xlii] are the full, complete, and comprehensive manual for the person. The person constantly engages with them in order to understand their own real selves, purpose, and goal in this short lifespan. If the person acts in the illusional dispositions of self-sufficiency, the person for sure wastes all this short life with the delusions of self-experiential discoveries. All these discoveries have authentic and true value as long as they are evaluated with the principles and guidelines of these scriptural and prophetic teachings[xliii].

367. The Dedication of the Book and the News

One day, the Sufi wrote a book. She dedicated it to one of her old friends who was living in another country. She submitted the book for publication. Then, the same day, she received a text message that her friend had died in a bike accident. The Sufi was in tears and changed the book dedication to include the date and put a note that read 'just a received a text that he passed away in a bike accident today'.

IN PRACTICE

It is important to constantly remember the reality of death. The discussion of death is a normal topic to be realized and practiced among all ages and all levels of learners. In this sense, death is not evil but it is going back to God as the person has been longing to do.

368. Being Present and Not Remembering the Past

One day, the Sufi was thinking... Being fully present in your time should require not remembering the past. The Sufi did not remember what she wrote and thought about yesterday. She said to herself, "Maybe, I am fully present now."

IN PRACTICE

Being fully present is the key. Yet, at the same time, planning for the future and for the afterlife is the main intention of life. The person on the path of God is a good businessman on the spiritual journey. The person invests in the afterlife as one's real goal. Yet, he or she gets the benefits immediately in this world on their spiritual journeys of heart, mind, and the body.

369. The Health of Faith & Practice

One day, the Sufi was reflecting on the difficulty of keeping one's *iman*, faith, and practice healthy as the person gets promoted in life in different worldly engagements. He said to himself, "Although you are trying, at any time your *iman* can become diseased. It is very disgusting to get these diseases constantly and one needs to put in effort in order to constantly clean it."

IN PRACTICE

Yes, it is very difficult to maintain the healthy state of *iman*, faith, and practice. It is not impossible with the grace and enablement of Allah, God. Yet, if one can detect the feelings of disgust as a symptom of these spiritual diseases, then that is a good sign. The person has the alertness and self-awareness of the incoming diseases. The next step should be to make an effort to clean them with *istigfar*, asking forgiveness, and making *ibadah*, engaging oneself with practice.

370. Effect of Clothes

One day, the Sufi took a walk in the rain. When he arrived at the mosque he was all wet. He found a pair of pants and a shirt. He put them on himself. The pants and shirt were small and very tight on him. He felt spiritually contracted and started feeling a headache. He said to himself, "This could be the effect of the clothes."

IN PRACTICE

What the person wears has an effect on the spirituality of the person. The term 'modesty' can reflect this similar idea in religions about the dress code. Sometimes a tight cloth, a colorful dress, wearing a cap, a turban, a headscarf, or a long dress can have a negative or a positive spiritual effect on the person. When a person makes an intention to follow a role model such as Virgin Mary or the Prophet Muhammad in their dress code, God rewards them and sends spiritual empowerment upon them as well.

Discussion Questions

▶ What do you base your decisions on for choosing your clothing each day?

▶ Do you notice a difference in the way you feel and behave based on what type of clothing you are wearing?

▶ What type of clothing do you like to wear when you are planning to pray or meditate and spend time with God? What is it about that kind of clothing that makes you choose it for this occasion? How does it make you feel?

371. Fine Lines of *Iman*

There was a Sufi who people used to love so much. They loved the Sufi teachings she shared with them. One day, the Sufi said to herself, "Allah does not reward? (I'm not sure what the missing word is here) my efforts of teaching the people about the genuine practices, yet I hope that it is an opportunity to be close to Allah."

IN PRACTICE

Sometimes, the arrogance of piety, religiosity, or the self-pride of teaching others about God can make the person lose on the path. Yes, it is valuable and encouraged to share with others what one finds as valuable. Yet, it is a means but not an end to please God.

372. Worldly & Spiritual-Seeming Achievements & Fatalities

One day, the Sufi was engaged in reviewing her life incidents. She was trying to play and re-play the incidents in her mind. There were cases of worldly and spiritual-seeming achievements. She said to herself, "From my life movie, it looks like I have had some fatal spiritual crashes in both arenas. In the cases when I lost the real goal, the ends got stuck in the false means."

IN PRACTICE

Anything or everything can be a test or trial. *Tayaqquz*, alertness with humble and full refuge in Allah SWT is the key for safety measures.

373. Two Crazy-Fools

There were two crazy-fools who used to come to the mosque to pray and hang around. One was old and the other one was young. The older one used to get angry at the younger one each time he entered the mosque and said to him, "Go and wash up yourself (wudhu) before you hang around in the mosque. Then come pray." The younger crazy-fool used to get upset about this. Yet, due to his respect for the older one, he would wash himself (wudhu) and then start praying. As this continued for some time, the younger one stopped coming to the mosque in order to not see the older crazy-fool. One day, the *imam* was leading the prayer. The cell phone of the older crazy-fool started ringing during the prayer. After the prayer was over, the *imam* gave a long lecture that people should turn off their cell phones during the prayer. The older crazy-fool got offended and stopped coming to the mosque.

In Practice

It is important to deliver a message without offending the other person. Although the person may be right, the wrong way of delivering the content can cause sometimes more damage than not delivering the correct content. Although it is difficult, one should train oneself in both perspectives. On another note, one can see the Just attribute of God in the above story. If we offend others, it is likely that someone can offend us as well.

374. Theoretical Physicist Sufi and Mind Wanderings

One day, there was a quantum physicist Sufi. She was thinking about her life when she was doing her PhD in theoretical physics. She used to immerse herself in a problem, and then could not get out of it for hours. As she advanced in her spirituality, she understood that mind wanderings can sometimes be fruitless when they do not have guidelines. She applied this notion from her spirituality teachings to her theoretical physics related mind journeys. Now, she was getting more efficient results in her problem-solving engagements related to the journeys of quantum physics.

IN PRACTICE

It is important to follow the guidelines. The Qur'an and the teachings of the Prophet Muhammad[59] can be those guidelines. It is important to involve oneself in reflection, critical thinking, and experiential journeys as long as these guidelines are followed preferably in the escort of a good and genuine teacher. On another note, one can witness a case of how the teachings of natural/social sciences can be related to teachings of spirituality in practice.

---

59. Hadith and Sunnah.

375. Not Dying After Death

One day, the Sufi was thinking, "How can I not die after my physical death?" She answered herself, "*Dua.*"

IN PRACTICE

It is important to make prayers in order to live after death. The Prophet Abraham is one of the examples of this case. In the Qur'an, it is mentioned that he prays to God in order to be remembered as good and to have virtuous offspring. As we can witness, his prayers are accepted and his legacy is still alive and much is remembered about his teachings.

376. The Crazy-Fool and the Cleaner in the Mosque

One day, the Sufi was sitting in the mosque when the crazy-fool arrived. The Sufi was the only friend of the crazy-fool. The crazy-fool was upset with everyone, even with his own blood relatives. As usual, the Sufi offered the crazy-fool some nice treats and coffee but the Sufi was acting very formally and was silent with the crazy-fool. Then, in came the cleaner of the mosque. His name was Habib, meaning "the lover." Habib was a nice guy and silent as well but did not think much of the crazy-fool. The crazy-fool started chatting with Habib about the weather and life. After a few minutes of nice conversation, the crazy-fool burst into his normal, real self and started complaining about life and people. Habib was not able to stop him. The crazy-fool was talking incessantly. Habib needed to go back to his job of cleaning the mosque. He wasn't able to do so because the crazy-fool was talking angrily without pause and shouting about people and life. The Sufi was watching this and he said to himself, "This is the reason why I am acting formally."

IN PRACTICE

It is important to try to understand the personalities of different people and their specific needs so as to know how to approach them. A person can help another person in different ways without exposing them in their weaknesses. The Sufi knew about the crazy-fool. He pretended to act formally in order to not put him in an uncomfortable situation of being humiliated by others. Yet, he still treated him nicely. The Sufi was his only friend in life. Allah has bestowed on the genuine Sufis the skills to be good friends with everyone including the people or animals who are disliked or scary. There are stories about Sufis being friends with snakes and lions as well.

377. The Realities and Short-Lifed Mind and Experiential Renderings

One day, the Sufi attended a gathering where people were emphasizing the experience and spiritual opening without much mention of the guidelines of the scripture, the Qur'an, and the Sunnah. They seemed to be discrediting the authentic knowledge. Then, later, the Sufi attended another gathering where the people were emphasizing the mind but not experience and genuine sincerity embodied with *adab*. They seem to discredit the genuine boost of sincerity. The Sufi said to herself, "The journey is so difficult. It is always important to respect both and to be in balance."

IN PRACTICE

One can witness a lot of groups who may emphasize the statements "If I experience..." or "If my heart is good and virtuous, I don't need to follow and practice genuine scriptures." On the other hand, others may not value the inner dispositions, but externalities with mind. Yet, balancing the internal and external is the key. This balance can reveal itself when the person follows and practices five-daily prayers and other required parts of the practice. Yet, at the same time, they try to infuse into themselves the deeper meanings of these practices.

378. The Realities, our Weaknesses and our Short Life

One day, the Sufi got some bad news about her work. Later that same day, she heard that her mother was put in the hospital having suffered a possible stroke. Then, she got sick. She said to herself, "We are so weak and our life is short. There is no one to take refuge in except Allah."

IN PRACTICE

Turning to God in both ease and difficulty is the key. Sometimes our weak willpower stops us from turning to God in our down moments. Yet, there is no real solution all the time, whether being in need or not, other than to turn to Allah.

379. The Angels and their Appearance

Abdullah Bin Masud in helping the lady (dead animal eating in the garbage) when going to pilgrimage. One day, one of the pious and famous Sufi teachers set on a journey for holy pilgrimage. While he was on his journey, he saw a woman looking through a garbage can for food. The Sufi teacher asked her what she was doing. She said that she was looking some food to feed her kids. The Sufi teacher gave all his money and sustenance to her and went back to his home after days of traveling. After the pilgrimage season was over, the pilgrims started coming back to their hometowns. They all came and visited the teacher about his emotional sermon during the pilgrimage. Everyone was crying. The Sufi teacher did not understand and did not say anything to anyone. He made *dua* and prayed Allah SWT to show him what was happening. Then, he slept. In his dream, he was told, Allah SWT was so very pleased with his action that an angel went on pilgrimage in his form and gave a sermon. Everyone's pilgrimage was accepted due to his sincere action.

IN PRACTICE

A simple and sincere act can boost the person in one's relationship with God. It may not be the mere quantity but the intense sincerity of the person can be the key in one's relationship with God.

380. Complaints & Lack of Appreciation

There was a Sufi who used to constantly receive complaints from his wife. His wife always said that the Sufi did not do anything around the house. She is the one always doing everything. The Sufi used to ask, "What do you want me to do? Please tell me explicitly." His wife used to give the 'to-do list' and the Sufi used to complete it to the best of his ability. Then, his wife used to be happy. After a while, the Sufi's wife again started to say same things. The Sufi again asked for the explicit 'to-do list'. Then, she was happy again. This cycle continued.

IN PRACTICE

Complaints do not add value but increase resentment for everyone. In family, professional, or other relationships, some people may do more work compared to others. This can be a fact. On the other hand, the ones who seem to do more work should not act as "the savior," and yet, at the same time, the ones who do less work should express their appreciation for the hard workers and try to contribute as much as they can regardless of the other party's complaints. Establishing relationships and doing things to please Allah can minimize or eliminate resentments when people do not appreciate the person's efforts.

381. Eschatology, Necessary and Unnecessary Engagements

There was a Sufi who was eating food with some friends. Her friends opened a discussion about the cases of eschatology, and the possibilities about the End of Days. Her friends were very interested in the topic, but not the Sufi. The Sufi said to herself, "Every learning engagement should have a good purpose. Mere curiosity of learning something without any purpose can induce fear, anxiety, and distraction in the mind and heart."

IN PRACTICE

It is important to learn and engage in any conversation or a lecture with a purpose and an aim. Mere engagements of chatting, or hanging around may make the person's mind wander and distracted. The Prophet asked for protection from the knowledge that does not benefit the person [51]. On the other hand, one can learn and inquire about topics such as eschatology with a purpose and an aim. These can be, for example, normalizing the occurrences and changes in societies through predicted prophetic miracles, and possibly using these avenues to explain to people that changes in our lives or societies are not random, but rather all are under the control and knowledge of God.

382. Real Teachers Don't Judge

There was a Sufi teacher who was so gentle, kind, and forgiving of people's mistakes. The Sufi used to learn from this teacher a lot. Yet, he was still making mistakes about not judging others and being kind and gentle similar to his teacher. The Sufi said to himself, "It is very difficult, yet I try to be like my teacher."

IN PRACTICE

As humans, we make mistakes. All the Prophets as genuine teachers had this non-judgmental quality. The Prophet Muhammad (PBUH) was a very kind and gentle teacher and implemented this gentleness and kindness in human relations constantly, whereas we tend to immediately rush to judge people in our relationships. This is the biggest difference between regular spiritual folks and the highest role models. Yet, we strive to be similar to our role models.

383. Headache, Arrogance & Prostration

One day, the Sufi had a severe headache. He didn't know what to do. He said, "Let me pray." He started praying and each time he put his head on the ground for prostration, he felt so good, his headache relieved and he kept his head on the ground for a long time. He said to himself, "Probably, this headache is due to my arrogance. Allah SWT wants me to humble myself with prostration so that this headache of arrogance can go away."

IN PRACTICE

It is important to relate the external diseases with the internal ones. Each occurrence in one's life is related to one's internal engagement. If the person is aware of oneself, it can be easy to treat both one's internal and external diseases with the help of God.

384. Silence, Smile & Sakina

There was a Sufi who wanted to be always in *sakina*, peace and tranquility from God. She used to constantly smile and keep silence. If she needed to talk she used to say it in a few words in a very nice and gentle voice and tone. Then, she used to stop talking and observe silence and smiling as it was most of her engagement. She used to always experience *sakina* as granted by God.

IN PRACTICE

Talking, harshness, and ungentle behavior in sound and voice can destroy one's spiritual honey of *iman*, belief. The taste of this honey is *sakina*, tranquility, peace and calmness as granted by Allah SWT. The Prophet Muhammad (PBUH) was embodiment of this trait. He (PBUH) used to smile much and talk less. When he spoke he used to utter few words with very deep and wisdom embedded meanings[xliv]. One of our problems today is that we don't how to stop talking once we start it.

385. Submission & the Sufi

One day, the Sufi had a desire of being in a position to the good. Then, he immediately restrained his emotions and thoughts and said, "Astagfirullah, Oh Allah!, Oh Allah, whatever You want, I am pleased with it. If You are not pleased with it, don't give it to me. You are my Decision Maker. I fully submit myself to You."

IN PRACTICE

There are different spiritual states and stations. Two of them are reliance and submission which may have close but different meanings. Reliance[xlv]

is making the necessary means and expecting the outcomes of these means from God. In addition to the requirements of Reliance, submission[xlvi] is not desiring or asking anything except submitting oneself to the One Who is the All knower, and holder of the good.

386. Marriage Proposal and the Sufi

One day, there was a Sufi who was not married. He happened to see a girl and fell in love with her. Then, after many days, and weeks of the pain of love, he tried to find a way to see if she was interested in getting married. Then, there was an arrangement made to meet with her. The Sufi said as soon as he saw her, "Can you please marry me? I love you so much." The girl said, "Yes." The Sufi started jumping up and down because of his happiness. The girl said, "I just want to say I have a sister who is more beautiful than me." The Sufi said, "Are you kidding me? Where is she?" The girl said, "Look there." The Sufi turned his face and died immediately. The girl said, "The real lover does not turn his gaze from the loved one even for a second."

IN PRACTICE

We claim to love God. Yet, our focus or gazes are all over the place expecting benefit and return from others. We prepare our spiritual death when we defocus ourselves from *La ilaha illa Allah.*

387. Coming Back to Earth and Social Problems

There was a Sufi who used to enjoy her time in solitude with God. One day, she realized that she needed to come back to earth realities to deal with the social problems in order to help people. She said, "*Alhamdulillah*, if I would please God, I would do it."

IN PRACTICE

The goal and purpose of everything is to please God but not to displease God. In this regard, worshipping in solitude is done to please God. Helping people in communal service is done to please God. The result is not important but the struggle on the path is valuable for God.

388. Love for the Last Child

There was a Sufi who used to have many children. She had a special love for her last child. This child was so nice in his character compared to the others. He had the utmost *adab*. If he made a mistake, he immediately said, "I am sorry." The Sufi was thinking about the wisdom behind it.

IN PRACTICE

Sometimes, being last can entail being inclusive of all the good traits. The Prophet Muhammad was the last one among all prophets. Yet, he was the most inclusive in all embodiment of good and virtuous characters.

389. The Sufi and the Inviter

There was a man who the Sufi used to call the Inviter. This man used to invite others for good and beneficial programs but he did not attend himself. It was again one of those days and the Inviter came to the Sufi and said, "There is a great beneficial lecture now in the other mosque if you want to go." The Sufi thanked him politely about the invitation and smiled that as usual the Inviter did not go to this great program himself but was inviting others to it.

IN PRACTICE

Actions come before words. Representation does not need words. People have minds to think and deduce meanings. Great orators do not have value as long as they do not practice. God values the sincere efforts but not cheap words.

390. Firing the Cleaner of the Mosque & Disappointment

There was an old man who used to clean the mosque. He did not speak English. Yet, he was good friends with the Sufi and they used to speak in sign language. One day, the old man came to the Sufi in a very sad way and told him that he received a letter from administration that his cleaning position would be terminated after 30 days. The Sufi felt sad and talked to the administration but unfortunately, there was no change in their decision. During these 30 days, the old man came to the Sufi a few times a week and said the same thing-that his position will be terminated by the end of the month. The Sufi felt very sad and he said to himself, "I wish we can only make our expectations from God but not from people."

IN PRACTICE

As humans, we expect recognition and encouragement from others, especially, if a person has been working in a place for a long time. Instead of recognition, the person is fired with only 30 days' notice. Due to the temporal and mortal nature of humans, their giving worth to other humans may have limited and temporal values. Humans can seem to applaud or congratulate others for their achievements but it is all time-based, superficial, and periphery. If the person expects recognition only from the Infinite God, then his or her achievement transforms to be infinite- and not time-based or temporal as compared to human achievement- in an infinite reward system of Heaven.

391. The Farewell Visit of the Mosque Cleaner

It was the last day for the cleaner of the mosque. After he finished cleaning the mosque, he came to the Sufi. The Sufi said to him, "Please forgive me" and the Sufi gave him a small gift. The mosque cleaner was surprised because for a long time spanning many months and even more than a year, the cleaner had never heard the Sufi talking and they had always communicated in sign language. The Sufi smiled and the man left and the Sufi was sad with all the good memories he shared with the mosque cleaner.

IN PRACTICE

It is important to ask forgiveness from the people with with whom we interact. The possibilities of backbiting and taking away the rights of others are serious engagements that require accountability in front of God in the afterlife. Therefore, it is traditional to ask forgiveness in farewell cases although there may not be an issue among the individuals.

392. Carrying Change

There was a Sufi who used to not like to carry change and cash in his pocket. He liked to have empty pockets without any weight. One day, a beggar came to him and asked him for money. He felt bad that he couldn't help him. The next day, while he was out another beggar came and asked him for money. He again felt bad that he couldn't help him. Finally, the Sufi said, "Maybe I should carry change in my pocket." The next day, he went out. He was happy that he had change if a beggar were to come and ask for money from him. All day went by and no beggar came. The Sufi felt sad.

IN PRACTICE

There are opportunities, times, and engagements for each place and time. There are five-times prayers that need to be performed during a certain time frame. People fast during a certain month. They go to pilgrimage at a certain time. If these times pass, opportunities to fulfill that good deed are missed. Similarly, in the above story, although the Sufi can get a reward from God due to his intention, it is always important to be prepared to catch the opportunities at the right times in one's relationship with God.

393. Troubles and Meanings

One day, the Sufi woke up and she had a headache. As usual, she started her day with her normal schedule. She started with her *dhikr*, meditation, and recitations of the scripture. As she was preparing to go to work, she thought, "I hope it is a fast and routine day as usual that passes quickly because my mind is all over the place and I cannot collect myself mentally and emotionally. I also have headache." With these thoughts, she went to her work. At work, she found herself in the middle of a mess with people blaming her about something. She was listening to the blames but did not have the energy to respond as her mental and emotional wanderings went further.

IN PRACTICE

It is important to constantly remember reliance on God. Sometimes, our routines or normalizations make everything normal, implicitly assuming self-sufficiency but not dependency on God. This can be called heedlessness[xlvii]. Yet, these moments of unexpected troubles, trials, or tests can pop up at any time and in any place. Our dispositions should be to seek forgiveness immediately from God for any possible mistake on our part as David (PBUH) did as mentioned in the Scripture[xlviii]. As soon as two people in dispute appeared in front of him to resolve their issue, David (PBUH) gave his judgment. Yet, as soon they left, he immediately rushed to ask forgiveness from them due to the appearance of this unusual case as a sign of reminder from God for him.

394. Virus & Precautions

There was a pandemic virus. Sufi heard the news and started taking the precautions as suggested by the doctors and officials. Yet, she reminded herself constantly that these are only and simply means and that God is the Real Doer.

IN PRACTICE

It is important to take the precautions as suggested by the experts. Yet, it is important to remind oneself that if these precautions do not work out, then the Decree of God[60] is the ultimate reason. One should never complain about this Divine Decree but still maintain the gratitude with the One during these difficult times. It is normal to grieve and be sad as a human as the Prophet [52] practiced. Yet, he never complained about the Divine Decree [52].

---

60. Qadar

395. The Quran and the Water Fountains

One day, the Sufi was traveling. He felt thirsty and stopped in a village. The village had a lot of water fountains for the travelers. As the Sufi entered the village he saw these different water fountains with different designs made for the travelers to quench their thirst without any payment. The Sufi went to one water fountain. He tasted the water. He said, "This tastes excellent and pure." Then, he said to himself, "I want to taste all the water from all of the different fountains." Then, he started trying all of them. He said, "*SubhanAllah*! They have all the same excellent and pure taste. Their source should be the same."

IN PRACTICE

The verses and chapters of the Qur'an are similar to different water fountains. If a person reads a verse, a chapter, or the entire Qur'an, one can realize that the Author is the Same, Allah (SWT), the Creator whether we say God, Adonai or the One. The themes are the same such as Oneness & Uniqueness of the Creator[61], accountability, justice, morality, and role model humans.

---

61. Tawhid

396. Nice Breezes of the Grave

It was the night fifteen days before Ramadan[62]. The Sufi went in the middle of the night to the graveyard to visit old friends as the Prophet (PBUH) did. He said as he had learned from the Prophet, [52] "Peace be upon you my friends, my teachers, and my family from the believers! You went before us. We will meet you soon inshAllah." Then, the Sufi felt a nice spiritual breeze as if hearing their response and they were happy that the Sufi visited them.

IN PRACTICE

Death of the body is only the death of the body but not the soul. We, with our souls are still alive in another reality or dimension called as *barzahk*. In this reality, the life continues. The Prophet knew and used to teach us how to engage with them as mentioned in the expressions of the Sufi above. The Prophet used to tell us their condition in the grave in their new life. If they needed help the Prophet taught how to help them [52].

---

62. Laylatul Bara'ah

397. Effects of the Society and Humanness

The Sufi as usual was practicing her life of solitude and minimal interaction with people. She sometimes used to think that I really don't care what is happening in the world as long as I maintain my relationship with God. One day, an epidemic disease came to the world. The news about it was everywhere every day. The Sufi still maintained her solitude with God without being much affected. Yet, as she was hearing the news in her minimal interaction with people, she said to herself, "As a human, it is very difficult to guard yourself from the effects of society although one can try to minimize all the social nearness."

IN PRACTICE

A person on the path is not disturbed with the daily occurrences of scandal perspectives of news. One can see a lot of people living with the news, sleeping with the news, and waking up with the news in front of them their TVs, cell phones, and computers. They let this news navigate their emotions up and down, cracking them apart and destroying them. Yet, a person on the path has a goal, meaning and purpose in life. Daily occurrences or scandal news do not navigate their emotions. Therefore, the people on the path engage themselves with the useful knowledge and information as suggested by the Prophet saw [52] (#2722) to help their lifelong goal on the path. This goal is to be happy, calm, and serene in this life by pleasing the One who is the Source of all happiness, calmness, and serenity.

398. Angels and the Sufi

One day, the Sufi was in the mosque for a prayer. There was no one to pray with him. So, he started praying by himself hoping that some angels would come pray with him in congregation. Then, from out of nowhere a butterfly came flying in. It was snowing outside and it was not the season for butterflies. The Sufi realized it and said, "*Alhamdulillah, I am not alone.*"

IN PRACTICE

If a person does something sincerely for the sake of God, God does not leave this person alone. God can send different forms of spiritual breezes to show the Divine Support for this person's genuine stance on the path. There is an understanding in the tradition that angels can change forms when they come to the human realm. They can come as humans or other beings. In the above story, the Sufi had a conviction that an angel came in the form of a butterfly as a Divine Support from God.

399. Bird and the Sufi

The Sufi used to go to the mosque to pray every day. As he was leaving the mosque, there was a bird that used to approach the Sufi and look at his face. The bird looked like a hoopoe. As this happened every day, the Sufi started thinking, "Maybe the bird wants to talk to me." Then, he started reading the verses from the Qur'an about the conversation between the hoopoe and the prophet Solomon. Then, the bird came much closer to the Sufi, looking at this face and started chirping and talking. The Sufi was thinking, "I wish I could understand what you are saying."

In practice

The people on the path can converse with other beings, animals, and plants. There are authentic reported cases that the people around the Prophet saw witnessed stones, trees, and animals talking and conversing with the Prophet Muhammad saw. The Qur'an mentions the conversation of the hoopoe and the Prophet Solomon.

400. High Expectations and Children

One day, there was a Sufi who had eight children. The Sufi used to love the seventh one so much. One day, the seventh one made a big mistake in his life. The Sufi was much disappointed and was not able to make peace with himself about this major mistake of his child. Then, he said to himself, "I should not really sanctify any human being, even my loved ones!"

IN PRACTICE

Humans are humans. Understanding this reality is important. If a person sanctifies or divinizes another human being, this is one of the highest mistakes that one can make in their life. *La ilaha illa Allah* requires only attaching oneself truly to God. One can love someone or something, yet true and correct valuation of everything is important. In the above story, one of the common mistakes is the parents' false and wrong assessment and valuation about their children. Then, when a parent witnesses the invalidation of their assessment, they can experience big frustration and devastation of their expectations. One should always expect from God. God is the only One Who does not leave the person with any frustration.

401. Good Intentions and Finding Yourself in a Mess

One day, the Sufi wanted to help her friend who was in need. The Sufi was trying to be extremely careful about how she should help her so that her friend does not get offended. Her friend was a type who did not want any help from anyone. The Sufi gently tried to approach her, yet she got angry and said some harsh words to the Sufi. The Sufi was upset and holding herself not to say anything back. The Sufi said to herself, "You never know how something can become a mess!"

IN PRACTICE

God rewards the person according to their intention but not according to the outcome of what they achieve or lose. Sometimes, a person with a good intention can find himself or herself in an unexpected situation. Yet, maintaining one's composure, calmness, and patience and not acting with anger can always be more fruitful in both spiritual and worldly affairs.

402. Winners and Losers

One day, a Sufi gained a lot of knowledge, piety, and respect. He started to have a lot of followers changing themselves with his teachings on the path of God. The Sufi's friends and family members were also benefiting from his knowledge and teachings. They said to themselves, "We are so lucky that we have the Sufi in our lives. What a great bounty of God! It is like winning a lottery!" Yet, a few of the Sufi's old friends and family members got jealous and said, "Why him? We are better than the Sufi. Why don't people follow us, but they follow him?" They have become increasingly jealous of the Sufi. They lost on the path of winning.

IN PRACTICE

It is important to detect our spiritual diseases before they kill us. A person on the path of God can be winning yet he or she can lose with jealousy. Satan is the primary example of this. On the other hand, an intelligent person can realize that if God chooses some people to be role models such as the prophets, and saints[63], then an intelligent person can make use of this to benefit their own spiritual growth. An intelligent person benefits from the people who are the source of light and guidance as the friends of God. Killing oneself with jealousy and self-destructive hatred is the worst foolishness, absurdity, and irrationality. When one reviews the life of the Prophet (ﷺ), everyone boosted their true spirituality with his pearl and diamond teachings. Yet, there were a few from his old friends and family members who blocked themselves due to their iron curtains built with jealousy, hatred, and arrogance in their hearts.

---

63. Awliyaullah

403. The Ban and the Sufi

One day, the Sufi heard that the town banned people going out at night due to expected protests and vandalism. She said to herself, "People will be in fear even if nothing happens." She spent her night in regular chants, prayers, and remembrance of God.

IN PRACTICE

It is important not to be trapped in current events. The maintenance of the relation with God can put the person in peace and calmness even during times when many people are in the states of fear and panic. At these times, it is a responsibility to give people hope and calmness once one takes care of oneself spiritually with one's regular engagements of one's relationship with God. The one who is already in the flow of fear and panic cannot help others already dragged down with daily and hourly news of magazines.

404. The Flies in the Dream

One day, the Sufi had a dream. Some of the dirty looking flies were stuck at home on the window screen trying to leave. The Sufi helped them to leave the house. There were a bunch of them. Then, she woke up from her dream. She said, "*Alhamdulillah*, my spiritual dirty flies will leave my house."

IN PRACTICE

Sound dreams are one of the means of communication between the seen and unseen realities [53]. Dirty flies in the above dream can represent one's spiritual sicknesses such as jealousy, arrogance, and anger causing one to oppress and abuse others. House can represent one's heart or soul, their real identity.

405. Head of the State & the Poor Man

There was a poor man in the mosque suffering from paranoia. Every day, he used to come to the Sufi in the mosque and tell him how everyone is planning against him in the mosque. One day, as usual, this poor man came to the Sufi in the mosque. He said to him, "Were you here when the head of the state came yesterday? He came here to plot against me with others in the mosque. I am a citizen of this country. They cannot kick me out." The Sufi did not say anything as usual and offered him a coffee.

IN PRACTICE

Sometimes, our ungrounded fears about others overwhelm us and make us dysfunctional. If this happens constantly, then it can become an illness referred to as persecution complex or paranoia which can lead to psychosis. Yet, it is important to diagnose it in its early stages before it becomes an illness. On the spiritual path, having a good spiritual teacher, a good collective meditation group, a good friend, and daily regular personal spiritual practices as *awrad* can be some of the means to detect and remove the seeds of these diseases before they grow further. Reliance on Allah ﷻ constantly with *La ilaha illa Allah*, removing and discharging oneself from all fears and anxieties with this chant, and regular daily prayers can be some of the practical remedies that can prevent building plaque on the heart and mind causing emotional and mental disorders.

- ▶ Sunnah or masnun duas.
- ▶ khayr
- ▶ Sunnah & Hadith
- ▶ The teachings of the Quran and Sunnah
- ▶ Jawamul Kalim
- ▶ Tawakkul
- ▶ Taslim
- ▶ Gaflah
- ▶ he Quran [38:24]

406. Religious Leaders, Institution, and Balance

One day, the Sufi attended a gathering. One of the priests of the mosque was proud to explain how one day a guy came to the mosque to pray but he did not want to follow the guidelines of the mosque. This person started arguing with the priest. The priest was firm about the rules. The guy left and did not come back again. Although the priest seemed to be following the guidelines of his institution, his confident way of narrating this incident to others made the Sufi uncomfortable.

IN PRACTICE

One should be always scared of breaking anyone's heart even though he or she may be right at the end of the argument. This attitude is so critical and can become deadly especially in the interactions with people coming to religious institutions and communicating with the representatives of the religion. In the above story, the Sufi was disturbed due to the self-assured attitude of the priest. The Sufi expected a sorrowful and empathy feeling (you might consider using the word compassionate) for the guy from the priest although he needed to implement institutional guidelines. One can find this often in the life of the Prophet ﷺ. When there was reparation of a person for his evil act, some people cursed the person. Upon hearing this, the Prophet ﷺ got very upset and said, "This person did such a repentance in front of Allah ﷻ that can be sufficient for all the city in Medina, [53]." Humbleness and humility requires having empathy for others.

407. Coldness in Attitude and Balance

One day, the Sufi happened to meet one of his friends that he had not seen for a long time. As soon as the Sufi realized that it was him, he ran to his old friend and said, "How are you? I hope everything is good. I didn't see you for a long time." His friend did not seem to be warm and welcoming. The Sufi replied, "Fine, thank you." The Sufi felt sad and said to himself, "Did I do anything wrong? I didn't see him for a long time. Therefore, I was excited. Why his attitude is so cold?"

IN PRACTICE

It is important to greet the person at least in the same manner as the greeter. The better is to greet the other with even more expressions of peace and even more excitement. This way is the way of the Prophet ﷺ [54]. Sometimes, a person's spiritual state can overcome the person. This can make the person not adapt to their surroundings easily. Yet, the person is expected to be aware of the realities and do their best effort not to offend people and disappoint people's expectations.

408. The Sufi and the Ant

One day, the Sufi was studying in the mosque. There was an ant walking on the carpet. The Sufi said, "Let me help her. It looks like she has lost her way." He took a paper towel to hold the ant. He was trying to hold the ant but she did not want to come. After a little struggle, the ant seemed to lose her energy. The Sufi screamed, "Please don't die! That wasn't my intention." The Sufi immediately rushed to bring some water and date pieces to give to the ant so that the ant can survive. The Sufi was crying and praying to God for the ant's life. After some time, the ant seemed to start walking again. The Sufi said, "*Alhamdulillah!*"

IN PRACTICE

Everything that has a life reminds of the One, al-Hayy, the Source of Life, Allah ☙. Everything makes *dhikr*, remembrance of Allah ☙. Therefore, everything is a real friend except some humans in loss who are not in remembrance of Allah ☙. Yet, one should even treat them as potential friends with their possible guidance by God.

409. The Sufi and "My Best Friend the Tree"

There was a Sufi who used to love all of the creation as connected to the Source of the Life, al-Hayy. One day, the people were arguing if they should cut the tree down adjacent to the mosque. They said, "We need to cut it down because its roots can damage the structure of the building." The Sufi opposed the idea and said, "We should not kill a tree that is alive." After a while, the discussion was over. Majority seemed to think that they should cut the tree. After a few weeks, it was a sunny nice day. The Sufi came to the mosque and while he was walking to the entrance, he fainted at the door. After a while people rushed to the Sufi. The Sufi woke up. He was crying about the tree that was cut. The Sufi said, "My best friend is dead."

IN PRACTICE

All the living beings remember and make the *dhikr* of Allah. Everything is a friend that connects the person with them. The Sufi was devastated in the above story by witnessing the death of one of his best friends, the tree.

410. Silly Things Turn Into Big Problems

One day, the Sufi was thinking about how simple and silly things can cause big problems if they are not handled gently and with wisdom and patience. He said to himself, "Anything at work, at mosque/temple, at home and even with friends. Wow! SubhanAllah! Very challenging, yet it looks like a piece of cake! Maybe, it should be called a "piece-of-cake looking minefield!""

IN PRACTICE

The notion of *fitnah* can be defined as chaos in societies, in families, and even in any type of relationship. The starting point of *fitnah* can be something silly and it can grow if it is not handled carefully and taken care of with wisdom and patience. Some contemporaries may refer to this as early stage cancer cells as compared to the ones in the later stages that can kill people as they kill relationships. They can cause social, family, kinship and friendship chaos, aggression, violence, animosity, and disconnected relationships or diasporas at group or community levels. Therefore, the person should not take anything easy or as a "piece of cake" in life but remain always in the state of uncertainty; yet at the same time, stay in the state of tranquility by praying to God for protection and striving to have a very strong relationship with God regularly.

Discussion Questions

- ▶ What do you do in your life to address small problems before they grow into big problems? At work? At school? At home? In relationships?
- ▶ How do you manage your stress as you strive to balance the many aspects of your life?
- ▶ Do you notice a connection between how much care you are putting into your spiritual life and how well you are able to manage your daily stresses?

411. Balance in Sharing What You Know

There was a Sufi who used to think about the personalities who like to share and go over their limits and the ones who don't care to share about what they know. Then, he said to himself, "What is the ideal model?" Then, he said, "The balance."

IN PRACTICE

There is a balance in sharing religious knowledge. The person does not try to proselytize to people. The Qur'an mentions that "there is no compulsion in religion." In other verses, the Qur'an mentions that if God wanted, everyone on the earth would believe in God. At the same time, if a person is benefitting from a spiritual knowledge, the person welcomes the people who want to learn in order to address their own problems. In classical Sufi writings, this is expressed as a caravan and everyone is welcome to join of their own choice.

412. Miracles, Randomness & Determinism

The Sufi was enjoying her new life. She was saying constantly, "*Alhamdulillah*" for the miracles in her daily life. She was trying to increase her knowledge about God constantly but trying to maintain humbleness, and humility with weakness by praying to God regularly so that she does not become lost on the spiritual path. Then, she thought about her old life much with misery, doubt, arrogance, hardship, and chaos. Everything seemed as random in those years of darkness. As she was comparing her past and present, she said to herself, "*SubhanAllah!*, This is the difference: As the person detaches oneself from God with doubt, ingratitude, and arrogance, then God leaves this person in that state with darkness, and depressive states of randomness and chaos. But, when the person realizes his or her real self with weakness, need, purpose, and connecting to the One, God with *iman*, belief and appreciation, then God opens all the doors of light, tranquility, easiness and even constant daily miracles to approve this correct and true disposition.

In practice

As the person sets off on the journey with humbleness and humility in one's relationship with God, then God opens all the doors of signs. One may call this miracles. Then, the person starts living a wonder and a heaven-like life in this world before she or he dies and goes to the heaven in the afterlife.

413. Levels and Tastes: Columbian Roast vs Breakfast Blend Coffee

The Sufi always used to drink breakfast blend coffee. She did not like other blends. One day, she realized that she had bought the wrong blend of coffee-the Columbian roast. She did not have time to go return it to the store. So she made a pot of coffee using the Columbian Roast. After the first sip, she said to herself, "*Alhamdulillah*, I didn't know I liked the Columbian roast as well!"

IN PRACTICE

As the person changes physically over the time, the person also changes spiritually. A thorough engagement with one spiritual state can be painful; but at another time, it can have a good taste and bring pleasure. Tasting differentiation is a skill. Different brews of coffee taste differently to different people at different times. For one, external appearances may look like suffering but internally there is joy.

Discussion Questions

- ► Describe a situation when you and someone else had different emotional reactions to the same event. What factors do you think played a role in how each of you experienced that event internally?
- ► Is there any significant experience in your life that you had a very different response to and perspective about when going through a second time? How about a third time?
- ► Have you been surprised by your own responses to some of life's surprises? What do you make of them?

414. Learning for a Purpose

One day, the Sufi was thinking about why people learn. She said to herself, "There are a lot of people who learn but they don't benefit themselves. Is this knowledge still useful? Is learning just any knowledge useful?"

IN PRACTICE

Knowledge can be distracting if there is no purpose and no application. The Prophet teaches and God asks us to learn useful and beneficial knowledge. In other words, knowledge can be distracting from one's relationship with God if there is no purpose to it, if there is no benefit, and ultimately, if there is no application of the acquired knowledge by the person.

Discussion Questions

- ► What kind of knowledge is useful to you in your life?
- ► What knowledge do you personally find to be without purpose in your life?

415. Child and the Parents

One day, the Sufi visited a family and witnessed an interaction between the child and parents. The child said to the parents, "You did not do anything for me. I don't care about you." The mom said, "Oh my son! Do you remember the days that I used to change your diapers, breastfeed you, and take you to your school? Do you remember the days that your dad used to take care of you, teach you, and get what you needed?" The child said, "I don't care. I don't want to know you in my life." The Sufi did not like the environment and said to herself, "What an ungrateful child! This is exactly the same and the worst case- when the person does not recognize God and is ungrateful to their Creator."

IN PRACTICE

It is required to respect, acknowledge, and appreciate the parents regardless of if they are good or bad. Even in disputes of religion, God orders their kind treatment in the scriptures [55]. The relationship of the person with their parents can be a measuring stick for the people to judge their relationship with the Creator. The Creator, God, has more rights on a person than the parents. Yet, there are a lot of people who tend to deny these rights.

416. Alien, the Sufi and Cutting Nails

There was an alien who came from another planet. God gave the alien different abilities not too similar to humans. For example, the alien could be cut into pieces and unlike humans, would not feel any pain, and then could be put back together into its full body again. The alien witnessed the humans suffering if something happened to their bodies. One day, the alien saw the Sufi on a Friday cutting his nails. The alien got shocked and said to the Sufi, "Are you an alien like me! I see that if humans cut any part of the body, they are in so much pain and screaming! Yet you are cutting your nails and seem to still be happy and not in any pain!"

IN PRACTICE

Our bodies are just bodies. It does not have much value compared to the value of soul. In other words, it has a value and deserves respect because God created it. Yet, the real purpose is not the bodily endeavors. If God wants, humans can be equipped with different physical frames called bodies similar to the alien's body in the above story. Perhaps, the body parts such as nails or hair are given to humans without any sensory awareness by God to remind us of this reality although all of the other body parts are surrounded by the nervous system and are capable of receiving pain.

Discussion Questions

- ▶ Do you ever have a sense that you are more than your body?
- ▶ Do you ever feel stuck in your body?
- ▶ Do you find that you take balanced care of your body and soul, or better care of one or the other?
- ▶ What can you do to take better care of your soul?
- ▶ How can you use your body to take better care of your soul?

417. Mission and Over

One day, the Sufi was thinking about her mission in the world. She was deeply thinking about the following questions: "Does death mean that the mission is over?" "If so, what is my mission?" "Can I decide when my mission is over?" or "Without my choice, is the mission over?"

IN PRACTICE

The mission in the world is to please God by working on oneself, by training one's ego with worship, gratitude, and joy. At the same time the mission is to serve humanity in order to please God. Some people can dedicate their entire lives and death comes indicating that the mission is over. They don't choose the end of the mission. Some elect people, like the Prophet Muhammad, are asked by God through angels, if they want to stay in the world longer for the mission or be with the Beloved, God [54].

418. Healthy Fear

One day, the Sufi was driving home on a Friday night passing a few bars where some people were drinking. On the street, there was a big billboard showing a crying parent who lost their children due to a drunk driver. Another billboard next to it was showing scary police and the imprisonment of a drunk driver with the huge fines for drunk drivers. The Sufi got scared and felt disturbed. After collecting himself from the scenes of drinking people in the bar and the billboard signs, he said to himself, "Fear has a place and it is not always evil."

IN PRACTICE

Sometimes, we go through different emotional cycles during the day. In some emotional states, we may not care about hurting others. At these times, as mentioned in the above story, if the person has the fear of consequences of his or her goofy actions, then he or she may stop doing it. Similarly, on the spiritual path, sometimes, the person can feel so pumped up with joy, self-satisfaction and certainty. If the person does not have the fear of accountability in front of God, then the person can have vanity and arrogance while being called a "religious person." Fear has different levels. Some people fear and stop their own evil in order to not be punished in Hell because they want to be in Heaven. This can be a good starting point. Yet, this can be a beginner's level. Some people have fear and stop their own evil in order not to displease God because they love and appreciate God so much. This can be the level of the elect on the spiritual path.

419. Heart & Mind

One day, the Sufi was enjoying her prayers, and fasting so much. She did not want to continue much learning and using her mind. Yet, she felt guilty about it. Another day, she was enjoying learning so much she did not much continue her prayers and fasting other than the required ones. Yet, she felt guilty about it. She said to herself, "I know the key is balance as the Prophet SAW suggested."

IN PRACTICE

The Prophet teaches us the balance between heart and mind. The Prophet was always in deep meditation, prayers and worship, yet the Prophet smiled, ate, and socialized nicely and kindly with his family members and people. Even during the journey of ascension[xlix], the Prophet was offered to be in Heaven where one's emotions and feelings can overpower the person. Yet, the Prophet SAW used the faculties of both his mind and heart, to come back to earth in order to fulfill and complete his mission. The balance is very difficult. Yet, it is the goal.

Discussion Questions

► How could I bring more balance into my life right now? Which 2 areas are being neglected and which 2 areas are taking most of my energy?
► Which relationships in my life need more attention right now?
► Does my relationship with God need more attention?

420. Our Role Model

One day, the Sufi was thinking about our role models. She was thinking about the life of the Prophet Muhammad and how he lived a life without breaking hearts. Everyone loved him. He was truthful. Then, the Sufi said, "*Alhamdulillah*, we are so lucky to have such role models so that we can realize that humans do achieve to become real humans although we have a lot of challenges and difficulties.

IN PRACTICE

It is important to have teachers who show and apply the teachings in their lives as role models. The Prophet Muhammad embodied all the teachings in his own life. Therefore, people practiced his teachings not due to experiencing a formal lecture format but by observing him and impersonating him as their role model.

Discussion Questions

- ▶ What has been the value in your life of living role models?
- ▶ Have you been inspired by legends of role models passed down? What inspired you?
- ▶ What important teachings have you absorbed in your life that you did not learn in a classroom?
- ▶ What important teachings do you strive to embody, allowing people to witness that there are people like you out there?

421. The Punishment of the Tree and the Sufi

There was a Sufi who used to drive a cool sports car. One day, he went to the mosque and parked his car under a tree. While he was closing the windows, the leaves of the tree were stuck in the windows. The Sufi saw this and said to himself, "When I come back I can open the windows to take the leaves out." After a few hours, the Sufi came to his car. As soon as he drove away, he heard a light scream. He looked around and said, "Oh my God! I forgot the branches stuck in my windows. I hope the tree was not upset with me." As the Sufi was driving the car, the Sufi saw light raindrops on his car's windshield. He turned on the wipers. The wipers seemed to not wipe away this rain. The Sufi said, "I don't understand. This is a new car. The wipers should be new, too." The Sufi could not see well and barely made it home. When he got out of the car, he touched the windshield and there was a sticky substance thickly smothering the car. The Sufi said, "The punishment of the tree!"

IN PRACTICE

Everything remembers God and chants in its own language except some humans and jinn. Hurting them for no reason can require compensation. There are rulings in practice not to cut tree branches. If people do it there can be some measures taken against the person. In the above story, the tree released some type of sticky substance on the Sufi's car due to its branch being cut unjustly.

422. Missing the Prayer & Marriage Problems

One day, the Sufi had an argument with her husband. She was upset with him and did not want to talk to him. He was also too proud to use wisdom. He said to himself, "If she doesn't want to talk, I am also not going to talk." They slept as usual together in the same bed. Both fell asleep and missed the morning (fajr) prayer. Both woke up very upset because of missing the prayer. The Sufi said to herself, "Possibly, this may be a sign of the displeasure of God about useless and purposeless argumentation between the couple leading to broken hearts.

IN PRACTICE

The one who has the upper hand is the one who can control his or her lowly selfish desires of anger, pride, and arrogance in human and especially marital relationships. Our egos naturally incline to show these signs if they are not trained or disciplined. One of the important displeasures of God is about the disputes and arguments between couples. In practice, divorce is permissible but one of the disliked options of God. The person is expected not to act childishly, especially in marital affairs. If one is acting in these manners, then the other should strive even harder to uphold the principles of marriage loved by God. In gender identities of marriage, man is expected to establish peace in the family moreso than the woman. If the wife gets angry, the husband is expected to be on the calm side, to smile, and to let it go. This is the underlying notion in the teachings of the Qur'an in different verses[64]. If one analyzes the relationship of the Prophet with women, it is in his extra gentle, calm, and soft manners [50].

Discussion Questions

 ► What could I say to my spouse when we are in conflict that might disarm the emotional state we have co-created and give us a chance to start anew?
 ► What prevents me from seeking peace when I know I want peace?
 ► How can I use my relationship with God to guide my conflict resolution practices?

---

64. Such as [4:34]

423. Vanilla Ice Cream and the Sufi

There was a Sufi from Turkey who had a hard time pronouncing the word vanilla and yet, he loved vanilla ice cream. In Turkish, there are no letters differentiating the sounds between w and v. Again, one day, the Sufi went to a drive-thru to buy ice cream for his kids and himself. He said, "Can I please get three baby cone vanilla ice creams?" The cashier on the speaker at the drive-thru said, "Sir, what did you want, could you repeat it again?" The Sufi repeated himself, but again, the cashier didn't understand. After a few times of going back and forth, the cashier, said, "Sir, sorry, I think we have some problem at our speaker system. Sorry for the inconvenience. If you could kindly pull up to the window, we can take your order there."

IN PRACTICE

It is always preferred to assume good for others. Although the person may know others' mistakes and spiritual diseases, it is a spiritual level and maturity to gently address these issues without directly pointing or blaming the person. In the above story, the cashier gently addressed the problem without making the Sufi feel bad.

Discussion Questions

- ► Give an example of how you might politely address someone's misbehavior without embarrassing the person.
- ► Give an example of how someone has politely addressed your misbehavior without embarrassing you.
- ► What is the benefit of assuming the good for others? How does that benefit others and how does it benefit you?

424. Computer Cord

One day, the Sufi was working on her computer. There was a bunch of books next to the computer. The computer was plugged in to the outlet for charging. There were books on the cord, covering it, and the Sufi had forgotten about them. After a few hours of studying, the Sufi wanted to take a break and wanted to unplug her computer. Then, she started pulling the cord. She applied force to pull the cord but for some reason the cord seemed to be stuck somewhere. Then, she realized the problem. She gently held the piles of the books to swiftly retract the cord. She did it and said, "*Alhamdulillah*, if I pulled the cord harshly, all the books would have fallen on the floor and made a big mess."

IN PRACTICE

It is important to use gentleness and wisdom when solving difficulties. Sometimes, we tend to apply more force with harshness to solve problems in human relations. Yet, this can aggravate the issue more, make a big mess, and even break relationships. The Sufi realized a similar trend in our physical interactions with the objects.

425. Loyalty to the Old Shoes

The Sufi had old shoes. He was still using them and liked them very much. His wife was getting angry with the Sufi about not throwing these old shoes in the garbage. One day, the Sufi was wearing other shoes and he was not home. His wife used this opportunity to throw away his old shoes. When the Sufi came home he couldn't find his shoes and asked his wife about it and she said, "I put them in a bag outside to be thrown in the garage. They will be thrown away." The Sufi smiled and did not say anything. He found the bag and retrieved his shoes and started wearing them again. His wife got angry but didn't say anything to the Sufi. After a few months, the Sufi was not home. His wife was cleaning the garage and again saw the Sufi's old shoes. She took then and put them at the bottom of the garbage can. After a while, the Sufi came and wanted to wear his shoes. He asked his wife about his shoes, she said, "They are in the garbage." The Sufi went to the garbage and started searching for his shoes. It was so difficult with the bad smell for the Sufi because Sufis are repelled by bad smells. With all his effort, he couldn't find his shoes. He was upset and it was garbage day.

IN PRACTICE

The loyalty to our old friends, teachers, and especially to our parents are critical. One should not dump old, good relationships with others as one changes in life. The Prophet also had relationship and appreciation with objects such as a hair brush that he was using. In the above story, the Sufi wanted to carry this perspective of loyalty for his old shoes.

Discussion Questions

▶ Who are you loyal to and who is loyal to you? What is important about the loyalty in these relationships?

▶ Do you have any things or activities in your life that you are loyal to as well? Why?

▶ What is it about your loyalty that makes it an important part of your life?

426. The Mirrors & the Kids

One day, the Sufi was thinking about which of her kids she is most similar to in character. She had three children. After a while of thinking hard, she said, "My childhood is similar to the youngest one. My present character is similar to the middle one. Perhaps, my old age character will be similar to the oldest one."

IN PRACTICE

It is important to realize that God is fair and just. God sends us people, events, or things to see our own selves. Yet, we don't seem to take lessons from them but rather see them as external events, or things related with others. One of the biggest mirrors among them is a person's own children.

Discussion Questions

- ▶ What have your children taught you about yourself?
- ▶ Who else in your life acts as a mirror for you?

427. Pain in the Eye & the Prayer

Mind of the Modern Sufi

427. Pain in the Eye & the Prayer

One day, the Sufi had a pain in his eye. He was thinking about what he should do. Then, he remembered the *dua*, the prayer of the Prophet about pains of the eye. He put his hand over his eye and read the *dua* as suggested by the Prophet. The pain was immediately gone.

IN PRACTICE

It is important to follow all the teachings of the Prophet. If one applies these simple-looking but very effective teachings then one can avoid a lot different kinds of pain in life easily and quickly. In the above story, the Sufi applied the Prophetic Teachings immediately instead of rushing to take a medicine from the pharmacy or calling a doctor.

Discussion Questions

► Do you ever use holistic medicines for common ailments?

428. Train Ride Nowhere

One day, the Sufi was riding on the train in Boston. It was rush hour in the morning. The Sufi was calmly sitting on the train, disconnecting from her surroundings and making her *dhikr*. She then for a second put her head up and realized everyone was looking at their cellphones and they were also disconnected from their surroundings. Then, the Sufi smiled and said to herself, "Orthodox and post-modern Sufi looking people."

IN PRACTICE

Disconnection from one's physical medium is a virtue as long as this is disconnection takes the person to a better spiritual state. If the disconnection aggravates the person's focus with more distraction, one should reconsider the effects of this disconnection. In the above story, cell phones can be tools for the representations of the modern Sufi-looking engagements.

Discussion Questions

► What are some ways the cell phone can be used to promote a better spiritual state?
► What are some other activities that could be done on a train ride to promote a better spiritual state?

429. Honoring the Guest

There were two Sufis, one liked having guests and the other did not as much. The one who liked the guests honored his guests and treated them so nicely. Then, the guests and the Sufi became lifelong friends in this world and even in the afterlife. The other Sufi did not honor his guests much. Although he knew and understood its importance, he did not honor his guests much for some reason. Then, the guests felt broken-hearted and not treated well. Later in life, they became evil-seeming enemies.

IN PRACTICE

Every trial, test, and difficulty can be a guest. If the person honors them by saying *Alhamdullilah*, and stays grateful and appreciative to God, then these evil-seeming incidents can become friends, as a means of salvation in this world and in the afterlife. However, if the person complains and severs relationship with God, then the person can lose happiness both in this world and in the afterlife.

430. The Mosque Administrators

One day, the Sufi was traveling. He visited a mosque during his travel. He said to himself, "Let me go to the early morning prayer and stay there for a few hours to do my *wird*." After the morning prayer was over the administrators of the mosque came to the Sufi and said that they needed to close the mosque.

IN PRACTICE

It is important to help the travelers and use the prayer places for their suggested purpose by the Prophet. Unfortunately, there are a lot of people who seem to follow the policies of institutions but not follow genuinely and mercifully the pearl and diamond teachings of the Prophet.

431. Bee Confident

There was a confident Sufi who used to give advice about bees. He used to say, "As long as you don't bother the bees they don't sting you." One day, he went out in the backyard with his wife to sit in the gazebo. There was a bee around his wife. His wife got very nervous and agitated. The Sufi said, "As long as you don't bother the bees they don't sting you." He smiled confidently and the bee left. One day, the Sufi was walking under a tree and he heard a buzzing sound around his neck. He got nervous and started thinking, "If this bee stung me on my neck, I could be hospitalized." Then, he panicked and put his hand on his neck, and immediately felt the pain. The confident Sufi was stung by a bee. He smiled bitterly to himself, changed slightly his usual motto and said, "As long as you don't fret and panic when the bees are around, *then* they don't sting you."

IN PRACTICE

In spiritual journeys, and life endeavors, sometimes rush or panic modes can cause more damage than an expected benefit due to rushing or panicking. Especially, the term *fitnah* can be translated as the panic times when there is uncertainty in engagements. The Prophet suggests to be passive and not active in those times even though there can be an expected benefit [52]. In the Qur'an, it is mentioned that the long-term harms of a *fitnah* can be more damaging than short-term explicit harms [2:191].

432. Lost Data on the Computer

One day, the Sufi was working on her computer. The computer shut down with an error. The Sufi started thinking the message behind it was that nothing happens randomly.

IN PRACTICE

It is important to personalize each incident in one's life. There are different signs that are sent to us constantly by God. Yet, if we seem to not care, then the magnitude of these signs can change until one understands and gets the message. Yet, there are ones who die without deciphering these meanings and applying them in their lives. They are shown the realities of everything without any full interpretation until immediately after death but this can be too late.

Discussion Questions

▶ What are you grateful to have already learned now while you are still living?

433. Monitoring the Heart

There was a Sufi who used to teach the elite of the society. The Sufi was trying to control her heart within the position and and among the prestigious identities of her students. As she was trying to monitor her heart for any type of disease, she felt some type of anxiety, fear, and uneasiness before and after teaching her students. She understood and detected this sickness and said to herself, "The viruses are entering into my heart. That is the reason why I feel uneasy and fearful. I need to practice more detachment."

IN PRACTICE

The person always makes one's intention to please Allah. If this intention is slightly affected by other means, then the person can be immediately diseased. The initial symptoms of this disease can be fear, anxiousness, and uneasiness. One should constantly go back to the embodiment of detachment phrases such as *La ilaha illa Allah* and physical prayers accompanied with tears to clean the filth. If this cleaning is not done regularly and immediately, the disease can spread in all spiritual faculties. Therefore, there is no guarantee of one's pure and full relationship with Allah until one dies. The person should be in a constant state of spiritual alertness and monitoring of their heart.

434. Password & Keeping Secrets

There was a small girl who used to tell others about her family life incidents related to her parents and siblings. The Sufi mother used to advise her that there are things that should remain only within the family and that others do not need to and should not know. One day, this girl's cousin came to see her. They used to be best friends. While the two girl-cousins were playing together next to the Sufi outside, the wind closed the door of the house. The guest-cousin needed to go inside the house to get a drink of water and asked her cousin, "Can you please tell me the passcode so that I can go inside?" The girl went to her mom and said in a whispering voice, "Should I tell her?" The mom smiled and said, "This is not a secret. She is your cousin. She can go inside the house."

IN PRACTICE

There are many secrets that one should keep with Allah. Exposing them can make the person lose that intimate, trust-based relationship. Similarly, in a family, among husband, wife, and children there can be some secrets. Exposing them to others can make the people lose the close relationships and break the trust among them. Secrets with Allah and others are all trusts that one should not betray.

435. Positions, Disgust & Need

One day, the Sufi was thinking about why the people take positions and titles for themselves in life. It is all responsibility, accountability, and yet at the same time, these things carry within them self-deceptions coming from arrogance, and desire for fame and recognition. Then, the Sufi was disgusted and said, "*Alhamdulillah*, I just want to be a normal, simple man for people but a man of value *inshAllah* known only by God."

IN PRACTICE

One of the diseases is the desire for recognition and applause by people. The person can be in certain positions to fulfill a need. Yet, it is very important to always control one's heart and replace himself or herself with the people of more worthiness.

436. Scratching the Body

One day, the Sufi was doing her meditation. As she was enjoying the *dhikr*, the tip of her middle toe felt tingly and the Sufi looked at her toe and touched it and started scratching it. While she was touching her toe, she was looking at it and reflecting on the shape of the toe, and its purpose on the body. After a few minutes she said to herself, "Wow, now I understand why we need to scratch different parts of our body. It is to realize what we have been given by God and appreciate it."

IN PRACTICE

It is important not to take things for granted. Most of the time we have a lot but we don't realize and appreciate it. We keep our heedlessness or 'I don't care' attitude with other fellows and especially with God. Sometimes simple things like scratching the body as in the above story can be sufficient for the ones who are trying to practice appreciation and awareness of God and other fellows. Sometimes, big things such as evil-seeming incidents of losses, trials, and tragedies are not sufficient to wake up the person from their sleep of heedlessness.

Discussion Questions

- ▶ Describe an experience you have had similar to the story which helped you realize how important every small part is to the whole being.
- ▶ Have you ever lost something and felt a greater sense of appreciation for the thing when it was returned to you? What was that like? Did you turn to God for help during that time?

437. Prescriptions for the Heart

There was a Sufi who used to have a hard time understanding people and treating them accordingly. It took him one year to understand a person. Another person, it took two years for the Sufi to understand. There are ones whom the Sufi still does not understand. The Sufi said to himself, "Once you understand them, then you can treat them accordingly."

IN PRACTICE

Sometimes, we don't understand our differences related to gender, age, and culture. We insist on our stance without contextualizing the differences and normalizing them. Once the person normalizes the seeming differences, then the empathy can develop. Genuine empathy can lead to genuine communication, helping others, and learning from others. The Prophet (PBUH) always used to give different answers to the same question for different people as the person who was the ultimate embodiment of empathy, kindness, and gentleness.

438. Signs & the Earthquake

It was early Thursday morning and the Sufi was reading her daily Qur'an in the mosque. She kept falling asleep while reading a page where there were some punishments mentioned about the ungrateful ones. The Sufi woke up and tried to read the same page again. She again fell asleep while reading the same page. This happened a few times. There was a heavy rain with darkness outside. The Sufi woke up one more time, glanced outside the window and said to herself, "Something is going on. May Allah SWT protect us and all of us." Shortly thereafter, the Sufi got a text message from her husband about news of a major earthquake in the city where her parents live.

IN PRACTICE

Everything is a sign from God in life. God does not give life without any purpose and goal. Each second or minute of a person's life has a meaning and a purpose. No occurrence in life is by chance or by luck. Everything has a meaning if the person understands. If the person does not understand, anything big or small does not make any difference for this person due to that person's heedlessness or 'I don't care' attitude.

439. The Signs

One day, the Sufi visited her friend around noon. Her friend asked the Sufi, "What is *ajal*?" The Sufi said, "It is the end time of a person, or expiration of their life." As the Sufi was leaving her friend's house, she was thinking to herself, "Why did she ask me that word out of nowhere? Was this a sign?" Later in the afternoon as the Sufi was working on her computer, she turned on her cell phone. She saw a text from an old friend that she had not spoken to for a long time. The text was about one of her close friends who had passed away in an accident. Her friend that she had visited in the morning and the one who had died did not know each other. The Sufi said to herself, "*Inna lillahi wa inna ilayhi Rajiun*, and now, I got the sign- *ajal*."

IN PRACTICE

Everything has a purpose. God sends different signs with different purposes. Sometimes, it is to comfort the person, sometimes to warn the person or to prepare the person for upcoming incidents and engagements. The expression "Inna lillahi wa inna ilayhi Rajiun" can translate as "We indeed belong to God; we indeed will go back to God."

440. See No Evil

The Sufi was watching a cartoon with her kids on a Saturday night. They were eating popcorn, ice cream, and melted nacho cheese with crackers. Everyone seemed to enjoy watching. Yet, the Sufi was critically thinking about the representations in the cartoon. She said to herself, "What if my kids see similar looking people on the street? They will all be scared. Representations!"

IN PRACTICE

Our memories are built through our minds and hearts and they are not garbage. We cannot watch things and then not think about their consequences. Every piece of spiritual garbage inhaled, seen, heard, or experienced will affect our lifelong memories in this life and in the afterlife. Looking, seeing, and watching are all *ni'mah*, bounty from God. If this bounty is not used with other ones in their proper prescribed ways then they will be witnessing against us as mentioned in the Qur'an [41:21], [56].

Discussion Questions

► In what ways has your media consumption negatively informed your views of stereotypes?

► Do you avoid any types of media as part of your spiritual lifestyle?

► How might you use media to enhance your relationship with God?

441. Our God First

One day, the Sufi attended an interfaith gathering. The Sufi said our God is the Same, One, and Unique Creator whether we say God, Elohim, or Allah. All the beautiful and perfect names belong to God. There were some who wanted to emphasize that their God was different. The Sufi said to herself, "I don't know why we are jealous of sharing our One and Unique Creator and getting into these lowly identity issues and problems."

In practice

First, it is important to find common ground and shared values and beliefs before one discusses the differences. Being so excited about talking about differences can indicate some spiritual diseases such as jealousy and arrogance. This can be very dangerous in the discourses of religious topics and discussions both in this world and in the afterlife.

442. Talking About or to God?

One day, the Sufi attended a spiritual retreat. The retreat was about relationships with God. One of the speakers said, "I think we have talked sufficiently about God. Now, let's talk to God through prayer." The Sufi said to herself, "Wow! SubhanAllah, this is an interesting statement." Then, she started thinking about this statement.

IN PRACTICE

It is interesting to realize that sometimes a person or especially a genuine teacher makes a statement and it really makes a mark on the person's heart and mind. This one simple-looking statement can lead to a lot of spiritual openings for the person. Most of the time, it is not due to the skills of an eloquent speaker but the power or heaviness of the words, phrases, or statements coming from the heart of the person and penetrating the hearts of others. As one looks at the life of the Prophet Muhammad, he said few words in his conversations [57]. Yet, it was sufficient to transform individuals and societies. The unfortunate ignorant and naive witnessed this transformation but they did not rationalize the power of this change and called the Prophet or genuine teachers magician [38:4], [56].

443. Spiritual Activist

One day, the Sufi attended a lecture. The lecturer said, "Spiritual activism is our solution to face the conflicts, problems, and evils in life and in the world. We should all be spiritual activists." The Sufi was thinking about the implications of this phrase.

IN PRACTICE

Spiritual activism can indicate the spiritual power of the person through prayers, recitation of the scripture and *dhikrs* by connecting via different means to God. If a person is spiritually active, then this can lead to genuine, sincere and effective individuals as social activists. There are a lot of social activists who die in their engagements due to not being fed correctly and regularly through the food of spiritual activism.

Discussion Questions

▶ How can a person activate spiritually in one's relationship with God?

▶ How can a person improve one's relationship with God through social activism?

444. Just a Face in the Crowd

The Sufi attended a deep and powerful retreat. Some were asking from Allah SWT for some spiritual openings. The Sufi was cautious and said to herself and prayed, "Oh Allah, I want to be a normal and ordinary human as long as You are pleased with me. I don't want any spiritual openings that may come with tests and trials."

IN PRACTICE

Anything given can come with tests and trials. The purpose of tests and trials is to ensure that the person still maintains a sincere, grateful, and appreciative relationship with God. There are a lot of individuals in practice who do not want extraordinary spiritual powers but only want to be normal, simple, unknown and ordinary human beings with whom God is pleased. In reality, this disposition can boost the person vertically in their relation with God. The Prophet Muhammad was the embodiment of this normality. When the Prophet was given the choice of being a king prophet or a normal human like others, the Prophet wanted to be the second option. This choice delivered him the highest attainment in spiritual journeys of God.

Discussion Questions

- What are some of the advantages of remaining unknown while you achieve your spiritual and worldly goals?
- How can these advantages help you ultimately thrive spiritually and in the world?
- What are some of the emotional and intellectual obstacles the ego-driven *nafs* presents that you must struggle to overcome even though you accept how valuable it is to remain humble and ordinary?

445. Being Loaded

One day, the Sufi was waiting for her bus at the bus station. Someone was watching a cowboy movie on their computer in the bus station while waiting for the bus. The Sufi saw a cowboy loaded with guns and other things walking in the Wild West, waiting to be challenged. The Sufi said to himself, "Wow, this is like walking with *wudhu*- loaded with the Qur'an on the right side of your jacket pocket, and *dua*/prayer/litany book on the left side of your jacket pocket, having *tasbih* on the right side of your pants and having *athar*/scent on the left side of your pants."

IN PRACTICE

To be loaded spiritually can be the readiness and constant fulfilling of one's daily award, regular chants/*dhikr*/prayers. At any time, an evil can come and hit the person. If the person is not loaded spiritually, he or she may easily die. In practice, one does not challenge and ask for evil but always asks from God easiness, blessings, and protection from the evil-seeming incidents. Yet, if it comes as a test, trial, or for any other purpose, then the person should be ready to take care of it.

446. Remembrance

The Sufi used to go to the Boston airport for work every Wednesday. The Sufi used to get a cup of hot water to make her own coffee with chants from a coffee shop at the airport. There was a cute Chinese bartender. Each time the Sufi went and offered money, she used to say, "That is okay. No money needed." The airport was extremely busy every day with thousands of people. After a few weeks, the Sufi went again on a Wednesday. She asked again for a cup of hot water and tried to hand over the credit card as usual although the bartender did not charge any money. This time the bartender said, "We can't give you this for free every day," but still she did not charge for the hot water. The Sufi smiled and left and said to herself, "The importance of regular prayers!"

IN PRACTICE

It is important to practice the prayers and rituals regularly. God accepts and gives the reward of prayers as if the person spent in one worship to another with the Divine Mercy and Grace. In the above story, although the Sufi went to the coffee shop every Wednesday, the bartender thought that she was coming every day due to the regularity. On a positive note, she remembered her among hundreds of people visiting the coffee shop.

447. The Man of Gratitude

The Sufi used to know a man for many years. He always used to say, "Alhamdulillah" or "Many thanks and all gratitude[65] is to God." One day, this man had a big accident and he was about to die. The Sufi saw the man. The man said to the Sufi, "Many thanks and gratitude to God." After a year, the Sufi saw this man again. He had brain surgery. He was almost going to die due internal bleeding in his head. The man said to the Sufi, "Many thanks and gratitude to God." After a few more years, the man got older. The Sufi saw the man again. The man had a stroke and he was hardly able to talk. The few words that the man was able to utter to the Sufi were, "Many thanks and all the gratitude to God." The Sufi started crying on the spot!

IN PRACTICE

It is important to embody thankfulness, gratitude and appreciation to God. This life is a test to reveal the levels of people in their degree of gratitude of God. Some of us can complain with a small pin pain on our body due to an accident and immediately blame God questioning why God did not protect us. Some exceptional people like the man in the above story can embody gratitude and thankfulness for God. God appreciates and prepares great rewards for the ones who excel in this test of recognition and remain always grateful to God.

---

65. Shukr in Arabic.

448. Leaving the Present and Forgetfulness

One day, the Sufi was enjoying his presence with God. Then, he forgot that he was teaching class. His phone was receiving texts from the students. He still did not understand why he was receiving texts. He continued his presence. After a while, when the class time was over, he remembered that he had a class that day. He called the students and apologized to them and said to himself, "It should be the case of full presence."

IN PRACTICE

It is important to aim to be in the full presence[1] of God constantly. This state can sometimes entail forgetting everything except fully embodying being in the presence of God. It may sometimes be difficult to transform from these spiritual states into humanly expected engagements and responsibilities.

449. Reminders & Blame

There was a Sufi who used to remind people before bad things happened so that people could do something to fix the issues before they happened. When a problem already happened, the Sufi used to not remind but rather try to console the people and make them feel easy. A friend of hers asked, "Why don't you remind them that you told them before about the possible problems?" The Sufi said, "If I tell after the problem occurs, then it is called blame, but not a reminder. The reminder is the advice before something happens so that people can take some precautions."

IN PRACTICE

The Prophet Muhammad never did blame people when people did not listen to his advice. He instructed them with reminders before but afterwards he did not blame them. There are many incidents of this principle. There were even cases[ii] when people faced very dire outcomes due to not listening the Prophet. After the incident, the Prophet did not say even once, "I told you but you didn't listen." In every aspect of life, our role models such as the Prophet teach us how to be a real human being without breaking people's hearts.

450. The Double Man

One day, there was a very pious Sufi sitting in a gathering with a very pious teacher. As he was sitting silently and with his eyes closed benefiting from the presence of this pious teacher, the Sufi for just a second opened his eyes and saw across from him his exact copy sitting in the same gathering. The Sufi was startled seeing exact his copy in front of him. Then, he started thinking about it.

IN PRACTICE

Allah SWT sometimes sends angels to encourage the person in their genuine and sincere efforts for God. Sometimes the angels can visit the person in the human form to test the person whether the person is on the path of God genuinely or not.

451. Real Sincerity & Fame

There was a writer Sufi. One day, the writer Sufi met another Sufi who was in practice. This new Sufi had a very interesting life story of change. He tried different ways of spirituality before becoming a Sufi. This Sufi said to the writer Sufi, "You can write my life story. Maybe, it may inspire others. In case it becomes famous and one of the top reads, I don't want to be known. Please don't use my name or any identifiers so that in case people want to backtrack to me, they won't figure out that it is my biography."

IN PRACTICE

Sincerity, *ikhlas*, is the key. Everything is performed to please Allah SWT. All the efforts of inspiration are performed to please Allah SWT. In this case, fame in the efforts of inspiring others can be poisonous. The natural human tendency can be eagerness to become famous to inspire others in order to please God. Yet, this can be one of the traps on the path. To avoid this trap, the person should really seek and ask, "How can I be unknown by all humans and known only by God, and yet inspire others towards goodness?" This is the real sincerity, *ikhlas*. Humanly recognitions, titles, and fame are valueless and even they can be a spiritual poison for the person. Unidentified, unnamed, and unknown engagements by humans are spiritually safer and more sincere than their opposite that attract other lowly intentions and motivations.

452. The Crying, the Mother and the Sufi

One day, there was a Sufi who visited his mom. He mentioned to his mom about the genuine practice. His mom got angry and cursed his teachers. The Sufi started crying and went to his teacher and explained what happened. The Sufi asked his teacher if he could pray for his mom. Then the teacher started praying for her. Then, the Sufi went to his home. He knocked on the door. The mom opened the door and apologized about what she did. She said, "Can you please teach me the spiritual practice? I need it in my life."

IN PRACTICE

The prayers of teachers for the students are very effective. God can easily answer these prayers compared to other relationships. There is no interest-based relationship between the teacher and student. In the genuine practice, they engage with their roles of teaching and learning in order to please God.

453. The Man of Astagfirullah

One day, the Sufi was traveling to Toronto, Canada. He stopped by a mosque to pray. A man from elsewhere led the prayer but not the imam. After the prayer, the man said from nowhere, "Please make abundance of *astagfirullah* and don't be angry." The Sufi said to himself, "He is talking to me."

IN PRACTICE

Allah can inspire people and even send angels in the form of humans to address their dilemma if they are trying on the path of God sincerely and trying to be aware of their inner voices or dialogues. It is not uncommon in the tradition that individuals show up from nowhere to address the need of a person. It is not uncommon in the tradition that the teachers or friends of Allah SWT address from nowhere the problems of the person in a lecture. Yet, one should take heed of it and change oneself and appreciate the One constantly Who sends these reminders.

454. The Wise Fool and the Locked Doors

There was a wise fool who used to sometimes act as a fool and sometimes as wise. When he used to act wisely, people let him enter the mosque. When he used to act foolishly, people did not let him enter the mosque. The Sufi was observing this incident. Each time the wise fool was on probation of not entering the mosque due to his foolishness, he used to come to the mosque and the mosque door would be locked. The Sufi was inside by himself in the mosque. Each time, the wise fool used to come the locked doors. Sometimes he opened them although the wise fool did not have the keys for these doors. The Sufi first used to get startled about it while observing this, but then he tried to normalize it and tried to understand the wisdom behind it.

IN PRACTICE

The people who are loved by Allah SWT are hidden. It is very critical not to treat any person harshly and break their hearts. Especially, if they are loved by God, then the person may take the risk of attracting the displeasure of Allah SWT on oneself. This can be very dangerous even this person who causes uneasiness for others is another Friend of God. Another point is that the places of worship are venues for people to discharge themselves and connect with God. We don't have authority to ban people from entering these places. In the above story, the wise-fool was a hidden person perhaps loved by God. God enabled him to enter this place of worship beyond the physical means.

455. Sufi and Escalator

One day, the Sufi used the escalator to go down. She remembered that she forgot to take something from her room. She ran back against the opposite moving direction of the escalator. Then, she fell down and hurt her hand. Then, she said to herself, "My sins." She immediately went to the room asking forgiveness from God.

IN PRACTICE

Nothing happens randomly. One's own thoughts and actions can be the cause of one's evil rendering toward their own selves to oppress themselves. Therefore, one should not blame anyone but immediately rush in solitude to ask forgiveness and help from God.

456. Injury and the Sufi

One day, the Sufi fell down and hurt his hand. She was thinking about the possible meanings behind this injury. She asked for forgiveness from God and asked for protection from the possible expected renderings in the destiny.

IN PRACTICE

It is important to realize that nothing happens randomly. There is an apparent, external and internal meanings to every occurrence. The person can ask protection from the possible outcomes of an incident from its internal meanings. God can change anything. God can transform an expected bad outcome to a positive outcome if one turns to God, makes repentance and asks forgiveness with humility and sincerity.

457. The Sleeping Man in the Kitchen

One day, the Sufi went to the mosque to pray the morning prayer at 6:45 am. After 10 minutes of prayer, everyone left except the Sufi. The Sufi stayed in the mosque for a few hours to do his work. It was peaceful and silent in the mosque. After working for a few hours, the Sufi wanted to go to the kitchen to get a cup to make coffee. The kitchen door was locked. This was unusual. As he was walking around the kitchen door, he heard a noise from the kitchen and the door suddenly opened. The Sufi was startled and said, "*A'uzu billahi min asshaytani rajim.*" A man came out from the kitchen and said, " I fell asleep while waiting for my bus." The Sufi said, "*Assalumu Alaykum.*" The man said, "*Alaykum Assalam.*"

IN PRACTICE

It is important to always ask refuge in God from unexpected incidents or events. There are seen or unseen beings that we may realize or not. Yet, we can constantly make the protection prayers as taught by the Prophet Muhammad saw in order to take refuge in God from everything.

458. The Best Time for Prayer

One day, the Sufi was looking for a best time to pray to God. As he was constantly searching for this best time, he realized that he has been not doing any prayers, but only thinking about this. He said to himself, "The best time is when you immediately remember to make prayer."

IN PRACTICE

It is important to optimize the results and expectations from God by selecting the best time for prayers. The Prophet Muhammad saw kept his special prayer for humans after death on the Judgment Day. All other prophets and messengers of God used their prayer for their people and followers in this world. Yet, if one would be affected with the whispers of laziness and heedlessness in the effort of searching for the best time and therefore not pray to God, then he or she should pray immediately as he or she feels the need for it.

459. Sharing and Caring: Food

There was a Sufi who had four kids. One of the kids did not want to share his food but if someone ate his food secretly he did not care. Another kid did like to share his food but if someone ate her food secretly, she got very angry and started screaming. There was another kid who did not like to share her food and became extremely angry when someone ate her food secretly. There was another kid who did like to share his food and did not care if someone ate his food secretly. The Sufi loved the last one the most and said to herself, "I wish even some adults can be like him, a very good quality. MashAllah!"

In practice

Our real character reveals itself when we are tested with the application of these sublime teachings on the path of God. There are a lot of people who preach and listen to preachers and even cry. Yet, when it comes to application they are not really aware of their own selves.

460. Oatmeal and Capacity

One day, the Sufi was making oatmeal. He put some hot water on the oatmeal. The oatmeal started sucking in the water and started becoming big. The Sufi was amazed with this oatmeal. The Sufi had a little bit of hot water left in the boiler. He said to himself, "Let me add this as well, so that the oatmeal can get bigger and this remaining hot water is not wasted." He added it and after waiting half an hour, the oatmeal did not suck in the extra water. The Sufi said to himself, "Everything has a capacity!"

IN PRACTICE

Knowledge and experience depends on the capacity of the person. Sometimes, giving more than what is needed may not have much use but it may affect the texture and quality negatively. One can always ask from God to increase one's capacity in spiritual engagements and knowledge in order to please God.

461. Galaxies and the Person

One day, the Sufi attended a gathering. There was an attendee who was discussing the galaxies. There was another attended who disagreed with the argument and she emphasized the importance of the self in one's own inner journey rather than the outer journeys of spiritual traveling. The teacher was watching the conversation and said, "Both are important to break the attitude of heedlessness and 'I don't care' for different people. It can also be important for the same person who may be going through different conditions with different spiritual states."

IN PRACTICE

It is important to recognize the different avenues given by God to break our attitudes of unrecognition and unappreciation in our relationships with the Divine. Sometimes, the realization of stars, the moon, and galaxies and sometimes a feeling coming from simple human engagement can help the person to break this heedlessness. A person in different states of spiritual engagement can benefit from each at different times. Different people with different spiritual tastes of engagements can benefit differently from each of the available resources.

462. Troubles and Meanings

One day, the Sufi woke up and she had a headache. As usual, she started her day with her normal schedule. She started with her *dhikr*, meditation, and recitations of the scripture. As she was preparing to go to work, she thought, "I hope it is a fast and routine day as usual that passes quickly because my mind is all over the place and I cannot collect myself mentally and emotionally. I also have headache." With these thoughts, she went to her work. At work, she found herself in the middle of a mess with people blaming her about something. She was listening to the blames but did not have the energy to respond as her mental and emotional wanderings went further.

IN PRACTICE

It is important to constantly remember reliance on God. Sometimes, our routines or normalizations make everything normal, implicitly assuming self-sufficiency but not dependency on God. This can be called heedlessness[lii]. Yet, these moments of unexpected troubles, trials, or tests can pop up at any time and in any place. Our dispositions should be to seek forgiveness immediately from God for any possible mistake on our part as David (PBUH) did as mentioned in the Scripture[liii]. As soon as two people in dispute appeared in front of him to resolve their issue, David (PBUH) gave his judgment. Yet, as soon they left, he immediately rushed to ask forgiveness from them due to the appearance of this unusual case as a sign of reminder from God for him.

463. The Medical Practices of the Prophet

One day, the Sufi heard news about a spreading, deadly virus. The Sufi immediately engaged herself with both spiritual and medical practices as suggested by the Prophet. Then, she looked into the modern medical advices as suggested by the doctors.

IN PRACTICE

The prophets receive divine guidance in the treatment of all spiritual and even bodily diseases. Therefore, one should first review the prophetic advice about prevention and treatment of diseases before seeking medical help from doctors. Both are means that God enables and God gives both the cure and treatment for diseases. One should follow the means as a form of prayer and respect to God. Laws and means are created by God to be followed. Therefore, medicine is a science as the law of God to be followed. Yet, one should always see them as means but not the real cause or effect. The Real Doer is God behind all the means.

464. The Sufi and the Water Fountains

One day, the Sufi was traveling. He felt thirsty and stopped in a village. The village had a lot of water fountains for the travelers. As the Sufi entered the village he saw these different water fountains with different designs made for the travelers to quench their thirst without any payment. The Sufi went to one water fountain. He tasted the water. He said, "This tastes excellent and pure." Then, he said to himself, "I want to taste all the water from all of the different fountains." Then, he started trying all of them. He said, "SubhanAllah! They all taste the same- excellent and pure! Their source should be the same."

IN PRACTICE

Allah SWT sends at different times different scriptures and prophets to all humans to remind them of their meaning, goal, and purpose in life. The commonalities of these teachings show that the Source is the same. We may refer to Allah SWT, Adonai, God, the One or other Beautiful Names and Attributes. The differences and contradictions may indicate impurity or human additions or alterations into the original, pure, authentic source.

465. Positive Group Association

One day, the Sufi was thinking, "Why do I take so much pleasure if I am involved and associated with doing something good although Allah SWT does not need it from me?" He was thinking about the answer to this question for many years. Then, one Friday morning, when he was doing his regular engagement with the Qur'ān, he had a little bit sparkling in his mind about this throbbing question and said, "If I claim that good thing is from me, then it will be arrogance. If I deny it, then it can be ingratitude or a lie. If I say *Alhamdulillah* and accept being part of it although it can be just a miniscule effort, then my association with it gives me joy, positive assurance and certitude on the path of Allah SWT."

IN PRACTICE

Real enablement of all the good things are from God, the One, Allah SWT. Yet, we may not know how to act when we realize these constant bounties showering on us. Allah SWT does not need any of these good deeds of ours. Yet, inclination for a good work by using our free will gives us solace, calmness, peace, positive and happy perspectives in life. Therefore, it is an honor to be used as a small insignificant tool on the path of God by doing good and virtuous acts. These acts are not our achievements but given to us as a Grace from God. Therefore, we say *Alhamdulillah* with gratitude for God to be the simple means but do not claim any of those achievements to be ours.

466. Spending Time with the Dead

One day, the Sufi visited Medina. Everyone in the tour group was saying, "*Alhamdulillah*, let's spend some time with the Prophet saw." There was a novice person in the group. He said, "How can we spend time with *Rasulullah* 🕌? He is not alive, but he is in his grave." The Sufi smiled and said, "Just spend a few days sitting and making your *dhikr* in *masjid* Nabawi next to the blessed grave of *Rasulullah* 🕌, then you will understand." A few days later, the novice man said to the Sufi, "Now, I understood!"

IN PRACTICE

Death is not anything but death of the body, yet not the soul. When there is a person next to a grave, there is the interaction of the souls. When a person spends a little time next to the Highest Soul, the Prophet 🕌, then there are the effects of this communication, presence, and interaction showering on the person from the Prophet saw with the permission of Allah SWT. If the person cannot visit the Prophet, similar effects from the Prophet can come on the person with *Salawat* with the permission of Allah SWT every day, especially on Fridays.

467. Humanness of the Prophet (Saw)

One day, the Sufi was thinking about the Prophet (saw). She said to herself, "What is the most unique feature of the Prophet saw?" She exclaimed, "His humanness!"

IN PRACTICE

God sends us prophets as humans as we are humans. Yet, the prophets are role models to show us how to be a real human being as our expected goal, purpose, and meaning in life is to please God. All the prophets including the Prophet eat, drink, go to the marketplace and get married to normalize our human needs. Yet, at the same time as narrated in the Qur'ān, they show us how to balance the life of a human with high goals, fulfilling intention and rewarding purpose to be happy and content in this life and after death. When one analyzes the life of the Prophet saw, one can be mesmerized with these human qualities of the Prophet saw with balance and the middle-way of kindness, gentleness, and care. Yet, at the same time, his spiritual level is higher than the angels.

468. The Sufi teacher of the Bird

Every day, as the Sufi was leaving the mosque, a bird used to approach the Sufi and stare at his face. Then, the Sufi took a moment to read to the bird from the verses of the Qur'ān on the hoopoe and the prophet Solomon. The bird used to carefully listen and fully focus without any chirping and come closer and closer to the Sufi as he was reading. Each day, after the Sufi finished the recitation of the Qur'ān, he said to the bird, "Assalamu alaykum, peace be upon you" and left walking to his car. The bird tried to escort the Sufi as much as possible to his car.

IN PRACTICE

It is important to have a relationship of *adab* between the student and teacher. *Adab* can be translated as the etiquettes of respect. Some of these etiquettes of the student of knowledge is to be always ready, wait, and be prepared for your teacher with *adab* and respect. The student should work around the schedule of the teacher but not the opposite. When the teacher starts teaching to give full attention to the teacher is another *adab*. When the teacher finishes the teaching, to escort the teacher when they are leaving with *adab*, respect and humbleness are some of these etiquettes. Animals can follow these etiquettes as mentioned in the above story. How about the humans?

469. The Absent Student: The Bird

The Sufi used to teach a bird about the conversation of the hoopoe and the prophet Solomon in the Qur'ān. Each time the Sufi used to leave the mosque, the bird used to come respectfully with *adab*, taking his lesson and then leave. One day, the Sufi did not see the bird attending the class. Then, he tried to look for the bird and was concerned about him. After some time looking for the bird, the Sufi said to himself, "I tried to do my part as a teacher."

IN PRACTICE

The teachers have a responsibility to look after their students. If the student is sick or if they are in need, the teacher should try to do their best to ask about them, help, and fulfill their needs. In the above story, when the Sufi did not find the bird attending the class, he was worried about the bird and put in an effort to look for him.

470. Good Company

One day, the Sufi was thinking about the reason for her fears, uneasiness, and feelings of insecurity. She was thinking about this for a long time. Then, she visited some good friends. They did a group chant and reading. The Sufi felt super happy, calm, and refreshed. All of her fears were gone. She said to herself, "My need for good company!"

IN PRACTICE

It is very critical to be around good company of friends and teachers from whom the person can benefit from their experiential knowledge on the path of God. A person can be a genius, a good reader, and a critical thinker. Yet, a human is a human. They need good people to receive different frequencies of goodness from their experience.

471. Dual Identities

There was a Sufi who used to immediately detect the ill feelings in himself towards others. One day, he felt the feelings of jealousy[66] towards some people. He immediately caught it and started the work, struggle, and process of terminating these feelings and transforming them into better and positive ones. Another day, a person came to the Sufi and praised him about how great he was. Then, the Sufi immediately caught his feelings of conceit, vanity, and arrogance. He then immediately engaged in the self-struggle of terminating them and transforming them into more positive ones. The Sufi was really getting tired from these constant struggles of the fight within himself between dual identities.

IN PRACTICE

The purpose of life is the struggle between the pure identity of soul as created by Allah ﷻ and raw ego, *nafs* which is pumped up falsely by Satan and with which we are constantly deceived. The struggle is to train this raw ego referred to as *nafs*. The soul should be decision maker but not the *nafs*. The purpose of existence is the life-long struggle between the soul and *nafs*. In this struggle, God is All Merciful. God sent us the scriptures, the Prophet ﷺ and all the other messengers as guidance and role models for us to define the nature of this struggle and how to win the game.

---

66. Hasad in Ar.

472. Assumptions & Laws

One day, the Sufi traveled to another country to visit his friend. The laws and norms of the country were different than the norms and laws in his home country. The Sufi was surprised how the laws were so detailed and different in this country, and asked his friend, "Why are the norms and laws in this country so very different than my home country?" His friend said, "In some societies, the norms and accordingly, the laws assume that humans are good, ethical, and moral and accordingly, expect initiatives from people. In some societies, the norms and accordingly, the laws assume that humans are evil, bad, and oppressive and accordingly, protects people from their harms."

IN PRACTICE

Contrasting and comparing different cultures and norms can make a person judgmental about the practices of others. The Prophet ﷺ was never judgmental about other cultures, norms, and teachings. There was an influx of different people from different cultures, understandings, and norms accepting the teachings of the Prophet ﷺ. Yet, he accepted them as they were and taught them the means to connect with God through worship, meditation, practices of individual rights, and justice.

473. The Squirrel and the Sufi

One day, the Sufi was taking a walk in the early morning and reading his regular routine from the scripture. As he was walking, there was a squirrel standing in the Sufi's path and eating a nut while looking at the Sufi. The Sufi started staring at the squirrel. The squirrel was eating and looking at the Sufi as well. The Sufi said to himself, "We are both connected with *imān* and *dhikr*. Therefore, the squirrel is my friend. We have the same goal."

In practice

Everything chants, praises, and prays to God in its own language. The perspective of *imān*, faith or belief in One Creator, God, Adonai, or Allah ﷻ gives a positive meaning to all of creation and to everything in the universe. In this sense, nothing is scary compared to the philosophies not emphasizing *imān*. In these worldviews, everything becomes scary because there is a disconnect among everything. There is no structure, system, a positive hierarchy. In these gloomy perspectives, everything is in chaos, fighting for their rights, freedom. Everything is enemy to each other. The powerful abuses the weak. Therefore, the weak are doomed to disappear due to so-called 'natural selection'. One has a choice in life- either continue with these 'assumptions of darkness' worldviews which increase one's depression; or embrace all of the creation with purpose, meaning, and friendship as the servants of God.

474. Modern Slaves

One day, the Sufi traveled to another town to visit her doctor friend. They were very happy to see each other. Although the Sufi was with the doctor, the doctor was constantly on her phone- sometimes talking or texting to her patients, or shopping, or engaging herself with social media in different chat groups. The Sufi felt uncomfortable. Although her friend was there physically, her mind and emotional states were not present. The doctor constantly had her head down looking at her phone while walking in the house and while outside. The Sufi felt bad about her friend. Yet, she seemed to be happy and not care about her engagements.

IN PRACTICE

Mental and emotional slavery can be worse than physical notions of slavery. Our modern slavery hides behind the popular terms of liberty and freedom. Yet, we don't have any self-focus times to engage ourselves with self-accountability. Self-engagements in focus take the person for self-discoveries. True self-discoveries lead the person to Allah ﷻ with the reality of *La ilaha illa Allah*. Modern slavery instigates a spiritual disease that 'the world is rotating around me'. This can mean that 'I am so important that if something happens to me everything is going to collapse.' Yet, God mentions in the scriptures often the mortality of all great humans indicating fully the reality of our upcoming demise. Intelligent is the person who focuses on *La ilaha illa Allah*.

475. Self-Destructive Group Identities

One day, the Sufi attended a gathering to benefit herself about collective engagements of spirituality. The lecturer was constantly giving examples of the greatness of her spiritual school. The Sufi felt uncomfortable.

IN PRACTICE

Group identities on the spiritual path should come with balance. A person can claim or say, "My group is the best, but it is not the only way." Considering one's spiritual path as the best is normal and expected, so that the person can follow the guidelines on that path from a teacher. Yet, it is wrong to assume and say, "My group is the ONLY way." This implies arrogance, falsehood, and deviation from the true path of God.

476. The Old Man and the Sufi

There was a man who spent almost all his life in evil and bad actions. As he was becoming very old, approaching ninety years old, one day, he met with the Sufi. The Sufi and the old man became good friends. As the old man was spending time with the Sufi, he started leaving his bad habits and wanted to learn more and more on the path. One day, the Sufi received a call from the old man. The old man was crying on the phone. He said, "Please come and pick me up, I can't drive due to my old age. Please take me to one of these chanting sessions." The Sufi felt so bad for the old man and went to pick up the old man. After picking up the old man, the Sufi was driving the car to their place of gathering for chanting. Then, while they were waiting at a red light, the Sufi said something about the angel of death and he immediately heard a big bang. The Sufi did not understand what was happening and fainted on the spot in the car. After a few minutes, he woke up to an ambulance, police car, and firetruck sirens. The Sufi and the old man were in a big car incident. They were hit from the side while waiting at the red light. The old man was dead in his seat in the car as he was holding on his lap, the book of chant.

IN PRACTICE

God values everyone's effort on the Divine path until the last minute before death. We don't know how, where, and when we will die. Yet, the way of ending is very critical. The way of ending life can be an indication how we would be welcomed or not for the next life. Therefore, a true person on the path should always be ready for the departure at any time and anywhere. The old man did not seem to live in piety for most of his life. Yet, his effort and genuine intention seemed to put him in a position to end his life on the Divine path.

477. The Mechanic & The Professor

One day, the Harvard Sufi went to a fast food place with his kids since it was Friday and the end of their school week. All of the kids were very happy to eat a nice and yummy chicken hoagie. As they were jumping around in the restaurant and impatiently awaiting their hoagies, there was a Sufi from Yemen eating his own food. The two Sufis did not know each other. While eating, the Yemeni Sufi was chatting with the Harvard Sufi's kids and mentioned that he was a mechanic and fixing the cars. The Harvard Sufi was checking to see if he parked okay on the street, going back and forth watching outside so that he didn't get a ticket. The Yemeni Sufi finished his food and called over to the Sufi and said, "Please, I want to pay for your food." The Sufi said, "No, that is ok, thank you." The Yemeni Sufi insisted so much and the Harvard Sufi accepted it. Then, the Harvard Sufi went to his car and got an expensive gift and gave it to the Yemeni Sufi. The kids were watching all this. They were amazed and asking questions to understand what was happening. The Harvard Sufi said to himself, "Throw the titles, Harvard, Phds and MDs in the garbage! Be a real man like this person!"

IN PRACTICE

It is very important to be generous. One of the cultures known for their trait of generosity is Yemen. The Prophet had a special praise for the people of Yemen. The Prophet highly encourages exchanging gifts, feeding each other and being generous so that there is the increase of love between brothers and sisters. In practice, it is important to embody the traits than the titles. There are a lot of unknown and secret people called *ahlullah*, loved by God. This is the real status and title.

478. Cupping and Going to ER

There were two friends in the mosque. One was trained in cupping. He used to do cupping on people. The other friend used to watch his expert friend while he was cupping others. The expert cupper needed to relocate to another town. One day, an old man came to the mosque and said, "I am looking for the expert cupper. I have a lot of back pain." The cupper's friend was there and said, "He moved from here. If you want, I can do it for you. It is not difficult." During the cupping, there was heavy bleeding. The ambulance came and took the old man to the hospital's emergency room. He almost died.

In practice

It is important to genuinely learn and apply the spiritual teachings under the guidance and mentor of a teacher. Sometimes, we cause spiritual deaths on others and on ourselves but we don't realize it.

479. Wishing "Peace" for Everyone

There was a Sufi who used to say, "Peace upon you" to whomever she used to meet. One day, she met another Sufi and she said, "Why do you always say 'peace upon you' to everyone? We only say it to our role models." The other Sufi said, "Why do you want to limit the peace coming from God to only certain people? Allah's peace is infinite."

IN PRACTICE

Some people may be confused when a person says "peace upon this person" if he or she is not one of the role models such as prophets or messengers. These are terminologies to differentiate among the most elect, the elect, and the pious. For example (PBUH) as "as" for the prophets or messengers, may God be pleased with them as "ra" and may God have mercy on them as "rh." All are good.

480. Simple is Better

There was a Turkish Sufi married to an American Sufi. One day, the Turkish Sufi was at home with her kids. She made macaroni for her children and made it in Turkish style with mint, diced tomatoes, olive oil and salt. After that she served to the kids. All the kids were asking for ketchup and hot sauce. The Sufi insisted that they needed to eat in the way that she made it with her style. The kids started crying and said, "If our dad was here, he would give us whatever we want. We don't want to eat plain macaroni." The Sufi said, "Either you eat it this way, or no food!" After the kids ate the food, they started saying among themselves, "Wow! This is the best macaroni we have ever eaten although it looked plain and it was much healthier!"

IN PRACTICE

Sometimes, we cry and ask something from God in such a way that we are very confident about our position. In the end, we got disturbed, and ungrateful in our relationship with God because the result was not in the way that we wanted. After many years, we start seeing the benefits of God-given results over the ones we deemed good and desired to have. Then, at that point in time, if we haven't lost our sense of gratitude, we apologize to and ask forgiveness from God. But, all those years between the disconnection from to the re-connection with God could have been wasted in misery and darkness. Yet, if we develop the attitude of gratitude and constant reliance on God, all the years, months, days and even minutes can be spent in constant sweetness and tranquility.

Discussion Questions

▶ Discuss a time when something worked out better than you had expected and you looked back at the time spent worrying and knew you had wasted that time feeling that way. How do you wish you would have spent that time instead?

▶ Was there ever something in life you really wanted only to find out later that it wasn't as good for you as you thought it was going to be?

- Have you grown to appreciate something in your life for becoming more than you expected it to be when it first came into your life?
- Have you had any experiences of feeling like you received just what you needed, right when you needed it, even if it wasn't exactly what you would have preferred?
- Have you ever had the experience of feeling, "That's just what I needed!" after something has happened to help take care of you, make your day better, or nurture you in some way that you didn't even know you needed until after it happened?
- How have these experiences affected your sense of gratitude to God and faith in God?

ENDNOTES

i. Shukr
ii. [14:7]
iii. This is a famous saying in sufism. The relationship between wird and waridat.
iv. Hadith 3:31
v. Zuhd
vi. Kabah, Mecca, and Madina.
vii. Nafs Ammarah
viii. Hurriyah
ix. Book 2:221
x. [13:28]
xi. Hadith 2678
xii. Hadith 81:53
xiii. [3, 8]
xiv. Hadith 218
xv. Hadith 292
xvi. Hadith 1325
xvii. Hadith 945
xviii. Fajr or morning prayer
xix. Hadith 7047
xx. Zuhd
xxi. Salawat
xxii. Hadith 2702
xxiii. Hadith 2704
xxiv. Hadith 2705
xxv. [18:24]
xxvi. For example, [34,13]
xxvii. For example, [23,78]
xxviii. Original term is majzub or majnun.

xxix. The experiential knowledge is critical. One can review Rumi's famous dialogue with his teacher about the importance of experiential knowledge.

xxx. The expression "spoiling the honey" comes from the statement of the Prophet Muhammad (saw) that anger spoils the faith.

xxxi. This story is a famous story passed especially orally in Ottoman culture.

xxxii. [49:2–4]

xxxiii. [49:13]

xxxiv. [39, 42]

xxxv. [41, 21]

xxxvi. [49:2]

xxxvii. [94:1–8]

xxxviii. [3,159]

xxxix. Called "sir" in terminology.

xl. Sunnah or masnun duas.

xli. khayr

xlii. Sunnah & Hadith

xliii. The teachings of the Quran and Sunnah

xliv. Jawamul Kalim

xlv. Tawakkul

xlvi. Taslim

xlvii. Gaflah

xlviii. The Quran [38:24]

xlix. Miraj

l. Khudur

li. The Prophet's suggestion about Uhud.

lii. Gaflah

liii. The Quran [38:24]

BIBLIOGRAPHY

[1] Al-Ghazzali, M. *Al-Ghazzali on Knowing Yourself and God.* Kazi Publications Inc., 2003.

[2] Vahide, S. *The Collection of Light.* ihlas nur publication, 2001.

[3] al-Ba'uniyyah, A. *The Principles of Sufism.* NYU Press, 2016.

[4] Kumek, Y. J. *Practical Mysticism: Sufi Journeys of Heart and Mind.* Kendall Hunt, 2018.

[5] Muslim, A. *Sahih Muslim,* translated by A. Siddiqui. Peace Vision. 1972.

[6] Al-Bukhari, M. *The Translation of the Meanings of Sahih Al-Bukhari.* Kazi Publications, 1986.

[7] Ozkan, T. Y. *A Muslim Response to Evil: S. N. on the Theodicy.* Routledge, 2016.

[8] Murad, K. *In The Early Hours: Reflections on Spiritual and Self Development.* Kube Publishing Ltd, 2013.

[9] U. P. Oxford, "Oxford Dictionaries," 2016, http://www.oxforddictionaries.com/us/definition/american_english/.

[10] Al-Ghazali, M. *Deliverance from Error.* Louisville: Fons Vitae, 2000.

[11] Ali, A. Y. *The Meaning of the Glorious Quran.* Islamic Books, 1938.

[12] Dawud, A. *Sunan Abu Dawud.* Darussalam, 2008.

[13] Ashraf, M. M. K. 'Ali Thānvi, *The Path to Perfection: An Edited Anthology of the Spiritual Teachings of Hakīm Al-Umma Mawlānā Ashraf 'Alī Thānawī.* White Thread, 2005.

[14] Ibn Qayyim. I. K. *The Soul's Journey After Death.* Noah, 2018.

[15] Vandestra, M. *Human Souls Journey After Death In Islam.* Dragon Promedia, 2017.

[16] Hanbal, A. B. *Musnad Imam Ahmad Ibn Hanbal.* Dar-Us-Salam Publications, 2012.

[17] U. P. Oxford, "Oxford Dictionaries," 2016. [Online]. Available: http://www.oxforddictionaries.com/us/definition/american_english/.

[18] Al-Ghazali, M. *Deliverance from Error,* Louisville: Fons Vitae, 2000.

[19] Salamah-Qudsi, A. *Sufism and Early Islamic Piety: Personal and Communal Dynamics.* Cambridge University Press, 2018.

[20] Muslim, A. *Sahih Muslim* (translated by Siddiqui, A.). Peace Vision. 1972.

[21] Hanbal, A. B. *Musnad Imam Ahmad Ibn Hanbal.* Dar-Us-Salam Publications, 2012.

[22] Kumek, Y. J. *Practical Mysticism: Sufi Journeys of Heart and Mind.* Kendall Hunt, 2018.

[23] Ansar, A. *Peace of Mind and Healing Broken Lives.* Universal Mercy, 2010.

[24] Smith, J. I. and Y. Y. Haddad. *The Islamic Understanding of Death and Resurrection.* Oxford University Press, 2002.

[25] Dorothy, G. and J. L. Singer. *Handbook of Children and the Media.* SAGE, 2002.

[26] Ring, N.C. *Introduction to the Study of Religion.* New York: Orbis, 2007.

[27] Ozkan, T. Y. *A Muslim Response to Evil: S. N. on the Theodicy.* Routledge, 2016.

[28] Al-Bukhari, M. *The Translation of the Meanings of Sahih Al-Bukhari.* Kazi Publications, 1986.

[29] Al-Ansari, A. B. "Ahadith al-Shuyukh al-Thiqat," vol. 2, no. 322, pp. 875–876.

[30] Tamer, Georges. *Islam and Rationality: The Impact of Al-Ghazālī: Papers Collected on His 900th Anniversary.* Boston: BRILL, 2015.

[31] Geoffroy, Eric, and Roger Gaetani. *Introduction to Sufism: The Inner Path of Islam.* Bloomington, Ind: World Wisdom, 2010.

[32] Shah, Idries. *The Sufis.* London: The Octagon Press, 1999.

[33] Jamal, Azim, and Nido R. Qubein. *Life Balance: The Sufi Way.* Mumbai, India: Jaico Pub. House, 2000.

[34] Shah, I. *Learning How to Learn: Psychology and Spirituality in the Sufi Way.* Octagon Press Ltd., 1978.

[35] Heer, Nicholas, Kenneth L. Honerkamp, al-Tirmidhī M. A. Hakīm, Muhammad -H. Sulamī, and Muhammad -H. Sulamī. *Three Early Sufi Texts.* Louisville: Fons Vitae, 2009.

[36] Singh, David E. *Sainthood and Revelatory Discourse: An Examination of the Bases for the Authority of Bayan in Mahwi Islam*. Delhi: Regnum International, 2003.

[37] Darimi, I. *Sunan Darimi*. Dar Al Kitab, 1997.

[38] Bukhari, M.I. I. *Moral Teachings of Islam: Prophetic Traditions from Al-Adab Al-mufrad*. Rowman Altamira, 2003.

[39] Schimmel, Annemarie, and Friedrich Heiler. *Deciphering the Signs of God: A Phenomenological Approach to Islam ; [to the Memory of Friedrich Heiler (1892–1967)]*. Albany: State Uni. of New York Press, 1994.

[40] Stowasser, Barbara F. *The Day Begins at Sunset: Perceptions of Time in the Islamic World*. I.B.Tauris, 2014.

[41] Al-Qahtani, S. B. W. *Fortress Of Muslim*. Darussalam Publishers, 2018.

[42] Abū, Dā'ūd S.-A.-S, and Ahmad Hasan. *Sunan Abu Dawud*. New Delhi: Kitab Bhavan, 2012.

[43] al-Qushayri, Abu -Q, and Alexander D. Knysh. *Al-qushayri's Epistle on Sufism: Al-risala Al-Qushayriyya Fi 'ilm Al-Tasawwuf*. Reading: Garnet Publishing, 2007.

[44] Ibn Qayyim, I. K. *The Soul's Journey After Death*. Noah, 2018.

[45] Khan, M. A. *Encyclopaedia of Sufism: Sufism and Naqshbandi order*. Anmol Publications, 2003.

[46] Adonis. *Sufism and Surrealism*. Saqi, 2013.

[47] Muhaiyaddeen, M R. B. *Dhikr: The Remembrance of God*. Narbeth, Pa: Fellowship Press, 1999.

[48] Abdullah, P. M. *ISLAMIC TASAWWUF: Shariah And Tariqah*. Adam Publishers & Distributors, 2001.

[49] Vaughan-Lee, Llewellyn. *Love is a Fire: The Sufi's Mystical Journey Home*. The Golden Sufi Center, 2000.

[50] I. Majah, *Sunan Ibn Majah*, Kazi Publications, 1993.

[51] A. R. A. Nisa, *Sunan Nisai*, Kazi Publications, 1997.

[52] A. Muslim, Sahih Muslim (translated by Siddiqui, A.), *Peace Vision*, 1972.

[53] M. Tirmizi, Jami At-Tirmizi, Dar-us-Salam, 2007.

[54] M. Al-Bukhari, *The translation of the meanings of Sahih Al-Bukhari*, Kazi Publications, 1986.

[55] M. i. '. A. K. Al-Tabrizi, Mishkat al Masabih, Beirut: Dar Ibn Hazm, 2003.

[56] SInternational, *The Quran*, Abul-Qasim Publishing House, 1997.

[57] S. Abu-Dawud, Sunan Abu Dawud, *Riyadh: Darussalam,* 2008.

GLOSSARY

A'bd: worshipper, servant, or slave

Accountability: liability, especially in Sufism and in Abrahamic traditions, everyone has a free will or agency in this world but accountability for their actions in the afterlife in front of God

Adab: good manners, esp. in the relationship with God in Sufism

Adjective: attribute, a phrase describing a noun

Adonai: name of God in Judaism

Affair: relationship

Agency: acting as an agent or a carrier with free will

Alhamdulillah: a chanted divine phrase of appreciation of God or Allah

Alienating: isolating, separating, disconnecting

Alienating Images of God: understandings about God that disconnects person to establish a regular relationship with the Divine or to follow a religion

Allah (ﷻ): Allah سبحانه وتعالى. The expression سبحانه وتعالى read as Subhānahu wa Tā'la also abbreviated as SWT and written as also Allah (SWT) is an expression of respect when the Name of Allah is mentioned. Among these expressions many English translations, one can be "Allah is One, Unique and Perfect with all the Divine Attributes and Names, far beyond human's negative and wrong constructions and imaginations. All Glory Belongs to Allah, the Most Exalted, the Most Respected, and the Most High."

Allude: explain, refer

Anger: uncontrolled and chaotic human spiritual state

Aphorism: sayings, proverbs in a culture, society, or belief

Appreciate: thank

Appreciative: with capital A, God

Arabic: language, especially the language of revelation of the Quran

Arrogance: feelings and actions of superiority

Ascension: rising, especially in Sufism increase of spiritual states in relationship with God

Assert: claim

Astagfirullah: a divine phrase of asking forgiveness from God and cleaning the heart

Attribute: adjective, a phrase describing a noun, especially in Sufism, attributes of God: divine phrases describing God

Authentic: original, genuine, true

Balance: modesty, especially in Sufism, following the middle way

Behavior: temporary nature of a person

Bismillah: a divine phrase of starting something with the blessing of God

Book of Chant: the Quran

Boost: increase

Bowing down: bending one's body, especially the act of respect by bending one's body, for God

Candy: hard delight, especially in Sufism, the pleasures or miracles given to the person on the path of God

Caution: carefulness, alertness, especially in Sufism, in spiritual manners not to be trapped by ego or self

Certainty: knowing without doubt, especially in Sufism, knowing and experiencing without doubt

Chanting: repeating, especially in Sufism, repeating the phrases with focus and experience

Chaos: disorder and confusion, especially in Sufism (spiritual) chaos being in negative states of anxiety, stress, and purposelessness

Charge: positive states of spirituality that makes the person happy, peaceful, and calm, especially in Sufism, filling oneself with divine knowledge and experience

Compassion: loving and caring

Confirming Book: the Quran

Confirming Scripture: the Quran

Conscience: internal instinct of distinguishing right or wrong

Consciousness: awareness

Constant: not changing, permanent, especially in practice, known as Reflective Attributes of God, where humans have an image but God has its source

Construction: formation of an abstract entity

Contract: squeeze

Convergence: similarity

Cookie: soft delight, small sweet cake, especially in Sufism, the pleasures or miracles given to the person on the path of God

Cosmology: knowledge about the origin and development of the universe

Covenant: agreement

Death: end of physical faculties of a person, especially physical versus spiritual death; the soul does not die but the body dies in understanding of physical death in Islam

Dedication: sincere constant effort

Deity: representation of the transcendent

Detox: discharge

Devout: pious, practicing

Dhikr: as one of the names of the Quran, or any type of chant to remember God

Discharge: negative states of spirituality that makes the person sad, stressed, and anxious, especially in Sufism, emptying oneself from all the temporal and worldly positive and negative attachments

Divine: transcendent

Doctrine: teaching

Dominance: control

Dream: visions when one is sleeping or awake

Ego: self, identifier of a person, especially in Sufism, raw and uneducated identifier and controller of a person

Elohim: name of God in Judaism

Embodiment, versus embody: making it part of one's character

Endeavor: engagement, activities

Epistemology: theory of knowledge

Ethical: moral

Ethnographic: based on observation

Etiquette: good manners and respect, especially in Sufism, respect in the relationship with God

Evil: anything that causes stress, sadness, or anxiety

Evil eye: the belief of unknown effects of the human eye across different cultures, traditions, and religions, especially in Sufism the evil eye effects due to extreme hatred, jealousy, or, oppositely, evil eye effects due to extreme veneration and love of someone

Expand: enlarge

Experience: internalization of knowledge

Experience or experiential knowledge: all types of learning except from a book or a teacher, internalizing and personalizing the formal learning

Figurative: unclear, secondary, and metaphorical

Free Will: free choice of a person in decision-making

Generous: with capital G, God

Genre: type

Genuine: sincere, original, authentic

Ghazali: philosopher, theologician, Sufi mystic, lived in 12th century

Glorification: the mental, spiritual, and maybe verbal act of describing God in an admirable way

Groundless: fake

Habitual: habit of doing something constantly

HasbiyaAllah: a chant with a meaning of "God is sufficient for me"

Healthy Cookies: beneficial extraordinary incidents, such as miracles in Sufism

Heaven: a place of all maximized pleasures of bodily and spiritual engagements while being with God

Hell: a place of punishment

Heretic: abnormal person, especially in Sufism, a desired state of being to experience and know the Divine

Humbleness: behavior of modesty in viewing oneself, especially in Sufism, accepting the weakness in one's relationship with God and not being disrespectful and arrogant to God

Humility: character or trait of humbleness

Illa Allah: "except Allah" or "except God"

Images of God: understandings and experiences about God

Imitation: trying without real understanding

Infinite: God, the Unlimited

Informant: a person who participates in anthropological research

InshAllah: God willing, hopefully

Intention: planning ideas before the action

Internalize: making it part of one's character, trait, or nature in Sufism

Intrinsic: internal

Islam: name of a religion that emphasizes believing in one God and Jesus, Moses, and Muhammad to be the human prophets of the Creator

Jihad: struggle, esp. spiritual struggle within oneself

Joseph: Prophet of God in Islam, Christianity, and Judaism

Journey: struggles of following guidelines of a mystical school

Khidr: mystical being who is sent by God at any time to help people in their problems; also believed to be the teacher of Moses in a mystical journey as mentioned in the Quran

Kitab: the Quran

Knowledge: theoretical understanding of something through education

La ilaha illa Allah: there is no God except Allah, a critical Divine phrase of chanting in Sufism implying a spiritual charge and discharge

Literal: clear and primary

Lord: God

Lucifer: Satan, mentioned in divine scriptures such as the Bible and the Quran

Majnun: crazy or, especially in Sufism, heretic

Mantra: a repetitive phrase or sound, especially used in Hinduism and Buddhism

Meditation: deep focus especially with reflection

Memorization: learning by heart

Mercy: compassion and forgiveness

Middle way: living a balanced life in spiritual and worldly engagements

Mimic: imitate

Mind: logic, reason, and rationality

Miracle: incidents against the law of physics and against all natural sciences

Mosque: temple of Muslims

Muhammad: the Prophet of Islam, referred as "the Prophet" in the text

Musaddiq: the Quran

Mystic: a person who adopts the teachings of mysticism

Mysticism: the knowledge of the transcendent

Nafs: self in its raw form

Neat: tidy and in order

Negation: denial, esp. in Sufism, emptying from the mind and heart the imperfect ideas and feelings about God

Neglectful: not giving the proper attention that is due

Notion: concept, idea

Ocean: a very large sea, especially in Sufism, represents God the Unlimited or God's Unlimited and Incomprehensible Knowledge

Odd: not even, unique, no equivalence

Olam: hidden, waiting to be discovered through experiential knowledge

One: with capital denoting the one and only Creator

Oppression: unjust action of the strong over the weak

Permanent: constant, not changing, not ending

Phenomenon: occurrence

Pious: devout, practicing

Poisonous Cookies: harmful extraordinary incidents, such as miracles in Sufism

Pollution: making something dirty

Popular culture: the ethnographic data gathered over the period of years among different Sufi communities

Preposition: a word that does not have a meaning by itself but has a meaning in relation to another word, especially in Sufism, prepositions having conceptual and terminological meanings when one describes the relationships with the Divine

Pronunciation: correct sounds of letters in a language

The Prophet: The Prophet *Muhammad (peace and blessings be upon him).* The *Arabic writing* ﷺ is read as "Sallahu alayhi wa salllam" abbreviated as "saws" when the name of the Prophet Muhammad is mentioned. The expressions ﷺ or saws are expressions and phrases of blessings and peace for the Prophet Muhammad. They are also the expressions and phrases of blessings and peace used for the other Prophets of Allah such as Abraham, Moses, and Jesus and others.

Prostration versus to prostrate: the act of respect by putting one's face on the ground, especially in Sufism, humbling oneself for God by putting the face, the noble part of the body, on the ground

Qibla: the direction where Muslims and Sufis turn when they pray

Quran: sacred text of Muslims

Rabbinic: related with the Rabbis, the priests, and teachers of Judaism Recitation, versus to recite: reading versus to read

Rasulullah ﷺ: The word Rasulullah can be translated as "the Messenger or Prophet of Allah." Rasulullah in its usage is the Prophet *Muhammad (peace and blessings be upon him)* (PBUH). PBUH: *Peace and blessings be upon Him*

Reliance: dependence

Repetition: repeating

Reverence: respect

Reward: prize, payment, especially in worldly and afterlife rewards in Islam

Ritual: practices in a religion or mysticism that have spiritual and divine value for a person

Ruku: bowing down

Rumi: great Sufi mystic

Saint: the person believed to be close to God

Sakina: peaceful and calm feelings

Salawat: names of the chants to remember teachers and their covenants with their students, especially the main teacher, the Prophet Muhammad and others, such as Abraham, Moses, and Jesus

Samad: the One who does not need anything, but everyone and everything needs God

Satan: the Devil, Lucifer, mentioned in divine scriptures such as in the Bible and the Quran

SAW: "Sallahu alayhi wa salllam" abbreviated as "saws" when the name of the Prophet Muhammad is mentioned. The expressions ﷺ or saws are expressions and phrases of blessings and peace for the Prophet Muhammad and other prophets such as Abraham, Moses, Jesus and others.

Scent: perfume, nice smell

Scholar: expert, especially in Sufism, the experts who practice what they teach (alim)

Scripture: sacred book or sacred text

Self: ego, identifier of a person, especially in Sufism, raw and uneducated identifier and controller of a person

Service: ethical action of doing good for others and society

Spiritual Journey: struggles of following guidelines of a mystical school

State: level, especially in Sufism, spiritual level

Struggle: efforts to achieve a goal

SubhanAllah: glorification of God, a divine phrase of chanting of spirituality implying a spiritual charge and discharge

SubhanAllahu wa bihamdihi: a divine phrase of glorification of God

SubhanAllahul Azeem: a divine phrase of glorification of God in the prostration posture

SubhanRabbiyalAzim: phrase of glorification for God in the bowing posture

Submission: natural acceptance of the uncontrolled and unseen

Sufi: follower of Sufism

Sufism: mystical path of Islam

Superstitious: fake

Surrender: involuntary state of acceptance of the uncontrolled and the unseen

SWT: Subhānahu wa Tāʾla also abbreviated as SWT and written as also Allah (﷽) is an expression of respect when the Name of Allah is mentioned.

Tahajjud: night prayer

Talismanic: unknown and indescribable effects of divine words and sounds

Taqwa: respect of God

Taste: pleasure, especially spiritual pleasure such as peace, calmness, joy, and happiness in Sufism

Temple: worship place

Temporal: ending

Temporary: transitory

Temptation: false ideas

The Curer: God

The Divine: God

The Forgiver: a name of God in Sufism

The Friend: a name of God in Sufism

The Helper: a name of God in Sufism

The Lover: a name of God in Sufism

The Peace Giver: God

The Prophet: Muhammad, the Prophet of Islam, referred as "the Prophet" in the text

The Real: God

The Real Maker: God

The Source: God

The Sustainer: a name of God in Sufism

The Reminder: the Quran

The Wise: with capital W, God

Throne: a figurative or metaphorical representation of dominion of God

Trait: permanent character or nature

Tranquility: peace and calmness

Transcendent: beyond human limits

Transitory: temporal

Transliteration: writing the sounds of words or phrases in one language with an alphabet of another language

Union: being together, especially in this book, goal and joy of being always in the presence of God

Unseen: anything five senses cannot testify in scientific methods

Weak: not having a physical strength to perform an action, especially in Sufism, not having spiritual strength to perform any action

Worshipper: a person who regularly follows and practices rituals, acts of prayers

ACKNOWLEDGMENTS

I would like to thank all my unnamed teachers, friends, and students for their input, ideas, suggestions, help, and support during and before the preparation of this book.

I would like to thank Professor David Banks, faculty of the Department of Anthropology, State University of New York (SUNY) at Buffalo, for meeting with me daily to go over the manuscript. Lastly, I would like to thank all of my family members for their patience with me during the preparation of this book.

AUTHOR BIO

Dr. M. Yunus J. Kumek is currently teaching at Harvard Divinity School on Islam. He has been religious studies coordinator at State University of New York (SUNY) Buffalo State and teaching undergraduate and graduate courses in religious studies at SUNY at Buffalo State, Niagara University and Daemen College. Before becoming interested in religious studies, Dr. Kumek was doing his doctorate degree in physics at SUNY at Buffalo published academic papers in the areas of quantum physics and medical physics. Later, he decided to engage with the world of social sciences through social anthropology, education, and cultural anthropology in his doctorate studies. He subsequently spent a few years as a research associate in the anthropology department of the same university. Recently, he completed a postdoctoral fellowship at Harvard Divinity school and published books on religious literacy through ethnography and practical mysticism: Sufi journeys of heart and mind. Dr. Kumek, who remains interested in physics—solves physics problems to relax—enjoys different languages: German, Spanish, Arabic, Hebrew, Urdu, and Turkish, especially in his research of scriptural analysis. Dr. Kumek takes great pleasure in classical poetry as well.

SUGGESTED READINGS

Al-Ghazali, M. *Deliverance from Error*. Fons Vitae, 2000.

Al-Ghazali, M. *Ihya 'Ulum al-Din.'* Dar al-Fikr, 2004.

Al-Ghazzali, M. *On the Treatment of Anger, Hatred and Envy*. Kazi Publications, 2003.

Al-Ghazzali, M. *The Alchemy of Happiness*. Routledge, 2015.

Ali, A. Y. *The Meaning of the Glorious Quran*. Islamic Books, 1938.

Anjum, Z. *Iqbal: The Life of a Poet, Philosopher, and Politician*. Random House, 2015.

Arberry, A. *Interpretation of Koran*. Macmillan, 1955.

Arberry. *Muslim Saints and Mystics: Episodes from Tadhirat al awliya of Faird al-Din Attar, Omphaloskepsis*, 2000.

Asad, M. *The Message of the Quran: Translated and Explained*. Al-Andalus Gibraltar, 1980.

Avery, K. S. *A Psychology of Early Sufi Sama: Listening and Altered States*. Routledge, 2004.

Awang, R. "Anger Management: A Psychotherapy Sufistic Approach," vol. 9, no. 1, 2014, pp. 13–15.

Barks, C. *Rumi: Bridge to the Soul*. Harperone, 2007.

Barks, R. N. C. with J. Moyne, Rumi, Jelaluddin. "The guest house." *The Essential Rumi*. Harper, 1995, p. 109.

Bayrak, T. *The Name & the Named*. Canada, 2000.

Berguno, G. & Loutfy, N. "The Existential Thoughts of the Sufis. Existential Analysis." *Journal of the Society for Existential Analysis*, vol. 16, no. 1, 2005.

Bowen, J. *A New Anthropology of Islam*. Cambridge University Press, 2012.

Clarke, M. "Cough Sweets and Angels: The Ordinary Ethics of the Extraordinary in Sufi Practice in Lebanon." *Journal of the Royal Anthropological Institute*, vol. 20, no. 3, 2014, pp. 407–25.

Cutsinger, J. S. *Paths to the Heart*. World Wisdom, 2010.

Douglas-Klotz, N. *The Sufi Book of Life: 99 Pathways of the Heart for the Modern Dervish*. Penguin, 2005.

Ernst, C. W. *Teachings of Sufism*. Shambhala Publications, 1999.

Esposito, J. *The Oxford Dictionary of Islam*. Oxford University Press, 2014.

Friedlander, S. *The Whirling Dervishes: Being an Account of the Sufi Order Known as the Mevlevis and its Founder the Poet and Mystic Mevlana Jalalu'ddin Rumi*. SUNY Press, 1975.

Geoffroy, E. *Introduction to Sufism: The Inner Path of Islam*. World Wisdom, Inc., 2010.

Gibran, K. *The Prophet*. Oneworld Publications, 2012.

Hanson, Y. H. "The Creed of Imam Al-Tahawi." Zaytuna Institute, California, 2007.

Hanson, Y. H. *Purification of the Heart*. Alhambra Productions, 1998.

Helminski, K. *The Knowing Heart: A Sufi Path of Transformation*. Shambhala Publications, 2000.

Izutsu, T. *Sufism and Taoism: A Comparative Study of Key Philosophical Concepts*. University of California Press, 2016.

James, W. "The Will to Believe." *New World*, 1896.

Jawziyyah, Q. *The Prophetic Medical Science*. Idara Impex, 2013.

Karamustafa, T. A. *Sufism*. Edinburgh University Press, 2007.

Katz, J. G. "Dreams, Sufism, and Sainthood." *Brill*, vol. 71, 1996.

Khan, Z. M. *Gardens of the Righteous*. Routledge, 2012.

Lewis, B. *Music of a Distant Drum: Classical Arabic, Persian, Turkish, and Hebrew Poems*. Princeton University Press, 2001.

Malak, A. *Muslim Narratives and the Discourse of English*. SUNY Press, 2007.

Morris, J. W. "Introducing Ibn 'Arabi's Book of Spiritual Advice." *Journal of the Muhyiddīn Ibn 'Arabī Society*, no. 28, 2000, pp. 1–17.

Pickthall, M. W. E. *Holy Quran*. Kutub Khana Isha'at-ul-Islam, 1977.

Ramji, R. *The Global Migration of Sufi Islam to South Asia and Beyond*. Brill, 2007, pp. 473–84.

Renard J. *Knowledge of God in Classical Sufism: Foundations of Islamic Mystical Theology*. Paulist Press, 2004.

Rumi, J. *The Essential Rumi*. Harper, 1996.

Schimmel, A. *Deciphering the Signs of God: A Phenomenological Approach to Islam.* State University of New York Press, 1994.

Siddiqui, A. "Sahih Muslim." *Peace Vision,* 1972.

Trimingham, J. S. *The Sufi Orders in Islam.* Oxford University Press, 1998.

Upton, C. *Doorkeeper of the Heart: Versions of Rabi'a.* Threshold Books, 1988.

Usmani, T. *An Approach to the Qur'anic Sciences.* Adam Publishers, 2006.

INDEX

Made in the USA
Middletown, DE
23 July 2022

69745094R00316